Harvard Economic Studies

Volume 148

Awarded the David A. Wells Prize for the year 1977–78 and published from the income of the David A. Wells Fund.

The studies in this series are published under the direction of the Department of Economics of Harvard University. The department does not assume responsibility for the views expressed.

EMPLOYMENT HAZARDS
An Investigation of Market Performance

W. KIP VISCUSI

HARVARD UNIVERSITY PRESS
Cambridge, Massachusetts
London, England
1979

Library of Congress Cataloging in Publication Data

Viscusi, W Kip.
  Employment hazards.

  (Harvard economic studies; v. 148)
  Based on the author's thesis, Harvard University.
  Bibliography: p.
  Includes index.
  1. Labor mobility. 2. Work environment. 3. Indus-
trial hygiene. 4. Industrial accidents. I. Title.
II. Series.
HD5707.V57   331.1′2   79-13149
ISBN 0-674-25176-8

PREFACE

This volume is based on my Harvard economics dissertation completed in August 1976 and submitted to the Wells Prize Committee in that year. Although I have added some new conceptual and empirical material, the essential results of this investigation have remained unchanged. Several of the issues considered in the volume, such as compensating wage differentials and determinants of quit behavior, have received a considerable amount of attention since the time of the completion of this dissertation. I will not discuss this subsequent research except in instances in which the work is very closely related to my main focus.

During my two years of dissertation research, a variety of individuals and organizations have enabled me to develop this analysis. The National Science Foundation provided financial support for the first year of the study and for my preceding two years of graduate work. The second year of the investigation was financed by the Manpower Administration of the U.S. Department of Labor. I would also like to acknowledge the General Electric Co., which employed me for two summers in a variety of assembly-line positions at their plant in Louisville, Kentucky. Even at this comparatively safe enterprise, there were sufficient occupational risks to stimulate my interest in the subject.

I am indebted to William E. Viscusi for drawing the figures for this volume. I would also like to acknowledge helpful discussions with Jerome Culp and Michael Spence, as well as the assistance of David Wise and Gregory M. Duncan, who made their logit computer programs available to me.

Beginning in 1975, I presented portions of this work in seminars at a variety of universities. In addition, two papers excerpted from the dissertation were given at meetings of the Econometric Society. I presented a preliminary version of Chapter 4 at the 1976 meetings in Atlantic City and portions of Chapters 4 and 13 at the 1977 Ottawa meetings. The reactions of many of the participants in these seminars and conferences were of value to me in my work. I would like to thank the *International Economic Review, Review of Economics and Statistics,* and *Public Policy* for allowing me to draw on work published previously.

My greatest debts are to my three thesis advisers. Professor Kenneth Arrow was instrumental in making the conceptual and empirical analysis more cogent and in highlighting the areas where additional research was required. Professor Richard Freeman encouraged me to make the conceptual analysis pertinent to real labor-market phenomena and was of particular assistance both in making data available to me and in providing close supervision of the empirical work. Finally, I would like to acknowledge my long-term debt to Professor Richard Zeckhauser, who served as the initial sounding board for many of the ideas in the thesis and who has contributed greatly to my academic development since 1970. Since I have not opted for the risk-spreading device of co-authorship, responsibility for the contents is my own.

CONTENTS

1

INTRODUCTION

How does one's work activity affect the quality of life? Man works to eat, to provide for his children, to better his social standing. It is an old truism to say that one labors to improve his leisure, and time has honored the notion that today's sacrifices bring tomorrow's rewards. But these morsels of folk wisdom give only the bright side of the coin. Perhaps most fundamentally, and perhaps least considered, a worker's present and future physical well-being, indeed his very life, may depend on his pattern of work.

This volume is concerned with the health and safety risks associated with employment and the implications of these risks for labor market performance. Many economic effects of occupational hazards extend beyond the participants in the labor market transaction. Society at large, for example, may have a stake in the health and safety impacts of employment both for altruistic reasons and because of a financial interest in the costs of social insurance programs. By neglecting these external effects of job risks, I do not wish to imply that they are unimportant.

Economists' interest in occupational hazards was prompted by the adverse working conditions during the Industrial Revolution. Adam Smith viewed these conditions as a competitive market outcome, observing that workers would be paid compensating wage differentials for jobs that are hazardous or otherwise unpleasant.[1] In contrast, Karl

1. Smith was cognizant of some of the problems associated with labor market risks. With respect to general occupational prospects, for example, he asserted that individuals would tend to overestimate their probability of success because of "the overweening conceit which the greater part of men have in their own abilities."

Marx took a less dispassionate view, as he considered employment hazards to be an integral part of the exploitation of labor. Engels likewise emphasized the inadequacy of market outcomes. In his study of the English working class, Engels noted such difficulties as worker ignorance of the hazards and inadequate insurance compensation for injuries.[2] Although Smith's general approach predominates among recent economic treatments of occupational risks, the criticism of market outcomes voiced by Marx and Engels is shared by many recent proponents of government intervention in this area.[3]

My investigation of occupational hazards bears a closer methodological relationship to the work of Adam Smith than to that of radical economists. Nevertheless, many of the most salient economic influences to be analyzed represent deviations from the standard competitive model. Most notably, the imperfection in the job risk information possessed by workers and enterprises has a considerable impact on market behavior and its implications for social welfare.

This book consists of three principal parts. The analysis of individual employment decisions in markets with potentially hazardous jobs is the focus of Part I. This portion of the study begins with two chapters that analyze the properties of individual choice in a world in which workers do not learn about the risks and subsequently revise their job risk assessments.

Utilizing the classic compensating wage differential analysis as the point of departure, I begin the analysis in Chapter 2 by ascertaining the minimal assumptions required to generate the standard compensating wage differential result. Although the economic underpinnings of the compensating differential theory are not particularly controversial, the fact that the most attractive jobs in society are also the highest paid may appear to contradict the theory, or at least suggest that other, more powerful economic forces are at work. Consideration of the impact of worker wealth on the job risk a worker will select permits one to reconcile these observations with the existence of wage premiums for hazardous jobs. Other matters considered in Chapter 2 include the optimal structure of workmen's compensation benefits, the effect of irreversible health effects on worker decisions, and the nature of the compensating differential results in dynamic contexts.

2. See, in particular, chapters 6, 7, and 8 of the recent translation of Engels' work (1958), which raises many of the key analytic issues.

3. The advocates of government intervention seem less inspired by Karl Marx than Ralph Nader. Occupational risks are not considered to be part of a general process of exploitation of labor, but instead are viewed as the labor market equivalent of a defective product. In his introduction to the Nader report on occupational hazards (Page and O'Brien [1973]), Ralph Nader emphasized his own disagreement with the classical compensating-differential arguments by noting that "merely compensating for such injuries or diseases is the sign of a catch-up, not a humane, society."

These multi-period effects are the primary focus of Chapter 3. Consideration of the influence of job risks on future welfare is especially important in analyzing long-term health effects, such as disability and death. In situations involving influences on the worker's future health, one might think that a worker would be willing to accept a greater risk as he grew older since less future well-being would be endangered. The analysis in Chapter 3 indicates that such a straightforward relationship does not always exist. It is even possible to observe such counterintuitive patterns as a worker preferring to incur a particular risk when he is either very young or very old, but not in the intervening years. Chapter 3 also addresses related dynamic issues, such as the influence on individual job choice of temporal fluctuations in the hazard posed by a job.

Although models in which workers do not revise their perceptions of job risks offer many profitable insights, they neglect an important feature of the individual choice problem. Workers seldom are fully informed of the hazards they face, but they can often learn about these risks through their on-the-job experiences and other forms of information acquisition.

The introduction of learning effects and the potential for making sequential decisions has a fundamental effect on the nature of individual job choice, as the adaptive models introduced in Chapter 4 indicate. Workers confronting a sequence of job risk lotteries will not avoid jobs with uncertain implications, but, somewhat paradoxically, will actually display a systematic preference for jobs posing risks that are dimly understood. If the worker's on-the-job experiences prove to be sufficiently unfavorable, he will quit. The analysis in this chapter provides the first formal theory of learning-induced quit behavior. Moreover, the methodology introduced will not only form the basis for much of the conceptual developments in subsequent chapters, but will also provide the theoretical impetus for the distinctive aspects of the empirical work.

Throughout the analysis of individual choice in the first three chapters of Part I, I make the conventional separability assumption that the worker's valuation of a sequence of lotteries is simply the sum of the discounted values of the expected payoffs in each period. A principal exception to this assumption is that lotteries not resolved immediately will affect worker welfare in the intervening periods. A coal miner facing the risk of brown lung disease or a worker in a nuclear plant risking leukemia might view his job quite differently if he knew the health impacts of his job immediately, rather than having to wait a decade or more for the implications of his current exposures to hazards to become apparent. The analytic implications of such influences, which are quite pertinent to occupational risks with deferred impacts, are explored in Chapter 5.

In Part II of the volume, the focus is shifted from individual behavior to enterprise decisions and the properties of market outcomes. The risk posed by a job often depends on the worker's personal characteristics, such as his agility, as well as on activities not directly related to work, such as cigarette smoking. If employers are unable to monitor differences in individual riskiness, one might hope that individuals would choose jobs in a fashion that would lead to efficient levels of workplace health and safety. This self-selection process is the subject of Chapter 6. The potential efficacy of market allocations depends on the severity of the health outcomes, the extent to which careless worker actions lead to accidents injuring their coworkers, and other economic factors. Perhaps most fundamentally, no stable economic equilibrium may exist in this situation.

Self-selection processes of a different nature are considered in Chapter 7. The enterprise's pool of prospective workers consists of individuals with diverse job risk perceptions that differ both in the level of the perceived risk and the precision of the probabilistic judgments. If worker turnover is costly to the firm, the enterprise will be concerned not only with the wage level but also with the turnover rate of its work force. The effect of different kinds of wage structures on the mix of workers attracted to the firm and on the costs of employment are explored in detail in Chapter 7. In this analysis the model of individual adaptive job choice is extended to the market context in which the enterprise's wage policy is responsive to the adaptive aspect of worker behavior.

The imperfect nature of worker information combines with the possession of superior, or at least different, knowledge on the part of the employer to create a potential role for enterprises as providers of job hazard information. Although limited information provision, such as safety training, is widespread, full information transfer is seldom observed. The impediments to information provision considered in Chapter 8 are quite diverse, with the most fundamental problem being that the employer has a vested interest in workers' use of this information.

If a firm provides job risk information to workers, the incentives of other firms to do likewise will be altered. The interdependence of enterprises in the information transfer process is explored in Chapter 9. This analysis not only has broad applicability to matters such as product advertising, but also provides insight into the appropriate strategy for publicly identifying the hazardousness of different enterprises if the policy objective is to promote similar work quality certification by other firms in the industry.

The analysis of enterprise behavior in Part II concludes with an investigation of the implications of employment hazards for the shape of the production function and the subsequent effect on enterprise decisions. Job hazards lead to injuries and illnesses as well as to workers' quitting, each of which introduces randomness into the firm's supply of labor. These stochastic effects alter the shape of the production function, introducing increasing returns in what would otherwise be a constant returns-to-scale technology. An analytic framework incorporating these stochastic features will be utilized to analyze such diverse and fundamental issues as the relation of job risks to the size of the firm and the impact of employment hazards on enterprise investments in worker training.

Although the absence of perfect information represents the most important deviation from idealized competitive conditions, other more familiar imperfections may be present. If there is concentration on either side of the labor market, either in the form of monopsonistic influences or monopolistic trade-union power, the level of employment will be affected. This economic result is well known. What has not yet been considered is the effect of this market power on the level of job risks and other work quality attributes. The principal concern of Chapter 11 is to consider the welfare implication of work quality outcomes in such situations and to investigate the circumstances under which unions may play a socially productive role.

Many of the implications of these models can be tested with available data. The empirical analysis in Part III utilizes both aggregative data and several large sets of survey data on individual behavior in an attempt to ascertain the validity and empirical importance of the most salient predictions of the conceptual formulations. The structure of the empirical model to be analyzed is summarized in Chapter 12.

The empirical work begins with an investigation of the determinants of worker quitting in Chapter 13. Unlike all previous empirical analyses, which considered only impediments to worker quitting, such as wage rates, my analysis focuses instead on quit behavior generated by an adaptive process in which workers switch jobs if their on-the-job experiences are sufficiently unfavorable. The matter of particular concern is the extent to which health and safety risks exert an independent influence on worker quitting. Other features of the adaptive models, including the influence of job risks on the length of employment at the enterprise, are also explored.

Underlying the adaptive framework is the assumption that workers learn about the hazards they face through their on-the-job experiences. Even in models without learning, workers' job hazard perceptions have an important influence on market outcomes since they affect the individual's employment decisions as well as the efficacy of the compensating wage differential mechanism. In Chapter 14, I investigate the extent to which workers' perceptions of the risks they face are influenced by objective indices of their industry's riskiness, direct experiences of injuries, and other sources of job hazard information. These findings cast considerable doubt on the common assumptions that workers systematically underestimate job risks or are typically ignorant of the hazards they face.

Chapter 15 considers the more familiar issue of whether workers receive financial compensation for job risks. The results are of particular interest not only because they disentangle job risk premiums from compensation for other aspects of the quality of work, but because they also provide comparisons of the levels of job risk compensation using both the worker's subjective assessments of the risk and objective job hazard indexes. Using these estimates, one can calculate the implicit dollar values workers attach to death and injury. Very small implicit values would cast doubt on the validity and economic importance of the theory of compensating differentials.

The analysis of health and safety risks in Chapter 16 is of a more exploratory nature. One would expect that the market would function somewhat differently for these two types of risk since health hazards raise greater informational difficulties. The differential economic influences of these hazards are explored as fully as the available data permit.

Chapter 17 summarizes the implications of the study for the performance of markets for potentially dangerous jobs. These markets do function, though in a manner that is quite distinct from behavior predicted by a perfect information paradigm. The dominant empirical characteristic of employment patterns is that workers accept positions whose health and safety implications are uncertain and later quit after unfavorable on-the-job experiences. This adaptive behavior has a fundamental impact not only on enterprise decisions, but also on the welfare implications of market outcomes.

PART ONE

Models of Individual Job Choice

2

Optimal Job Risks

2.1 Introduction

Workers choosing among alternative jobs consider a multitude of pecuniary and nonpecuniary job characteristics. Wage rates, pension benefits, convenience of work hours, and health and safety hazards are but a few of the pertinent job characteristics. Almost inevitably, a worker must trade off some valued characteristics for other job attributes when selecting from his employment opportunities.

In this chapter I will present a stylized version of this trade-off process in which the only two characteristics considered are the monetary wage rates and the health and safety hazards. From an empirical standpoint, these are likely to be the most important job components to workers considering potentially dangerous jobs, while theoretically there is little that can be said about a fully generalized multi-attribute case that does not represent a straightforward extension of the two-attribute case.[1]

Adam Smith observed two centuries ago that "the whole of the advantages and disadvantages of the different employments of labor and stock must, in the same neighborhood, be either perfectly equal or continually tending to equality." This compensating wage differential result forms the basis of several recent economic analyses of job hazards, including those of Oi (1973, 1974) and Thaler and Rosen (1976).

---

1. Perhaps the most important implication of a generalized model is that a worker should be cognizant to the entire portfolio of risky actions and should not make piece-meal decisions when strong interdependencies are involved. This issue is considered in the time allocation model in Appendix A.

The analysis in this chapter also can be viewed as a probabilistic generalization of Adam Smith's analysis, although the issues considered and the structure of the model are quite different from those in previous investigations.

The health state-dependent utility function approach that I will utilize is introduced in Section 2.2. This framework will first be used to analyze the minimal assumptions required to generate Adam Smith's compensating wage differential result. I will then consider the effect of worker wealth and income taxes on the level of the optimal job risk. If the worker can purchase insurance, he can diminish some of the welfare losses associated with adverse job outcomes. The optimal level of insurance coverage is investigated in Section 2.2D. As I will indicate, these results have important ramifications for the appropriate structure of workmen's compensation benefits.

Although the implications of single-period models of individual choice are instructive, many important ramifications of job risks are associated with their impact on the worker's future welfare. A worker incurring the risks of permanent disability or death, for example, is likely to be quite concerned about these risks. Section 2.3 generalizes the compensating differential analysis to consider issues of a dynamic nature, such as whether the worker will opt for more or less hazardous employment in multi-period contests. The Markovian decision framework that I introduce to structure this multi-period choice problem will also be used in Section 2.4 to analyze the role of irreversible health impacts and potential misallocations.

2.2 OPTIMAL JOB RISKS IN A ONE-PERIOD MODEL

A. Compensating Wage Differentials and the Health State Approach. The static models in this section illustrate the properties of the optimal job choice of a worker who is choosing from a set of job opportunities that involve the same number of work hours but have differing probabilities of adverse consequences. This approach does not appear to be unduly restrictive, since most job opportunities offer little individual leeway in the choice of hours. To facilitate comparison of the job risk results with time allocation models, Appendix A examines the implications of job risks in situations in which the hourly wage for different jobs is constant and there is complete leeway for workers to mix various job activities.

For simplicity, assume that there is no income uncertainty associated with any particular job. Although the wage rate is known, the health state resulting from one's activities is uncertain. In this simple model, one's health does not affect one's earnings. Two health states will be considered. State 1 refers to good health, while state 2 refers to ill health, such as being injured or dead. The shape of the worker's utility function u^j is dependent on his health state j. In particular, I will assume that a given level of consumption yields a greater total utility and a larger marginal utility when the worker is healthy than when he is not.[2] Nondiscretionary insurance benefits, such as workmen's compensation, are subsumed into the functional forms of the state-dependent utility functions.

The principal alternative format is to view an injury as being tantamount to a drop in wealth. If the utility function is of the usual concave form, this approach in effect assumes that workers have a higher marginal utility of income when they are in ill health than when they are in good health. Analyses along these lines have generated many profitable insights.[3] However, the health state approach imposes fewer restrictions on the shape of worker preferences and also affords greater insight into the particular issues considered in this chapter.

The notation I will use is as follows:

u^j = the utility function in health state j, where $j = 1, 2$
x = the composite consumption good whose price equals 1
p = the probability of the unattractive state 2 occurring
$w(p)$ = the wage for a job offering probability p of state 2 occurring
A = initial assets
λ = the shadow price of the goods constraint

Letter subscripts on the u^j and w terms indicate partial derivatives. The u^j and $w(p)$ functions are assumed to be continuous and twice differentiable. The wage schedule $w(p)$ represents the highest wage available for a job with probability p of injury. For the static models considered, p can either be the actual job risk or the worker's subjective assessment of the risk. Worker updating of their subjective assessments becomes important in multi-period contexts, as the analysis in Chapter 4 will demonstrate. I also assume that the worker receives the same wage for his job irrespective of the actual health impact.

Suppose that workers must select from a range of job alternatives that are equally attractive in terms of their time allocations but which offer different probabilities of unfavorable state 2 occurring. This range

2. The assumption that individuals reap a lower marginal utility of wealth when injured or dead might seem to be contradicted by purchases of life insurance, typically bought at actuarially unfair rates. However, substantial death duties lower the value of one's wealth after death, boosting the marginal utility of wealth and making the purchase of insurance potentially attractive even within the context of the health state model.

3. This technique is used by Oi (1973, 1974) and Thaler and Rosen (1976). Thaler and Rosen also analyze the use of a bequest function to reflect the preferences of workers who are killed. The treatment of a decline in health as a drop in wealth has a long and distinguished history. Arrow's classic analysis of the welfare economics of medical care, which is reprinted in Arrow (1971), utilized this framework.

is assumed to be continuous and to span all values of p. The set of alternatives that must be considered can be restricted to the efficient set of jobs that offer the highest value of w for any value of p. The hours of work are fixed and identical for all jobs.

The worker's objective is to select the job and consumption level that maximize his expected utility. In particular, he will choose the value of p and x that maximize the Lagrangian given by

$$L = (1 - p)u^1(x) + pu^2(x) + \lambda[x - A - w(p)].$$

The job with the optimal risk p is determined by solving the following first-order conditions for a maximum (as well as the budget constraint):

(1) $$L_x = 0 = (1 - p)u_x^1 + pu_x^2 + \lambda,$$

and

(2) $$L_p = 0 = -u^1 + u^2 - \lambda w_p.$$

Solving for w_p produces the result

(3) $$w_p = \frac{u^1 - u^2}{(1 - p)u_x^1 + pu_x^2} > 0.$$

The necessary condition for an interior maximum is that marginal increase in the wage as a result of the increased job risk be positive and equal to the difference in the two states' utilities divided by the expected marginal utility of consumption.[4] Thus, the job market equilibrium function $w(p)$ is necessarily an increasing function of p if workers are employed at each level of p. Jobs with identical stochastic properties will be rewarded equally in equilibrium. The positive sign of w_p is a result of the nature of the job choice problem. It is not an assumption. The derivation of this result did not require that workers be risk averters. The only key assumptions required are that the good health state be more desirable than the ill health state and that the marginal utility of consumption be positive.[5]

4. Throughout the rest of this chapter, I will consider interior solutions only. The no-risk corner solution is not particularly interesting. Little can be said about it other than what is mentioned in Appendix A. The case in which the unfavorable outcome has a probability of 1 occurs in only exceedingly rare circumstances, such as "suicide missions" during wartime.

5. If one uses a conventional model with a single utility function (not conditional on one's health) in which job risk outcomes are viewed as monetary equivalents, w_p is positive so long as $u' > 0$ and the argument of u is greater when the worker is not injured on the job. This property is quite unrestrictive and implies nothing whatsoever about the risk aversion, or lack thereof, of the worker. For this single argument case, the worker is said to be risk averse if $u'' < 0$. The second-order conditions for a maximum impose other restrictions, but do not require risk aversion. For simplicity, I will assume that the marginal utility of consumption is diminishing.

To assure that a solution to equation (3) is indeed a maximum, the second-order condition also must be fulfilled. In mathematical terms, the marginal rate of change of w_p with respect to further increases in p must be either negative or positive, but not too large:

$$(4) \qquad w_{pp} < \frac{-(w_p)^2[(1-p)u^1_{xx} + pu^2_{xx}] - 2w_p[u^2_x - u^1_x]}{pu^2_x + (1-p)u^1_x}.$$

The right side of equation (4) is positive, assuming plausible restrictions on the utility function. In particular, I assume that the marginal utility of comsumption is diminishing (that is, $u^1_{xx} < 0$ and $u^2_{xx} < 0$) and that the marginal utility of consumption is greater in the healthy state than in the injured state $u^1_x > u^2_x > 0$).

The compensating wage differential result in equation (3) implies that the curve relating w to p must have a positive slope if workers are to be attracted to jobs along it. The choice of a job will satisfy the second-order conditions for an optimum given by equation (4) if the wage premium per unit of risk declines with the level of p, is constant, or increases with p at not too great a rate. The empirical evidence for death risks presented in Chapter 15 is consistent with these assumptions, since the available evidence indicates that w_{pp} is negative.

B. Wealth Effects and the Optimal Job Risk. Casual observation suggests that the best jobs in society also tend to be the highest paid. This pattern does not necessarily imply that compensating wage differentials do not exist, but it does indicate a need to extend the scope of the analysis. In this section I will investigate the role of worker wealth in influencing the optimal job risk.[6]

To determine the relationship of one's assets to the optimal probability of injury, one can totally differentiate the first-order conditions for the basic model (equations [1] and [2] and the budget constraint), and solve for dp/dA using Cramer's rule, producing the result that

$$(5) \quad \frac{dp}{dA}$$

$$= \frac{-[(1-p)u^1_{xx} + pu^2_{xx}]w_p - [u^2_x - u^1_x]}{w^2_p[(1-p)u^1_{xx} + pu^2_{xx}] + 2w_p[u^2_x - u^1_x] + w_{pp}[pu^2_x + (1-p)u^1_x]}.$$

Since the numerator is clearly positive, the sign of dp/dA is the same as that of the denominator. Hazardous jobs will be an inferior occupational pursuit, as is plausible, if

---

6. The positive relation between the quality of a worker's job and his wealth has long been a matter of speculation by economists, such as Reder (1962). Weiss (1976) considers such a relationship for nonstochastic work quality attributes. Thaler and Rosen (1976) found an ambiguous relationship between property income and the death risk selected by a worker.

(6) $\quad w_p^2[(1 - p)u_{xx}^1 + pu_{xx}^2] + 2w_p[u_x^2 - u_x^1]$
$$+ w_{pp}[pu_x^2 + (1 - p)u_x^1] < 0.$$

But if this equation is solved for w_{pp}, the condition reduces to equation (4)—the second-order condition for a maximum.[7] Consequently, the extent of the job hazard one chooses necessarily decreases with one's wealth. The problem features guaranteeing this result are the requirements that the worker be at an interior maximum and that the utility function satisfy the seemingly mild restrictions specified in the previous section.

Since worker income and wealth exhibit a strong positive correlation, it is not surprising that individuals in the highest paying occupations do not incur particularly severe hazards. Rather, this pattern is a direct consequence of the health state model of individual choice. The presence of wealth effects and compensating wage differentials will be analyzed on an empirical basis in Chapters 14 and 15, respectively.

C. Taxes and Other Shifts in the Wage Schedule. In addition to exhibiting a negative response to worker wealth, the optimal job risk will also be influenced by the rate of remuneration for job risks. Consider the case in which the wage schedule $w(p)$ becomes $kw(p)$, where k is a positive constant. The proportional shift in the wage rate for different jobs changes the budget constraint to

$$x - A - kw(p) = 0.$$

After substituting this new budget constraint into the Lagrangian employed earlier, one can determine the new first-order conditions, which, in addition to the budget constraint, are:

$$L_x = 0 = (1 - p)u_x^1 + pu_x^2 + \lambda,$$

and

$$L_p = 0 = -u^1 + u^2 - \lambda kw_p.$$

The only difference from the earlier results is that $w(p)$ is replaced by $kw(p)$ in the budget constraint, and kw_p replaces w_p in the second of the first-order conditions. Solving for w_p produces the result that

$$w_p = \frac{u^1 - u^2}{k[(1 - p)u_x^1 + pu_x^2]},$$

which is positive, as before. The second-order condition is altered only slightly by the change in the form of the wage schedule and is now

---

7. The appearance of the second-order condition in the denominator of the term on the right side of equation (5) is not a coincidence, but rather is an inherent feature of optimization problems of this general type.

given by

$$w_{pp} < \frac{-k(w_p)^2[(1-p)u^1_{xx} + pu^2_{xx}] - 2w_p[u^2_x + u^1_x]}{(1-p)u^1_x + pu^2_x}.$$

The principal analytic issue of interest is the effect of changes in k on the optimal job hazard. Following the procedure used earlier, one can totally differentiate the first-order conditions and solve for $\partial p/\partial k$, yielding

(7) $\quad \dfrac{\partial p}{\partial k} = \dfrac{-w_p[(1-p)u^1_x + pu^2_x]}{D}$

$$+ \frac{w\{-[(1-p)u^1_{xx} + pu^2_{xx}]kw_p - [u^2_x - u^1_x]\}}{D},$$

where D is the negative term given by

(8) $\quad D = [(1-p)u^1_{xx} + pu^2_{xx}][k^2(w_p)^2]$
$$+ 2kw_p(-u^1_x + u^2_x) + kw_{pp}[(1-p)u^1_x + pu^2_x].$$

The sign of $\partial p/\partial k$ depends on the relative strength of the two effects resulting from a shift in the wage schedule. The first term in equation (7) is necessarily positive and represents the substitution effect from a change in k. The second term consists of w multiplied by the value of $\partial p/\partial A$ for this problem and thus captures the wealth effect of a shift in the wage schedule. Its value is always negative. The parameters specific to the worker's optimization problem determine the relative magnitudes of the two effects. If the magnitude of the wealth effect is quite small, the substitution effect will be dominant.

The analysis of wage schedule shifts takes on its greatest practical significance with respect to taxes on worker income. For simplicity, assume that workers pay a proportional tax t on all of their earnings and that the available wage schedule does not change in response to the effect of taxes on worker choices. The constant k thus takes on the specific value $(1-t)$. The first- and second-order conditions for a maximum are identical to those presented above once $(1-t)$ is substituted for k in each of the equations.

The impact of a marginal tax increase on the optimal job hazard can be determined in the same manner in which $\partial p/\partial k$ was ascertained, yielding

$$\partial p/\partial t = w_p[(1-p)u^1_x + pu^2_x]/D$$
$$- w\{-[(1-p)u^1_{xx} + pu^2_{xx}](1-t)w_p - [u^2_x - u^1_x]\}/D,$$

where the negative denominator D is given by equation (8) above. The first term reflects the negative substitution effect of a tax increase. The second term represents the wealth effect, which is positive since a decline in a worker's wealth increases the job hazard he is willing to incur. The net impact remains theoretically ambiguous. For very small wealth effects, an increase in taxes will reduce the job risk an individual will select.

D. *Optimal Insurance Coverage*   Individuals who incur job risks may find insurance coverage attractive. For example, they may purchase medical insurance in order to defray the costs of medical care if they are injured.[8] The economic issues raised by health insurance have been considered by Arrow (1971), Zeckhauser (1970), and others. Here I will focus on purchases of income insurance to reallocate the funds available for consumption in the two health states.

Consider a model in which workers can select an income insurance and wage compensation package subject to an actuarial constraint that the expected value of the consumption in the two states not exceed the worker's resources, or

$$(1 - p)x_1 + px_2 - A - w(p) = 0,$$

where x_1 and x_2 represent the levels of consumption in states 1 and 2, respectively. The optimality conditions for this revised problem are that

$$w_p = \frac{-u^1 + u^2 + \lambda(-x_1 + x_2)}{\lambda},$$

and

$$\partial u^1/\partial x_1 = \partial u^2/\partial x_2 = -\lambda.$$

This second condition is the principal matter of interest. Since the marginal utility of income is equated in each state, the worker allocates more funds to the healthy state 1 than to the unhealthy state 2, given the assumption that $u_x^1 > u_x^2$ for any particular level of consumption for each state. In practice, the selection of the *ex ante* and *ex post* compensation mix is complicated by problems of adverse incentives and adverse selection, which make it impossible for the worker to participate in actuarially fair schemes such as this. Nevertheless, the model correctly suggests that it may not be in the worker's interest to allocate more funds to himself when he is injured, because of the diminished impact these allocations have on expected utility. This conclusion contrasts with the results produced by a more conventional model in which job injuries are viewed as being equivalent to a de-

8. Analytically, medical expenditures can be viewed as having a twofold function: (1) to alter the worker's welfare in the ill health state (for example, treatment modes that reduce pain and suffering); and (2) to increase the probability of returning to the good health state. A multiperiod model such as the one presented in the next section is well-suited for analyzing such issues.

crease in wealth. A worker with an opportunity to purchase actuarially fair insurance in that situation would provide himself with the same post-lottery wealth level irrespective of the job outcome.

The optimal insurance results are particularly instructive in assessing the adequacy of workmen's compensation benefits. One can gain insight into the optimal policy intervention by asking how the worker himself would structure the insurance program if he were given a lump sum transfer and allowed to design the utility-maximizing plan subject to the actuarial constraint that the plan break even. The preceding results indicate that the optimal plan would provide for a lower level of consumption after an injury so that the marginal utility of consumption in each of the two states can be equated.

In contrast, models in which injuries are viewed as losses in income imply that the optimal insurance plan would equate the absolute levels of utility and consumption in each state, since this traditional approach assumes that the marginal utility of wealth is invariant with respect to the worker's health status. Workmen's compensation benefits are usually limited to a maximum of two-thirds of the worker's gross income, with actual benefit levels being much less, on average.[9] This income maintenance function is clearly inadequate from the standpoint of analyses that treat injuries as pure income losses, whereas the health state approach implies the direction of the income discrepancy is optimal.

2.3. JOB RISKS AND FUTURE WELFARE

In the interest of economic simplicity, a harried analyst might wish to limit his analytic attention to static models such as those in the previous section and in Appendix B. Indeed, all existing economic treatments of occupational hazards make such a simplification. However, it seems particularly ill-advised to abstract from the dynamic implications of job risks, since the forward effects of health and safety hazards on the worker's future welfare often appear to be critical determinants of a job's attractiveness.

Permanent disability, cancer, and death are but a few examples of health impacts that affect the worker's present and potential future welfare. The central analytic issue for this section is how workers' optimal choices differ when such temporal considerations are included. For example, is a worker necessarily going to choose a less risky job when the future implications of job hazards are included in the decision problem?

Since the worker's choice problem involves decisions that will influ-

9. For a summary of workmen's compensation benefit levels by state, see the annual Chamber of Commerce publication, *Analysis of Workmen's Compensation Laws.*

ence his lifetime welfare in a complex probabilistic fashion, the dynamic problem may seem difficult to write down, much less to solve or to analyze the properties of its solution. As one might expect, substantial simplifications are required to make the problem amenable to analysis.

For the purposes of this chapter, health state transitions are assumed to be immediate if they are to occur at all. Thus, I am assuming that the worker's job risks can be captured by a one-stage Markov process. A second simplification is that the Markovian decision model does not utilize a fully general lifetime utility function, but rather views the worker's objective as the maximization of the sum of discounted expected period utilities. The justification of this separability assumption is based on convenience rather than realism. A major exception to separability—anxiety experienced with regard to lotteries not resolved immediately—is the subject of Chapter 5. The principal advantage of Markovian decision models over a more elaborate lifetime decision tree model is that the latter technique tends to be computationally unwieldy. After analyzing the situation with two health states, we will investigate the properties of more complex Markov structures in the following section and in Chapters 3 and 4.

The dynamic version of the job choice problem involves considerable new complexities. Suppose that there is only one action the worker can take while in state 2, and that the probability of returning to state 1 on the next transition is $1 - q$. These probabilities are assumed to be time-invariant, that is, there is no updating of one's initial assessments. Then, if we let p_{ij} be the transition probability from state i to state j, the transition matrix is given by

$$(9) \qquad P = \begin{bmatrix} 1 - p & p \\ 1 - q & q \end{bmatrix}.$$

The reward vector for the two states will be denoted by

$$(10) \qquad \mathbf{v} = \begin{bmatrix} v^1(p) \\ v^2 \end{bmatrix}.$$

The more detailed formulation used in the static models in which p influences utility through wages and subsequently one's consumption has been simplified by making the valuation of the state dependent on p directly. The payoff for remaining in state 1 while working on a job with probability p of being injured is given by $v^1(p)$, while the reward for state 2 is given by v^2. Assume that $v^1(p)$ is greater than v^2 for all p. This reward structure implies that the worker receives a wage premium for the hazardous job only if he remains uninjured.[10]

10. The alternative approach of giving the hazardous job's wage to the worker even if he is injured would require that I add a third state or make rewards dependent on both one's present and previous state instead of the present state alone.

Let u^i be the maximum discounted expected reward that can be achieved by a worker starting in state i, or

(11)
$$\mathbf{u} = \begin{bmatrix} u^1 \\ u^2 \end{bmatrix}.$$

All workers start in the healthy state and use a discount rate of r equal to 0.08 in discounting future rewards.

The decision problem for the worker is to choose the optimizing value of p in each period. Thus, he must select the first row of the transition matrix and its associated reward. In finite time horizon problems this task is especially difficult, since the optimal p will depend on the time period. In an infinite time horizon model, the appropriate work choice for state 1 is time-invariant. I will employ the infinite time horizon version in this section, largely because the solution to this case is far more tractable than are the iterative solutions to finite problems.[11] For problems with a large number of periods, the infinite period solution is identical to that for the finite case except for the very last periods. Time horizon effects will be analyzed in detail in the next chapter.

To simplify the problem, assume that there is only a single strategy available for state 2—perhaps a treatment mode for work-induced disability. The principal analytic issue is how recognition of the dynamic nature of the problem alters the optimal job choice for the type of problem considered in the previous section. This issue is confronted in its general form in Appendix B. The discussion in this section deals with specific numerical examples and the simpler economic issue of whether one can ascertain in general whether a worker will choose a more or less risky job when he recognizes the dynamic implications of his actions.

Let v^1 equal $ln(1 + p)$ and v^2 equal zero. The optimal policy for these reward functions in a static model is to select the job with a value of p equal to 0.46. Consider the infinite time horizon analogue of this situation. If p is constrained to equal q, the infinite time horizon problem consists of a series of repetitions of the single period lotteries, as equation (9) indicates. The optimal p is the same as in the static problem—0.46.

Matters change substantially if the lotteries faced in each state are not identical. Since the optimal value of p will no doubt vary substantially with the value of q (the probability of remaining in the undesirable state), consider the optimal job hazard for the entire range of probabilities of remaining in state 2. Figure 2.1 shows that variation of the optimal job risk with respect to q. If the probability of remaining in

11. Though the time horizon is infinite, this does not assume that workers live forever. For example, a finite probability of death in each period can be incorporated into the discount factor. Or state 2 could represent the trapping state—death.

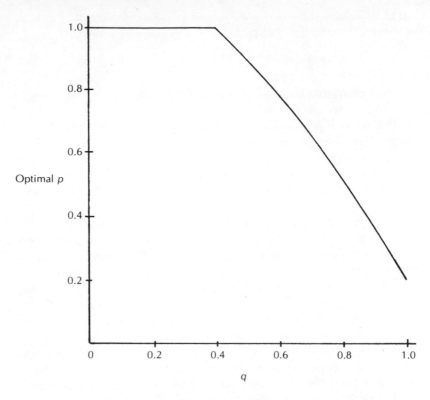

Figure 2.1 Variation of Optimal Job Risk *p* with Value of *q*

state 2 is less than 0.39, it is optimal to take the most risky job available by setting *p* equal to 1. As *q* increases to higher values, the optimal value of *p* decreases in a fashion that is slightly nonlinear. If *q* is an absorbing state, the optimal value of *p* reaches a minimum value of 0.18.

If *q* is less than or equal to 0.84, the optimal dynamic strategy calls for a greater job hazard than does the myopic strategy. Otherwise the myopic strategy results in the choice of a more hazardous job. As examples in subsequent chapters will demonstrate, the relationship between present-mindedness and the optimal job hazard is even more ambiguous when more complex Markovian decision models are considered. A principal implication of this result is that analysts and policymakers may be incorrect when they promote efforts to reduce job hazards on the grounds that such measures necessarily increase workers' long-term well-being. If workers can recover from job injuries quickly, the optimal risk from the standpoint of one's lifetime welfare may be greater than if only the immediate effects were considered.

2.4 IRREVERSIBILITIES AND POTENTIAL MISALLOCATIONS

In addition to providing a workable structure for risky job choices, the Markovian decision framework is especially helpful in illuminating special economic issues of interest. This section utilizes the Markovian framework to examine irreversibilities and potential misallocations.

Perhaps the most distinctive analytic feature involved in human resources investments is that the individual is dealing with stock characteristics that are nontransferable or transferable at only a large cost. This observation forms a central part of the recent human capital theory, although classical economists such as Alfred Marshall (1949) probably should be given much of the credit for this conceptualization. Within the context of job risks, these particular Marshallian "peculiarities of labor" imply that many job outcomes involve irreversible effects. Death, the loss of a limb, and lung cancer are among the least attractive irreversible outcomes that might result from a job. The main economic issue is what special effect—if any—the presence of irreversible impacts has on the worker's optimal job choice.

The structure of a Markovian decision model such as the one discussed in the previous section can be used to distinguish two types of irreversibilities.[12] First, at the broadest level, all job lotteries involve irreversibilities to the extent that present job risks have a probabilistic impact on the worker's future well-being. The health status and job skills of virtually every worker depend at least in part on his past.

The second type of irreversibility is defined more narrowly and differs from the conventional definition of irreversibilities, which is close to that discussed above. This second class of irreversibilities is defined in terms of Markov chains within the worker's transition matrix. Trapping states or collective trapping states will be used to correspond to irreversible effects. Trapping states are those states that cannot be left once they are entered.

Consider the transition matrix B given by

$$(12) \qquad B = \begin{bmatrix} .5 & 0 & .4 & .1 \\ 0 & .8 & .2 & 0 \\ 0 & .5 & .5 & 0 \\ 0 & 0 & 0 & 1 \end{bmatrix}.$$

For concreteness, let state 1 be the healthy state, state 2 represent partial rehabilitation from work diability, state 3 represent partial disability, and state 4 represent permanent disability. The worker in state 1 is incurring a 0.4 chance of partial disability and a 0.1 chance of perma-

---

12. This approach to irreversibilities was introduced in the context of environmental problems by Viscusi and Zeckhauser (1976). See the references contained therein for other analyses of irreversible impacts.

nent disability. State 1 is a transient state for this problem. Once disabled, the worker is in state 3. He may be rehabilitated to the partial disability state 2, but still may suffer a relapse to state 3. States 2 and 3 comprise a chain. The disability induced by a job represents an irreversible effect, since the worker cannot return to his former healthy condition. Somewhat analogously, state 4 comprises a chain. Permanent disability appears as the irreversible condition that it is. The number of irreversible conditions cannot exceed the number of states. The Markov system with the greatest number of chains is the identity matrix, for which each state is a trapping state.

Structuring the worker's choice problem in this manner highlights irreversible effects that may not be of consequence for some time. A vinyl chloride worker who has contracted liver cancer can never return to his former healthy state, although his welfare may not be reduced significantly until the disease reaches its advanced stages. In instances such as these, the immediate outcomes of job lotteries might not be consequential except for their influence on future transitions.

Some states are irreversible for all worker choices. Other "irreversibilities" may be reversible at a cost, as in the case of surgical operations that can return the injured worker to his former healthy condition.

Rather than pursue categorizations of this kind and analyses of different types of irreversibilities, let us determine first whether irreversibilities raise special analytic issues. Suppose that a new treatment mode has become available and that it offers a small probability of total recovery from permanent disability. The last row of matrix B given in equation 10 is now $(10^{-5}, 0, 0, 1 - 10^{-5})$ so that state 4 is no longer irreversible. For concreteness, let the interest rate be 8 percent and the payoff vector for the states be $(200, 100, 50, 0)$. The discounted expected value of starting in state 1 is now 1011.27, as compared with 1011.25 when state 4 was irreversible. Only a minor change in worker welfare is obtained by transforming an irreversible state to a reversible one that differs only slightly in its probabilistic structure.

Much of the analytic attention devoted to irreversibilities derives from using deterministic models in which altering the probability of an unfavorable outcome from zero to one causes a discontinuous drop in individual welfare. Use of the Markovian framework demonstrates that irreversibilities are not fundamentally different from other probabilistic structures and do not create special difficulties.

Reference to irreversibilities and closely related probabilistic structures nonetheless may be helpful in analyzing the long-term implications of job risks. This function is particularly important in discussing allocational mistakes. A worker might misassess the job risks, perceive irreversible situations as being reversible, or assume incorrectly that he can switch jobs with no long-term health effects once warning signs of his ailment become apparent. These misallocations have long-run impacts when irreversibilities are involved or when there are high probabilities of long-term losses. The notion of irreversibilities captures the permanency of the effects. However, it is the fact that irreversibilities are coupled with sizable losses in utility that make them important in analyzing individual welfare. A major cause of misallocations— imperfect worker information—will be discussed in Chapter 4. The analysis in that chapter will indicate that the presence of irreversible effects may complicate the worker's attempt to acquire information about job risks.

2.5. CONCLUSIONS

The static and dynamic models developed in this chapter generalize Smith's classic theory of compensating wage differentials to the probabilistic context. Workers will demand wage premiums for hazardous employment, assuming that they prefer being healthy to being injured. If workers are also risk-averse and if certain other mild restrictions are satisfied, the job risk they select will necessarily decrease with their wealth. If workers are permitted to buy insurance at actuarially fair rates, they will provide for a lower level of consumption in the ill health state. This result suggests that present levels of workmen's compensation are not necessarily inadequate. More ambiguous economic effects include the impact of taxes on optimal job risks and the relation of the optimal job risk in a static model to the optimal risk in an infinite time horizon situation. The next chapter considers a closely related analytic issue—the dependence of the optimal job risk on the worker's age.

3

LIFE CYCLE EFFECTS AND JOB RISKS

3.1 INTRODUCTION

Though the analysis of the preceding chapter did not neglect the dynamic implications of job hazards, variations in optimal job risks over one's lifetime were not considered. The reason for this omission lies with the simplifications built into the Markovian decision models. First, the key parameters of the worker's choice problem (that is, the probabilities and health state payoffs) were assumed to be time-invariant. Second, the assumption that the worker's time horizon was infinite simplified the analytics, but eliminated any time variation in the optimal job choice for different states. Each of these restrictions is relaxed in this chapter.

Section 3.2 retains the time-invariant problem structure, but imposes a finite time horizon on the analysis. The principal matter of interest is how a worker's attitude toward hazardous jobs will alter as he ages. Does the fact that an older worker has a shorter expected lifetime than a younger worker imply that he will be inclined to engage in more hazardous activities?

Section 3.3 delves into the area of varying probabilities of job hazards over time. This modification of the problem probably reflects typical rather than aberrant situations. The hazards posed by a particular job may vary with seasonal influences, the worker's experience on the job, or with more mundane factors such as the amount of sleep the worker got the preceding night. In which situations is it appropriate to employ the average transition probabilities over the period considered, and how is this average obtained?

Finally, Section 3.4 explores the influence of changing probabilities and preferences over a worker's lifetime on the choices he makes. The illustrative examples considered in the following sections will demonstrate that few unambiguous statements can be made about life cycle effects on job risks.

3.2 TIME HORIZON EFFECTS

The infinite time horizon models in the preceding chapter were instructive and realistic for workers optimizing over a very long period. However, as individuals age, their expected future lifetime becomes shorter. In such situations, it seems unrealistic to operate with a framework in which the time period is irrelevant for the worker's choice problem. The models in this section remedy this deficiency by imposing a finite lifetime on the worker. Other life cycle effects will not be considered until subsequent sections, so that the effect of the shortening time horizon will not be compounded with other influences associated with the aging process.

In some situations, there will be no temporal variation in the optimal strategy, as one job dominates the other irrespective of the time horizon. Throughout the remainder of this chapter, the discount factor b will be set at 0.9, where b is the reciprocal of 1 plus the interest rate. Suppose that a worker must commit himself to a particular job for all remaining periods. How is the appropriate commitment affected by the number of periods remaining?

Consider the two-state decision model in which the payoff vector $\mathbf{v}$ is given by

$$\mathbf{v} = \begin{bmatrix} 100 \\ 0 \end{bmatrix}$$

and is identical for each job. Suppose that job 1 is associated with transition matrix P, and job 2 is associated with transition matrix Q, where

$$P = \begin{bmatrix} .5 & .5 \\ 0 & 1 \end{bmatrix} \text{ and } Q = \begin{bmatrix} .4 & .6 \\ 0 & 1 \end{bmatrix}.$$

The worker starts in state 1. Job 1 offers a higher probability of remaining in the attractive state 1, while neither job offers any chance of emerging from the trapping state 2, which might be thought of as permanent disability. The optimal choice in this situation is clearcut.[1] Job 1 dominates job 2 for all time horizons, since it always offers a higher probability of being in the favorable state and a lower probability of being in the trapping unfavorable state.

1. One can solve the optimization recursively or by using z-transform analysis to obtain a closed-form expression giving the present value of the job as a function of the number of periods remaining. See Howard (1960) for a description of these techniques.

As the results of the preceding chapter might suggest, even within a 2×2 context there may be a reversal of job preferences for different time horizons. Suppose that the disability associated with job 2 is not permanent, but instead lasts for a single period. Transition matrix Q becomes

$$Q = \begin{bmatrix} .4 & .6 \\ 1 & 0 \end{bmatrix}.$$

Job 2 now offers a higher initial probability of entering state 2, but a much greater chance of returning to the healthy state 1. This latter advantage is so great that job 2 is preferred, provided that there are at least two remaining periods in the worker's choice problem.

It is this type of temporal variation that one might expect to be the norm in all situations in which there is no strict dominance of one job. As the worker ages, job risks that impinge on his future well-being do not produce as much of a long-term welfare loss as they did earlier. Consequently, a wage premium sufficient to make the hazardous job attractive in the short run will eventually produce a switching in the optimal risk incurred as the worker nears the end of his life.

As intuitively appealing as such a result might be, in general there actually may be multiple switches in the optimal job risk as the number of time periods remaining is varied. To see how reswitching of the optimal job commitment may occur as the time horizon is increased, consider a three-state choice model. The payoff vector is now given by

$$\mathbf{v} = \begin{bmatrix} 200 \\ 100 \\ 0 \end{bmatrix},$$

while the job's transition matrices are

$$P = \begin{bmatrix} .5 & .5 & 0 \\ .6 & 0 & .4 \\ 0 & 0 & 1 \end{bmatrix} \text{ and } Q = \begin{bmatrix} .52 & .48 & 0 \\ 0 & 1 & 0 \\ 0 & 0 & 1 \end{bmatrix}.$$

As before, the process begins in state 1. A permanent commitment to job 1 is preferred if the remaining number of periods is two or three. Otherwise job 2 is optimal.

Inspection of the transition matrices makes the reason for this reversal clear. Job 2 offers the initial advantage, since it provides a higher probability of remaining healthy in the immediate future. In the intermediate periods, job 1 is preferred, since job 2 offers no chance of exiting from state 2. In the long run, work at job 1 leads the worker to reside in the least desirable state, state 3, thus producing a reswitching in the optimal job commitment as the number of remaining periods is increased.

Similar ambiguity may result in a four-state model in which a worker is selecting the optimal job for a particular state. The worker is allowed to vary his job in each successive period. Let the payoff vector be

(1)
$$v = \begin{bmatrix} 200 \\ 100 \\ 50 \\ 0 \end{bmatrix},$$

and the transition matrices be given by

(2)
$$P = \begin{bmatrix} .5 & 0 & .5 & 0 \\ 0 & .9 & 0 & .1 \\ 0 & 0 & 1 & 0 \\ 0 & 0 & 0 & 1 \end{bmatrix} \text{ and } Q = \begin{bmatrix} 0 & 1 & 0 & 0 \\ 0 & .9 & 0 & .1 \\ 0 & 0 & 1 & 0 \\ 0 & 0 & 0 & 1 \end{bmatrix}.$$

For the worker entering in state 1, job 2 is the preferred job for that state provided that the number of remaining periods is not less than five or greater than nine. Otherwise job 1 is optimal. Job 1's inferiority in the intermediate periods derives from its high chance of entering the trapping state 3. Job 2 avoids this unfavorable outcome, but offers lower immediate payoffs and a greater chance of residing in the worst state 4 in the long run.

Those familiar with the widely accepted result that human capital investment declines with age might have expected a similar relationship between job hazards and worker age, such as an increase in desired job riskiness as the time horizon shortens.[2] The examples provided in this section demonstrate that the effect of aging per se on the optimal job choice may not be at all clear-cut. When a worker is confronting multiple hazards—not just one—reswitching the optimal job may be observed with increases in the time horizon. Somewhat paradoxically, a worker may prefer job lottery 1 to job lottery 2 when he is very young and very old, but not in the intervening years. Selection of more elaborate examples can produce even greater numbers of switches in the optimal job choice.

The examples provided suggest that when considering different hazardous jobs, it may be impossible to say that one job reflects a greater concern for the worker's future welfare than does another.[3] There may be no unambiguous ranking of jobs in terms of their influence on the worker's future well-being.

2. See Ben-Porath (1967) for an analysis of the relation of human capital investment to life cycle effects.

3. The reswitching of the optimal job hazard with increases in the time horizon is analytically related to the reswitching of optimal environmental policies discussed by Richard Zeckhauser and myself. There the reversal was obtained by increasing the interest rate in an infinite time horizon model. See Viscusi and Zeckhauser (1976).

3.3 TIME-VARYING PROBABILITIES

A. *Stochastic and Independent Changes.* Most job risks vary so frequently that the time-invariant structure may seem to be an unrealistic framework for analysis. This section considers random changes in the transition probabilities. A construction worker's accident risks may be affected by rain or by the amount of traffic he encounters on his way to work. A newly hired factory worker may face risks that vary daily and unpredictably as he is shifted from job to job depending on who is absent from the plant. In the extreme case, a worker might be confronted with continual fluctuations in the probabilities of job outcomes as his alertness or speed of operation vary. In situations such as these, is the worker correct in utilizing some average transition matrix for his choice problem?

To analyze this issue, consider the following valuation problem. Suppose that $\mathbf{u}(n)$ is the vector of present values of job payoffs for the worker when there are n periods remaining. In any period there is a probability s that the transition matrix will be P and a probability $1 - s$ that the matrix will be Q. The vector of discounted expected job rewards when there are $n + 1$ remaining periods consequently is given by

$$\mathbf{u}(n + 1) = s[P\mathbf{v} + bP\mathbf{u}(n)] + (1 - s)[Q\mathbf{v} + bQ\mathbf{u}(n)],$$

or

$$\mathbf{u}(n + 1) = [sP + (1 - s)Q][\mathbf{v} + b\mathbf{u}(n)],$$

which yields

$$\mathbf{u}(n + 1) = R[\mathbf{v} + b\mathbf{u}(n)],$$

where

$$R = sP + (1 - s)Q.$$

When fluctuations in job hazards are random, the transition matrix that is the simple weighted average of the alternative matrices yields correct results.

B. *Periodic Hazards.* Job hazards often vary systematically rather than randomly. Those who work outdoors, such as farmers and construction workers, may face job risks that vary seasonally. Changes in weather as well as changes in job operations may alter the probabilities of various outcomes. White-collar and other workers who might be unaffected by shifts in the weather could be incurring job risks that have other kinds of periodic variations. A tax accountant may run a greater risk of a heart attack near the mid-April peak season, while an assembly-line worker might have slower reflexes on Mondays.

Periodic job hazards can be analyzed by generalizing the problem structure. Suppose that the hazards in the first half of the year are described by the $n \times n$ matrix Q. The states are assumed to be identical for each, and the n-state payoff vector is $\mathbf{v}$. In solving job choice problems, one simply uses the $2n \times 2n$ transition matrix given by

$$\begin{bmatrix} 0 & P \\ Q & 0 \end{bmatrix},$$

where the $n \times n$ elements in the upper left and lower right corners are zeros. The payoff matrix is the $2n$-element column vector

$$\begin{bmatrix} \mathbf{v} \\ \mathbf{v} \end{bmatrix}.$$

This format can be generalized to analyze multiple periods, periods with different lengths, and instances in which transitions combine both periodic and random elements. However, the purpose of this section is not to scrutinize all of the possible intricacies that can be incorporated in the Markovian framework. The principal concern is whether, as in the case of random variations, a worker is correct in ignoring the periodic aspects of the structure by simply considering average transition probabilities.

Consider the following two-period example. Suppose that transition matrices P and Q are given by

$$P = \begin{bmatrix} 1 & 0 \\ 0 & 1 \end{bmatrix} \text{ and } Q = \begin{bmatrix} 0 & 1 \\ 1 & 0 \end{bmatrix}.$$

Also let b be the discount factor and the rewards vector $\mathbf{v}$ be

$$\mathbf{v} = \begin{bmatrix} 10 \\ 1 \end{bmatrix}.$$

The value of the job with two remaining periods is

$$\mathbf{u}(2) = \begin{bmatrix} 10 + b \\ 1 + 10b \end{bmatrix},$$

where the appropriate entry depends on the starting state.

Alternatively, suppose that the worker had employed the average transition matrix $0.5P + 0.5Q$, which is

$$\begin{bmatrix} .5 & ..5 \\ .5 & .5 \end{bmatrix}.$$

This approach would yield the result that

$$\mathbf{u}(2) = \begin{bmatrix} 5.5 + 5.5b \\ 5.5 + 5.5b \end{bmatrix}.$$

Clearly, when there is any discounting at a nonzero interest rate, it is incorrect to employ the average transition probabilities. Also, with a small number of periods, the average risk format gives incorrect results for odd numbers of transitions (except in degenerate cases when P and Q are identical).

However, this example might lead one to expect that in situations in which the number of transitions is large and they occur over a short enough period for discounting to be unimportant, use of average transition probabilities would be a correct procedure. In analyzing this possibility, let us simplify the analysis by considering only mono-desmic Markov processes, that is, those in which the limiting multistep transition matrix has identical rows.[4] This case should be particularly amenable to averaging techniques, since the long-run transition probabilities do not depend on the state in which the process originated.

Let P be the transition matrix for even-numbered transitions and Q be the transition matrix for odd-numbered transitions. Then the average transition matrix R is given by

$$R = 0.5P + 0.5Q.$$

The problem is to determine whether in the long run the average reward on transitions is identical using either R or P and Q on alternate trials.

In the case in which R is used, the average reward is $\bar{\pi}v$, where $\bar{\pi}$ is the limiting state probability vector for matrix R.[5] Let π^e be the limiting state probability vector for even-numbered transitions and π^o be its counterpart for odd-numbered transitions, where

$$\pi^e = \pi^e PQ,$$

(3)
$$\pi^o = \pi^e P,$$

and

$$\sum_{i=1}^{n} \pi_i^e = \sum_{i=1}^{n} \pi_i^o = 1.$$

The average reward on odd and even transitions is obtained by using the average limiting state probability vector—$0.5\pi^e + 0.5\pi^o$. The analytic question is whether this average is identical to the limiting state probability vector obtained when P and Q are averaged beforehand.

While one can manipulate a general model to demonstrate that these expressions are not equivalent (although they are quite similar), a numerical example is sufficient to indicate the difference. Let

$$P = \begin{bmatrix} .01 & .99 \\ .01 & .99 \end{bmatrix} \text{ and } Q = \begin{bmatrix} .4 & .6 \\ .8 & .2 \end{bmatrix}.$$

4. A sufficient condition for a transition matrix to be monodesmic is that it is possible to make transitions from any one state to any other state.

5. In other words, for large n, each row of $(R)^n$ is equal to the row vector π.

Multiplying these expressions yields

$$PQ = \begin{bmatrix} .796 & .204 \\ .796 & .204 \end{bmatrix}.$$

The value of π^e clearly is

$$\pi^e = [.796 \quad .204].$$

From equation (3), the value of π^o for odd transitions is

$$\pi^o = [.796 \quad .204] \begin{bmatrix} .01 & .99 \\ .01 & .99 \end{bmatrix} = [.01 \quad .99].$$

Consequently the vector used to calculate average rewards is

(4) $$0.5\pi^e + 0.5\pi^o = [.403 \quad .597].$$

Consider the average transition matrix R, which is given by

$$R = \begin{bmatrix} .205 & .795 \\ .405 & .595 \end{bmatrix}.$$

By inspection, one can determine that

(5) $$\bar{\pi} = [.338 \quad .663].[6]$$

Since equations (4) and (5) are numerically different, it is clear that periodic job hazards cannot be equated with the weighted average of the transition probabilities.

The initial examples in this section demonstrated that it is not correct to utilize the average probabilities for a period structure when the number of transitions is small or discounting is important. Now it is clear that even with a large number of undiscounted transitions, averaging of this type is incorrect. This result for job hazards is particularly surprising, since such a procedure would be correct if one were dealing with monetary payoffs.

Consider a man who is sufficiently wealthy to remain solvent over a large number of bets. There are two types of lotteries—lottery A, which involves the toss of a fair coin, and lottery B, which involves the roll of a die. For both lotteries the stakes and odds are fixed for all gambles. The expected payoff for a long series of bets is identical whether the lotteries are varied periodically on odd and even transitions or whether there is a 50 percent chance of selecting each lottery on every round of play.

The aberrant nature of job hazards can be traced to the irreversibilities involved. The outcome of past job lotteries has a permanent effect on worker welfare. This effect must be probabilistic, as the mono-

6. For a 2×2 monodesmic matrix A with elements a_{ij}, π equals

$$(a_{12} + a_{21})^{-1}[a_{21} \ a_{12}].$$

desmic systems involve no Markov chains other than the entire transition matrix. The irreversible nature of job hazards not only raises inter-
pretive issues, such as those discussed in the preceding chapter, but
may also undermine the appropriateness of the optimization techniques employed.

3.4 CHANGES IN PROBABILITIES AND PREFERENCES WITH AGE

Another source of variation in the worker's choice problem is that
the job risks and his attitudes toward them may change with age or
work experience. Probabilities of accidents on the job may increase to
the extent that a worker's muscle strength and alertness decline as he
grows older. To see how the Markovian framework can be altered to
include such effects, let us return to the four-state decision problem
summarized in equations (1) and (2). Suppose that recovery from an
unfavorable job 2 outcome now becomes less likely as the worker
grows older. This phenomenon is characteristic of professional football
players, who typically require more days to recuperate from the previous week's aches and bruises as they grow older. Let

$$Q = \begin{bmatrix} 0 & 1 & 0 & 0 \\ 0 & .8 + .01n & 0 & .2 - .01n \\ 0 & 0 & 1 & 0 \\ 0 & 0 & 0 & 1 \end{bmatrix},$$

where n is the number of periods remaining and n is less than 21. The
worker now selects job 2 only when there are five periods remaining,
whereas previously job 2 was optimal when there were five to nine
periods left. Job 2's transition matrix is less attractive than before except when there are 11 or more periods left, but in that range the
long-term risk of residing in state 4 is sufficiently great to undermine
the job's attractiveness.

Changes in worker preferences also can be included in the framework. Suppose that the transition matrices are given by equation (2),
but that state 4 decreases in value as one ages, perhaps because increased family obligations make death or permanent disability less
attractive. Let the payoff vector be

$$\mathbf{v} = \begin{bmatrix} 200 \\ 100 \\ 50 \\ -10 + n \end{bmatrix},$$

where n is the number of remaining periods. Whereas formerly, job 2
was optimal for five to nine remaining periods, it is now superior to job
1 so long as there are at least five periods left.

Using modifications such as those listed above, one can incorporate other changes in worker preferences and hazards into the analysis. In terms of systematic patterns, it seems reasonable that unfavorable job effects should become less attractive as workers grow older. Increased wealth and increased family obligations would affect preferences in this manner. Moreover, bodily deterioration with time would seem to reinforce the age-linked tendency toward safer employment.

However, such speculations are unlikely to suggest systematic life cycle variations in job hazards. Particularly when one is dealing with multiple risks, determining the direction of various effects—much less their magnitude—will remain beyond the capabilities of conceptual analysis. For example, suppose for the choice problem described in equations (1) and (2) that all states other than state 1 (the healthy state) decreased in value as the worker aged. Without knowing more about the magnitude of the variations, it is impossible to ascertain whether worker job choices will be altered.

More generally, even if the ordinal rankings of job outcomes are known, it will be the rare case in which jobs with multiple outcomes can be labeled more or less risky than one another even with a fixed time horizon. Once time horizon effects are included, reswitching of job choices over the life cycle becomes possible, further invalidating attempts to label one job as being more risky than another.

3.5 CONCLUSIONS

This chapter has two principal ramifications. First, the complexity of job hazards suggests that one should avoid statements about the relative riskiness of various occupations since such determinations require more detailed knowledge of the worker choice problem than any analyst is likely to possess. Second, the case for empirical determination of life cycle effects on job risks is especially strong since theoretical investigations are of little assistance in suggesting systematic directions of influence.

4

ADAPTIVE MODELS OF JOB CHOICE

4.1 INTRODUCTION

Workers seldom have perfect information about the health and safety implications of their jobs. For many hazards, the true probabilities of being killed or injured are not known by anyone. Owing to the retarded state of occupational medicine, even the underlying medical ramifications of different exposures to hazards of the workplace such as radiation, noise, high temperatures, and chemical vapors are little understood.[1] This uncertainty is compounded by uncertainty with regard to the characteristics of the work situation, for example, the concentration of asbestos fibers in the air.

The past experiences of other workers are likely to be of little assistance in eliminating this uncertainty. Unlike wage rates, which can be compared in relative and absolute terms, there is no single recognized metric for measuring health and safety hazards. Differences in individual preferences for varying risks limit the usefulness of any summary index. More fundamentally, the job outcome information that would be used to evaluate past injury or illness frequencies is inadequate, since many ailments are difficult to monitor or occur so infrequently that only the weakest of inferences can be drawn from the small samples available. These shortcomings are particularly acute for hazards that do not have immediate and recognizable effects. Finally, any assessment of the probabilities of job outcomes must take individual differences into account.

---

1. Indeed, it may not even be feasible for the worker to acquire perfect job risk information at any cost.

The imperfect nature of worker information implies that workers will base their job choices on their subjective assessments of the risk rather than on a definitive objective index. If the worker has no opportunity for information acquisition and updating of these probability assessments, the subjective probability assessments can be analyzed in the same manner as objective measures of the risk of the worker's job, so that the results in the preceding chapters would be equally applicable to both kinds of probabilities. However, if the worker's probabilistic judgments are modified by his on-the-job experiences, his subsequent employment decisions may be altered after he revises the assessed probabilities of different outcomes.

The worker's lifetime job choices in situations in which there is the potential for learning and sequential decision will be treated as the resolution of an adaptive control process. The outcomes of past job choices become a permanent part of the history of the worker's problem. They influence future employment decisions by altering one's probabilistic judgments and, in some instances, by influencing one's productivity.

The two major ingredients of the adaptive process are the presence of worker uncertainty about job characteristics and the generation of information during on-the-job experience that enable him to revise the initial assessments. Most pecuniary reward uncertainties fulfill both of these requirements. The assessed likelihood of being promoted, receiving an increase in pay, or earning a high wage under a piecework system is likely to be influenced by one's experience, apart from any effect on one's productivity that such experience may have.

Nonpecuniary rewards tend to involve more initial worker uncertainty than do monetary payoffs. A factory worker may have a fairly good idea of his immediate wage prospects, but have only a vague notion of whether he will get along with his coworkers, find the job too wearisome, or simply not enjoy the repetitive nature of assembly line work. Possible sources of information include personal experiences, observation of the job outcomes of other workers, and observation of various job characteristics such as the noise level, presence of noxious fumes, and the speed of operation.

The adaptive models used to structure the worker choice problem can be viewed as offshoots of the two-armed bandit (2AB) model, which is named after the gambler's choice problem involving the optimal sequential play of slot machines. A modified version of the analysis of this classic problem is ideally suited for analyzing the worker's sequential choice among potentially hazardous jobs. Although the exposition concentrates mainly on health and safety hazards, most of the results are applicable to monetary reward uncertainties and, more generally, to uncertainty with respect to pecuniary and nonpecuniary reward bundles. This framework provides not only a methodology for analyzing conditions under which workers will accept jobs with uncertain implications, but also provides an adaptive theory of worker quit behavior.

Although the role of job shopping and worker learning in affecting worker turnover has not gone unnoticed by labor economists, the economic implications of this learning process have never been analyzed.[2] Moreover, as I will indicate in Chapter 13, all prior conceptual analyses of worker quitting have focused on impediments to quit behavior, such as higher wages, but have never articulated a model that generates worker quits through adaptive behavior.

Section 4.2 presents the fundamental aspects of the 2AB model and illustrates its applicability to a variety of economic issues. Although it will be shown that hazardous jobs command wage premiums, the mean value of the probability assessment is not sufficient to determine a job's relative attractiveness. The degree of worker uncertainty will have an important effect both on his reservation wage rate for accepting a job initially and the likelihood that he will quit.

Section 4.3 generalizes the model to analyze irreversible consequences, such as permanent disability and death. Although adaptive behavior through job changing may not be possible in these instances, the precision of workers' probabilistic beliefs nevertheless has fundamental and perhaps surprising implications for worker behavior. Job changing also may be impeded by various transactions costs, such as the foregoing of pension benefits and seniority rights, which I consider in Section 4.4.

An important economic issue is whether workers should acquire information prior to work on the job or whether they should rely solely on their on-the-job experiences. This trade-off problem is the subject of Section 4.5. An alternative form of worker learning on the job, other than direct job experiences, is the observation of job outcomes for other workers and of characteristics of the workplace that can be used in revising one's probabilistic beliefs. The possibility of indirect experience of this type is analyzed using a three-armed bandit (3AB) model in Section 4.6. In Section 4.7, I relax the assumption that the worker faces a discrete set of job alternatives, by considering a multi-armed bandit problem in which there is a continuous range of prior assessments associated with available jobs. The implications of the adaptive

2. For example, Reynolds (1951) briefly notes that worker quitting is related to a job-shopping process. Mortensen (1975) analyzed the macroeconomic implications of learning-induced quits, but did not investigate the underlying individual choice process generating this behavior, since he was concerned with different types of issues than those considered here.

framework for the efficiency of market outcomes and for the economic analysis of employment patterns over one's lifetime are considered in Sections 4.8 and 4.9. Appendix D generalizes many of the principal results of this chapter to situations in which workers infer that higher-paying jobs are more hazardous and to analytic contexts in which worker preferences are characterized by state-dependent utility functions such as those employed in previous chapters.

4.2 The Two-Armed Bandit Model

A. Introduction to the 2AB Model. The worker's multi-period employment choice problem bears a strong analytic resemblance to the classic two-armed bandit (2AB) problem, which was first formulated by Thompson (1933) in an analysis of the optimal testing strategy for drugs. Bellman (1956) derived the dynamic programming solution to this general class of problems and analyzed the solution's properties.[3] Whereas the conventional 2AB model is concerned with the optimal sequence of plays for two slot machines, the models developed here focus on sequential choices between two job alternatives and the level of wages required to lead workers to select particular jobs at different points in time. The analytic structure of the variant of the 2AB model to be considered is as follows.

Suppose there are two machines, I and II. If machine I is played, there is a probability p of success and a probability $1 - p$ of failure. If II is played, the probability of success is q, while the probability of failure is $1 - q$. The value of q is known and constant for all trials, while the value of p is uncertain. The machines are independent. Successive trials on each machine also are independent, identically distributed, and invariant over time.[4] I assume that the outcome of each trial is known with certainty by the individual. The objective is to select the machine in each period that will maximize one's discounted expected

---

3. The rather voluminous 2AB literature includes contributions by Thompson (1933), Bellman (1956, 1961), Yakowitz (1969), DeGroot (1970), and Berry (1972)—all of which are principally of mathematical interest. An interesting economic application of the 2AB methodology to pricing can be found in Rothschild (1974). None of the structural modifications of the 2AB model that I present below have been discussed in the literature. The principal mathematical features are unaffected by the variations I consider, since they do not alter the problem's Markovian nature, that is, the payoff function is separable and transitions at time k depend only on the present state of the system and the individual decision.

4. Thus, I am ruling out the types of temporal interdependencies that produce streaks of successes or failures, deterioration over time, or worker learning about how to alter the probabilities of adverse outcomes.

rewards.[5] This objective function is separable; preferences are independent of consequences on other dates.

The employment choice problem corresponding to this 2AB format is that a worker must choose between two jobs in each period of his life. Uncertain machine I corresponds to a potentially hazardous job whose properties are unknown, while machine II corresponds to a job with known properties. The restriction to a single job in each period reflects the corner solution nature of most employment decisions. In Sections 4.6 and 4.7 the analysis is generalized to consider the choice of a job from groups consisting of more than two alternatives.

The payoff for a successful trial of the machine can be thought of as the reward when the worker remains uninjured, while the payoff for a failure corresponds to an unfavorable job outcome, such as temporary disability or loss of income due to illness. Work on job II only yields a possible payoff, while work on job I produces a possible payoff as well as information about the properties of that job. The conventional 2AB assumption that a success on either machine is valued equally is relaxed in order to accommodate the possibility of compensating wage differentials.

The learning in this model occurs only through the observation of the outcomes on the unknown job. This assumption makes the mathematics less unwieldy, but it is not essential. More complicated models, such as those developed in Section 4.6, could include worker observation of other forms of information regarding the job's characteristics. For the basic 2AB model, the information pattern for job I consists of the number of successes and failures on that job. The order of the payoffs does not matter.

For concreteness, subsequent discussions will concentrate on the updating of prior assessments that belong to the Beta family of distributions.[6] As Pratt, Raiffa, and Schlaifer (1965) have emphasized, this distribution is ideally suited for analyses of Bernoulli-type processes such as this. By adjusting the parameters of the distribution, one can obtain a wide variety of shapes. If an individual starts with a prior given by the Beta function $B(d, e)$ where d and e are the two parameters of

5. While the 2AB structure makes discussion in terms of monetary rewards convenient, all payoffs need not be financial. What I do assume is that a multiattribute utility function converts the evaluation of alternative states into a single utility index, for which the consumer maximizes the discounted expected value. While this approach does not require risk neutrality, it does make strong separability assumptions. Anticipatory effects and other exceptions to separability are the focus of Chapter 5.

6. A detailed description of the distribution and formal proofs of its properties can be found in Chapters 9 and 11 of Pratt, Raiffa, and Schlaifer (1965) and in Chapters 7 and 9 of Raiffa and Schlaifer (1961). The latter volume provides a detailed discussion of the superiority of Beta distributions to normal approximations in analyzing Bernoulli-type trials.

the distribution, the expected probability of success on the first trial is

$$E_B(\bar{p}|d, e) = d/e.$$

After a history of m successes and n failures, the revised probability of success on job I is determined using $B(d + m, e + m + n)$. Thus, m and n are sufficient statistics. The probability of success on I posterior to observing (m, n) is given by

(1) $p(m, n) = E_B(\bar{p}|d + m, e + m + n) = (d + m)/(e + m + n).$

B. *Illustrative Examples.* The economic properties of worker choices can be illustrated using a simple ten-period example. In finding the solution to the 2AB problem, one uses the procedure for updating probabilities given by equation (1) in conjunction with conventional dynamic programming techniques. Before writing down the form of the solution, we need some additional notation. Let y be the number of successes thus far on job I. The periods for the problem will be indexed by k, where $k = 1, \ldots, 10$. The reward function is given by v. To facilitate the subsequent analysis, the following specific payoff function will be employed. A failure on either machine is valued as zero, while a success on job II receives a payoff of 1. These two payoff levels in effect determine the scale in which other rewards are evaluated since von Neumann–Morgenstern utility functions are unaffected by a positive linear transformation. A success on unknown job I receives a payoff w, which can be thought of as the wage rate for that job, where the metric is not necessarily dollars but rather a scale defined with respect to the payoffs that were arbitrarily assigned values of one and zero. The interest rate r produces a discount factor b equal to $1/(1 + r)$. Finally, let a_k be the optimal job choice in period k.

An important result that facilitates the solution of the problem is that once the individual switches to the known job, he will never switch back.[7] The recursive form of the solution is given by

(2) $E[v(m, n, y, k, a_k)]$

$$= \max \begin{cases} p(m, n)\{w + bE[v(m + 1, n, y, k + 1, a_{k+1})]\} \\ \quad + b[1 - p(m, n)]E[v(m, n + 1, y, k + 1, a_{k+1})] \\ \quad = G(m, n, y, k, \text{I}), \\ q\{1 + bE[v(m, n, y + 1, k + 1, a_{k+1})]\} \\ \quad + b(1 - q)E[v(m, n, y, k + 1, a_{k+1})] \\ = q \sum_{i=k}^{10} b^{i-k} = G(m, n, y, k, \text{II}), \end{cases}$$

7. See Yakowitz (1969) for a formal derivation. This result means that the problem is one of optimal stopping—when, if ever, to switch to job II. The three-armed bandit discussed in Section 4.6 is not of this type.

where p is revised according to equation (1) if the Beta distribution is used. As equation (2) indicates, the present state of the system can be described by four state variables—m, n, y, and k. Transitions depend only on the state of the system and the decision selected.

The recursive solution given by equation (2) satisfies and can be derived from Bellman's Principle of Optimality. While the dynamic programming produces a unique maximum value, the solution need not be unique since there may be more than one optimal strategy.

More detailed specification of the problem is helpful in illustrating the properties of the solution. Suppose the prior distribution for unknown job I is given by the uniform distribution—the Beta function $B(1, 2)$, which imples that $p(0, 0)$ equals 0.5.[8] The probability of success on the known job II is 0.8. If the value of r is 0.4, how high must the wage w be in order for the individual to accept job I in the first period?[9] The minimum value of w that will compensate the worker for the greater chance of adverse consequences on job I is 1.33.[10] As in static models of job choice, there is a positive wage differential for the more hazardous job.

The problem's solution is in the form of a sequential strategy. The individual starts on job I, but will switch to job II once his assessment of job I's characteristics becomes too unfavorable, given the level of wage compensation. The worst histories (those giving rise to the lowest values of $p[m, n]$ consistent with the individual remaining on job I) are given by the second column of Table 4.1. For the wage 1.33, which was just sufficient to make the worker start on job I, the outcomes on I must be very successful for the individual to remain on the job. The greatest instability in the worker's attachment to job I is in the early periods, when a single adverse outcome will be sufficient to lead him to switch to job II.

Employers wishing to decrease turnover in such situations could increase the wage. If w equals 2, there is considerably less sensitivity to adverse outcomes on job I, as Table 4.1 indicates. The worker's discounted expected reward now equals 2.54. Although job I is more attractive than job II in all but the most unfavorable experience situations, use of a sequential strategy enables the worker to reap expected rewards more than 5 percent higher then he can obtain with the best pure strategy (job I), which offers a discounted expected reward of 2.41. Far less attractive is the randomized strategy, in which the

8. Appendix C discusses the sensitivity of the results to the worker's prior assessments.

9. A value of 0.4 for r for periods of approximately five years is equivalent to 7 percent compounded annually.

10. The discounted expected reward for the ten-year period problem is 1.94. This and all subsequent numerical values are discounted to period zero. I assume a one-period lag before any rewards are received.

Table 4.1. Worst Histories Consistent with Choice of Job I

Period	w = 1.33 (m, n)	w = 2 (m, n)
10	6, 3	4, 5
9	5, 3	3, 5
8	5, 2	3, 4
7	4, 2	2, 4
6	3, 2	2, 3
5	3, 1	2, 2
4	2, 1	1, 2
3	2, 0	1, 1
2	1, 0	0, 1
1	0, 0	0, 0

worker in effect flips a fair coin in each period in order to select his job. This option's discounted expected payoff totals only 2.17.

If the problem is modified by raising the probability q for job II, the wage needed to get the worker to accept a job in period I increases. Similarly, a decrease in q reduces the required value of w. Figure 4.1 illustrates the linear variation of w with q for two different interest rates, 0.4 and zero. This schedule shifts counterclockwise as r is increased.

As the diagram suggests, when the wages for successful outcomes on the two jobs are equal, the worker prefers the uncertain job I even in some instances in which $p(0, 0)$ is less than q. He must be paid a compensating wage premium to accept job II even though it offers a higher initial probability of success. The reason for this result is that there is the possibility that his experience on job I will be quite favorable and, if it is not, he can switch to job II in costless fashion. As the analysis throughout the rest of this chapter will indicate, this finding can be generalized beyond the confines of this numerical example. Workers faced with a sequence of job risk lotteries will prefer uncertain jobs to positions whose implications are known with precision.

C. The Two-Period Case. The implications of this numerical example can be formalized using a simple two-period model. Job I is characterized by the prior $B(d, e)$, while the probability of a successful outcome on job II is q. The payoff for a success is w for job I and 1 for job II. A key analytic question is how the level of wages required to attract the worker to job I is affected by the adaptive structure of the problem.

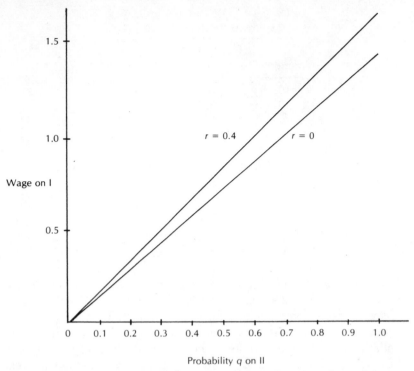

Figure 4.1 Wage Needed to Start on I as a Function of q and r

Since the worker will never leave job II after beginning work at that position, the discounted expected value of starting on job II is

$$G(0, 0, 0, 0, II) = [q(1)] + [q(b)],$$

where the first bracketed term is the expected initial period payoff and the second term is the discounted expected payoff in the second period. The discounted expected rewards from starting work on uncertain job I are given by

(3) $G(0, 0, 0, 0, I) = [w(d/e)] + (d/e)[(d + 1)/(e + 1)]bw$
$\qquad\qquad\qquad + b[1 - (d/e)]\max[wd/(e + 1), q(1)],$

where the first term is the expected first period reward, the second term is the discounted expected reward in period 2 after a success in period 1, and the third term is the discounted expected payoff after an initial period failure. The job choice in period 2 cannot be ascertained in general. However, the matter of concern here is the economic determinants of the minimal wage that will lead the worker to accept job I in period 1. It will be shown below that for that wage rate the worker will always switch to job II after an adverse outcome, so that the value of job I simplifies to

$$w(d/e)\{1 + [(d + 1)/(e + 1)]b\} + b[1 - (d/e)]q = q + qb.$$

The minimal wage that will lead the worker to accept job I in the initial period must be sufficient to make the worker indifferent between the two jobs or

$$w(d/e)\{1 + [(d + 1)/(e + 1)]b\} + b[1 - (d/e)]q = q + qb$$

Solving for w, this condition is that

$$(4) \quad w = \frac{q + qb - [1 - (d/e)]qb}{\{(d/e) + (d/e)[(d + 1)/(e + 1)]b\}}$$

$$= \frac{q[1 + (d/e)b]}{\{(d/e) + (d/e)[(d + 1)/(e + 1)]b\}}.$$

As indicated by the last term in equation (3), the worker will quit his job after an unfavorable outcome unless

$$[d/(e + 1)]w \ge q,$$

or

$$(5) \qquad\qquad w \ge q(e + 1)/d.$$

This wage rate exceeds the minimal wage to attract the worker to the job initially. In particular, it is always the case that the term on the right side of equation (5) is greater than the minimal w defined by equation (4), or

$$q(e + 1)/d > \frac{q[1 + (d/e)b]}{(d/e)\{1 + [(d + 1)/(e + 1)]b\}},$$

which after some simplification reduces to the requirement that

$$1 + b > 0,$$

which must necessarily be the case, since b is always positive for finite, nonnegative interest rates. The initial reservation wage rate is never sufficient to prevent worker turnover after an unfavorable job experience.

The properties of the reservation wage defined by equation (4) are similar to those described earlier within the context of the ten-period example. As was illustrated in Figure 4.1, the wage rate is a positive linear function of the probability of success q on job II, since

$$\partial w/\partial q = \frac{1 + (d/e)b}{(d/e) + (d/e)[(d + 1)/(e + 1)]b} > 0.$$

The positive relationship between the compensating wage differential and the attractiveness of alternative jobs is not altered by the adaptive structure of the problem.

The main addition to conventional analyses is in the roles played by the interest rate and by the uncertainty of workers' initial judgments. If equation (4) is differentiated with respect to the discount factor b,

$$\frac{\partial w}{\partial b} = \frac{\begin{array}{l}(d/e)q\{(d/e) + (d/e)[(d + 1)(e + 1)]b\}\\ - (dq/e)\{[(d + 1)/(e + 1)] + (d/e)[(d + 1)/(e + 1)]b\}\end{array}}{\{(d/e) + (d/e)[(d + 1)/(e + 1)]b\}^2} < 0$$

Since b equals $(1 + r)^{-1}$, this result implies that uncertain job I becomes more attractive as one's future orientation increases, that is, as r decreases. The lower compensating wage differential that is required reflects the fact that the potential gains from experimentation with job I are positive and necessarily deferred.

The most important implication of equation 4 is that the wage required on job I decreases as the worker's uncertainty about the job increases, that is, as d and e decrease for any given ratio of d/e. The influence of the precision of workers' prior assessments is through the $(d + 1)/(e + 1)$ term in the denominator. This result can be seen more clearly if job I and job II offer the same initial expected probability of success. If d/e equals q, equation (4) reduces to

$$w = \frac{[1 + (d/e)b]}{\{1 + [(d + 1)/(e + 1)]b\}} < 1.$$

Even though the jobs are equally attractive in the initial period, the worker is willing to accept a lower wage for job I because it offers the chance of greater expected rewards in period 2 if the period 1 outcome is successful, and it offers equal expected period 2 rewards after an unsuccessful outcome, since he can switch back to job I. An increase in the worker's uncertainty implies that he will accept a lower wage since the effect of information on the worker's probability assessment is greater for loose priors. The joint influence of on-the-job learning and the potential for adaptive behavior will lead workers to prefer jobs associated with imprecise probabilistic judgments.

Subsequent sections of this chapter will introduce additional complications that capture some of the pertinent features of the employment context. However, the most salient economic and mathematical properties will not be affected by these modifications. Lifetime job choice will continue to be viewed as an adaptive process in which past job experiences influence current job choices, and in which workers will prefer jobs whose implications are not fully understood.

If a worker had perfect information he would never switch jobs; he would always choose the job with the highest probability of success. Whenever a worker switches jobs, he must be doing worse than in the perfect information case.[11] There is an irretrievable loss incurred during the adaptation process. Yet, the optimal strategy is not a pure strategy or a randomized mix of pure strategies, but a sequential strategy that exploits the information generated by one's employment experience.

The job outcome at each moment is given by a probability distribution, not a number. Similarly, the discounted value of one's lifetime employment is a random variable. Workers are never perfectly informed. Even if workers with identical priors started on the same uncertain job I, their employment histories might vary if the outcomes of the job reward lotteries differed. The failure of workers' probability assessments to correspond to the true probabilities would be even greater if I had incorporated into the model the disruptive influences of changes in technology and operating procedures.

A particularly important result is that the minimum wage employers must pay to attract workers to jobs with identical stochastic properties may not be identical.[12] There is no reason why the market equilibrium must converge on a single wage, since differences in prior judgments and on-the-job experience may result in different required wages for each job. The employer who is forced to pay a higher wage for the equivalent job may be unable to alter a worker's judgments since he too may be uncertain about the job's characteristics and may be unable (or unwilling to incur the cost) to convey information that might alter the worker's assessments. In a world of uncertainty, the wage for jobs of equal underlying attractiveness may be characterized by a wage distribution rather than a unique wage.

These nonuniqueness problems are likely to be created more by nonpecuniary hazards than by income uncertainties. As I have already indicated, one's prior assessments of wage rewards tend to be sharper, since wage measurements are easy to make using a single metric that provides a comparable basis of evaluation for workers with diverse preferences. Even when the future income stream is fairly uncertain, the initial salary is usually known.

Nonpecuniary job aspects typically cannot be evaluated precisely until one is assigned to a job and can observe the job characteristics through experience. This learning process is complicated by the fact that experiencing the job outcome may provide the worker with information, but there may be little opportunity for adaptive behavior when

11. I am excluding, of course, the possibility of equally attractive jobs.
12. This result is similar to that produced by Rothschild (1974) for the pricing context.

the adverse outcome is an irreversible consequence such as death—a problem I will examine in the next section.

4.3 IRREVERSIBLE CONSEQUENCES: PERMANENT DISABILITY AND DEATH

Health and safety hazards entail risks that may influence one's future health and productivity. In many instances, adverse consequences are irreversible. The loss of a limb, the onset of liver cancer, and death are a few such irreversible effects. This section will attempt to incorporate such irreversibilities in the 2AB framework.

A. Partial Disability Suppose the outcomes on job II have no permanent physical effects, as in the case of lotteries on income, whereas unfavorable outcomes on the uncertain job I result in partial disability. If each failure on job I results in 10 percent disability, the fraction of the individual's remaining productivity after n failures is given by

$$h(n) = 1 - 0.1n.$$

For simplicity, assume that productivity and wages are decreased uniformly by $1 - h(n)$ for all jobs.

The recursive solution to the ten-period optimization problem now becomes

$E[v(m, n, y, k, a_k)]$

$$= \max \begin{cases} p(m, n)\{wh(n) + bE[v(m + 1, n, y, k + 1, a_{k+1})]\} \\ \quad + b[1 - p(m, n)]E[v(m, n + 1, y, k + 1, a_{k+1})] \\ \quad = H(m, n, y, k, I), \\ q\{h(n) + bE[v(m, n, y + 1, k + 1, a_{k+1})]\} \\ \quad + b(1 - q)E[v(m, n, y, k + 1, a_{k+1})] \\ = qh(n) \sum_{i=k}^{10} b^{i-k} = H(m, n, y, k, II). \end{cases}$$

For the parameters of the 2AB paradigm (r equals 0.4, p is given by $B(1, 2)$, and q equals 0.8), the minimum wage needed to get the worker to accept job I in the initial period increases to 1.45 from its former value of 1.33. The compensating wage differential must be larger when job hazards involve permanent decreases in welare.

B. Death and Other Outcomes that Terminate Employment. The risks of death and permanent disability alter the structure of the adaptive choice model, since the worker's employment at the enterprise does not continue after an unfavorable outcome. Any informational content of such experiences is of no use to the worker if his subsequent decisions do not include the possibility of work at that firm. In the case of death, the worker's decision problem is terminated after an unfavorable outcome. Similarly, if job injuries compel the worker to leave his former place of employment, this modification in the problem would seem to undermine the preference of workers for uncertain positions, since any adverse information obtained cannot influence any decision over which the worker has discretion, and any favorable information cannot alter his initial decision to have accepted the job.

I will treat death as a termination of the employment process, that is, a payoff of zero in the period of death and all subsequent periods. In utilizing this format, I am not ignoring the pain and nonmonetary consequences associated with an unsuccessful outcome—death. Rather, the payoff for death, which is zero, and the payoff for a successful outcome on job II in effect define the metric in which the value of the wage rate w for job I is given. If an unfavorable outcome on either job results in death, the recursive solution is given by equation (2), with the added condition that

$$(7) \qquad E\{v(m, n, y, k, a_k\} = 0$$

if

$$m + y < k.$$

Consider the implication of death risks within the context of the ten-period model in Section 4.2. Suppose that w equals 1, r equals 0.4, and q is 0.8. What is the optimal strategy for this employment situation in which both jobs offer the same payoff structure? Should the worker opt for the job with known probability 0.8 even though $p(0, 0)$ may be slightly higher? Since an optimal policy would never require that one switch jobs, one's intuition might suggest that a myopic policy is optimal, that is, pick the job with the highest probability of success in the initial period.[13] For concreteness, suppose that the prior distribution of p is given by $B(d, 2)$. What is the minimum value of $p(0, 0)$ or $d/2$ that is sufficient to get the worker to choose uncertain job I? For the parameters of the problem, this value is 0.73. Thus, the uncertain job is preferred even though it offers a lower initial probability of success.

The economic influences responsible for this result can be investigated utilizing a variant of the two-period model in Section 4.2. Let the assessed probability of a successful outcome (life) be given by $B(d, e)$ for job I and q for job II, while the reward for a successful outcome on job I is w, as before.

---

13. Indeed, this strategy is optimal if there is no switching of jobs and if the unfavorable outcome pays zero but does not result in death.

Using equation (2) coupled with the condition imposed by equation (7) implies that the discounted expected value of job II is

$$G(0, 0, 0, 0, II) = q + q^2b,$$

while the comparable value for job I is

$$G(0, 0, 0, 0, I) = w(d/e) + wb(d/e)(d + 1)/(e + 1).$$

The worker is indifferent between the two jobs when $G(0, 0, 0, 0, I)$ equals $G(0, 0, 0, 0, II)$, or when

(8) $$w = \frac{q + q^2b}{(d/e) + (d/e)[(d + 1)/(e + 1)]b}.$$

The properties of the required wage in the sequential life-and-death lotteries case are somewhat different from the work-injury model presented earlier.

Whereas the required value of w formerly was a linear function of q, the incremental change in the wage rate following an increase in q is now given by

$$\partial w/\partial q = \frac{1 + 2qb}{(d/e) + (bd/e)[(d + 1)/(e + 1)]} > 0.$$

Although the sign of $\partial w/\partial q$ is unchanged, the required wage rate in the death risk model rises at an increasing rate with the probability of a successful outcome on job II. In similar fashion, one can show that the value of $\partial w/\partial d$ is negative and $\partial w/\partial e$ is positive. Parameter changes that alter the probability of success on job I have the expected effect.[14]

The role of one's temporal orientation differs from the job injury results. Partially differentiating equation (8) with respect to b implies that

$$\frac{\partial w}{\partial b} = \frac{q^2[(d/e) + (bd/e)(d + 1)/(e + 1)] - (q + q^2b)(d/e)(d + 1)/(e + 1)}{[(d/e) + (bd/e)(d + 1)/(e + 1)]^2}$$

$$= \frac{(qd/e)\{q - [(d + 1)/(e + 1)]\}}{[(d/e) + (bd/e)(d + 1)/(e + 1)]^2}.$$

Increasing the value of b, which is the weight placed on period 2 payoffs, raises the wage level required for job I if q exceeds the updated probability of success on job I, and conversely. Unlike the work injury case, there is no opportunity for job changing after an adverse outcome, so that the gains from experimentation and adaptive response do not enter. The influence of changes in b on the required wage level depends on which job offers the greater chance of avoiding an adverse outcome in period 2.

14. The increase in the value e is undesirable, not only because it lowers the mean value of the prior, but also because it increases its sharpness.

The final and most important issue pertains to the effect of worker uncertainty on the worker's employment decisions. Even though there is no opportunity for adaptive behavior after an unfavorable outcome, the worker is not indifferent to the precision of his probabilistic judgments for different jobs. Inspection of equation (8) indicates that greater worker uncertainty (that is, lower values of d and e for any given ratio d/e) increases the value of $(d + 1)/(e + 1)$ and consequently diminishes the wage required for uncertain job I. The attractiveness of jobs with uncertain implications is perhaps most clearcut when both jobs offer identical initial probabilities of success, that is, q equals d/e. In that instance, equation (8) becomes

$$w = \frac{(d/e) + (d/e)^2 b}{(d/e) + (d/e)[(d + 1)/(e + 1)]b} < 1,$$

implying that the worker is willing to accept a lower wage on uncertain job I. When a worker is confronting a sequence of life-or-death lotteries with identical payoff structures, he will always choose the uncertain job if $p(0, 0)$ is not less than q and may choose the uncertain job even though it offers a lower initial probability of success.

The reason for this counterintuitive result is as follows. The worker never switches jobs. Since the process terminates with an unfavorable outcome, the only information generated about uncertain job II is favorable. This asymmetric provision of information always makes the uncertain job more attractive than a certain job with an equal or lower initial probability of success, and more attractive than jobs with slightly higher known probabilities of survival. A worker confronting a sequence of such job lotteries cares about the shape of the probability distribution, not just the initial probability of success. The uncertain job offers the greatest chance for an uninterrupted streak of successful outcomes and hence the greatest opportunity for long-term survival.

This conclusion generalizes to all situations in which the worker must leave the uncertain job after an unfavorable outcome. Suppose that the payoff structure is the same as before, except that if the worker experiences an unfavorable outcome on either job in the initial period, he must switch to a job with an expected reward of q' in the second period. In the case of permanent physical impairment or other health impacts that affect either the worker's employment prospects or his physical well-being, one would expect that q' would be below q. This restriction is not necessary, since q' could equal q so long as the worker left job I after the injury. In the death case, q' was set at zero.

After making these modifications, one can obtain the generalized version of equation (8), which indicates that the minimal wage w that will attract the worker in the initial period must satisfy

$$w = \frac{q + q^2b + bq'[(d/e) - q]}{(d/e)\{1 + b[(d + 1)/(e + 1)]\}}.$$

If both job I and job II have the same initial probability of a successful job outcome (that is, if d/e equals q) or if q' equals zero, the value of w is the same as in equation (8). As before, the job with uncertain implications will be preferred if both jobs offer the same initial probability of success. Moreover, for any mean value of d/e, the required w is reduced by a proportional decrease in the magnitude of d and e, which in effect reduces the sharpness of the worker's prior assessment.

In all situations in which employment on the uncertain job terminates after an unfavorable outcome, the worker will display a preference for the uncertain position when he confronts a sequence of job risk lotteries. Unlike the job risk situation considered in Section 4.2, this preference is not due to the ability of the worker to switch jobs if his experiences are unfavorable. It derives instead from the asymmetric provision of information that assures that all lotteries on the uncertain job after the initial period will be on more favorable terms.

4.4 TRANSACTIONS COSTS OF SWITCHING JOBS

A. Increasing Transactions Costs. Few job switches can be achieved in the costless fashion considered thus far. Usually, there are substantial transactions costs to job switches. These costs include moving costs, search costs, forgone pension benefits, and forgone wage increases linked to seniority and specific skills. Since most of these costs increase with the length of employment, I will treat transactions cost t of leaving job I as being a linear function of the length of time spent on that job.[15] Thus, if a worker at period k has been on job I for the past $k - 1$ periods, and if α is some constant cost per period,

$$t(k) = (k - 1)\alpha.$$

Subsequent numerical examples set α equal to 0.1.

The transactions costs of leaving job II are assumed to be zero, but actually their value is irrelevant since a worker will never switch from job II (with known properties) once he is on it. If we let j be the job in the last period, where j equals 1 for job I and j equals 2 for job II, the recursive solution to the modified ten-period choice problem from Section 4.2 is

15. This, of course, is a substantial simplification. For example, costs such as those of job search are uncertain. While such complications could be incorporated in a general model, the main results would be unaffected. Two seminal search papers are the efforts of Stigler (1961), who used a fixed sampling-size approach, and McCall (1970), who used sequential strategy models that are closer to the spirit of this investigation.

$$E[v(m, n, y, k, a_k, j)]$$

$$= \max \begin{cases} p(m, n)\{w + bE[v(m + 1, n, y, k + 1, a_{k+1}, 1)]\} \\ \quad + b[1 + p(m, n)]E[v(m, n + 1, y, k + 1, a_{k+1}, 1)] \\ \quad = J(m, n, y, k, I, j), \\ q\{1 + bE[v(m, n, y + 1, k + 1, a_{k+1}, 2)]\} \\ \quad + b(1 - q)E[v(m, n, y, k + 1, a_{k+1}, 2)] + (j - 2)t(k) \\ = q \sum_{i=k}^{10} b^{i-k} + (j - 2)t(k) = J(m, n, y, k, II, j). \end{cases}$$

The principal economic effects of transactions costs are twofold. First, unless the probability of ever incurring positive transactions costs is zero, the worker will demand a greater wage to accept job I than he would if job transfers were costless. The minimum wage needed for the basic paradigm modified with transactions costs is increased to 1.38 from 1.33, thus boosting the necessary wage differential by 0.05.

The second effect of imposing transactions costs is that workers are less responsive to unfavorable information about job I. Compare the third column of Table 4.2 with the third column of Table 4.1. For the same wage on job I (w equals 2), the history of outcomes on job I must be considerably more unfavorable to get the worker to switch jobs, particularly in the later periods. Even at the minimum wage needed to get the worker to accept job I (1.38 for Table 4.2 and 1.33 for Table 4.1), the decision to switch to job II requires that job I's characteristics be more unfavorable when transactions costs are imposed. The quit rate and transfer rate for a hazardous job with uncertain characteristics consequently should decrease as the costs of such job switches are increased.

These results can be formalized with a modified version of the two-period model. Let t be the transactions cost of changing from job I to job II.[16] The inclusion of transactions costs in the worker's optimization problem changes the discounted expected value of job II to

$$G(0, 0, 0, 0, II) = [dw/e] + (d/e)[(d + 1)/(e + 1)]bw$$
$$+ b[1 - (d/e)]\max[dw/(e + 1), q(1) - t].$$

The role of t can be seen most clearly in the situation in which the jobs would be equivalent in a one-period situation, that is, w equals 1 and job I is described by the probability distribution $B(d, e)$ where d/e equals q. Job I is preferred initially so long as

$$t < (d/e) - d/(e + 1).$$

For very large transactions costs that make job changing economically

---

16. The transactions costs of leaving job II are irrelevant since a worker would never leave this position with known and invariant properties.

Table 4.2. Worst Histories Consistent with Choice of Job I, Transactions Costs Model

Period	w = 1.38 (m, n)	w = 2 (m, n)
10	0, 9	0, 9
9	2, 6	2, 6
8	3, 4	2, 5
7	3, 3	2, 4
6	3, 2	2, 3
5	2, 2	1, 3
4	2, 1	1, 2
3	1, 1	1, 1
2	1, 0	0, 1
1	0, 0	0, 0

unattractive, all that matters is the expected initial probability of success. Job I, with a prior assessed probability of success given by $B(d, e)$ is equivalent to job II, which is described by a value of q equal to d/e.

If the cost of changing jobs is sufficiently large, the job choice problem resembles the death lottery situation, insofar as there is no opportunity for learning-induced job switching. The principal difference is that the worker incurs the subsequent job I lottery irrespective of the previous job outcomes in the transactions costs model. This difference undermines the superiority of jobs with uncertain probabilities, since the attractiveness of all jobs is captured by the expected initial probability of success.

B. Cyclical Effects. Transactions costs of switching jobs, such as search costs, vary with the state of the economy, decreasing during economic upturns and increasing during downturns. The main effect of temporary increases in transactions costs due to cyclical influences is to decrease job switching during that period. To conceptualize such changes, modify the ten-period numerical example by letting job switching costs increase temporarily by an additional value of 0.5 in period 4. I assume that this increase is totally unanticipated.[17] If w equals 2, there is no pattern of successes and failures on job I that will lead a worker to switch to job II, while if w equals 1.38, all previous outcomes on job I must be failures to lead a worker to switch to job II. However, inspection of Table 4.2 indicates that such a pattern could

17. This simplification enables one to abstract from backward induction influences of expected future costs of job switching. A more realistic model in which transactions costs are stochastic and not totally unanticipated is easy to construct and to solve, but does not substantially alter any of the analytic results.

never occur, since it requires a failure in the first period, which would have led the individual to switch to job II in period 2.

The temporary increase in transactions costs consequently eliminates job switching in period 4 for these two cases. The worker will observe another outcome of the job I lottery. Even if he would have switched to job II in period 4 if there had been no transactions costs, he need not decide to switch to job II in period 5, since favorable information provided by the additional experience on job I may increase job I's attractiveness.

Anticipated transactions costs, such as nontransferable pension benefit rights, and transaction costs that are determined probabilistically, such as those dependent on cyclical factors, both should diminish workers' quit propensities. This prediction will be examined empirically in Chapter 13.

4.5 Prior Information Acquisition versus Learning by Experience

The models considered thus far have treated experience on the job as the only method by which workers can acquire information about its characteristics. Actually, one can acquire information in other ways throughout one's work life. Discussion with fellow employees and research into past injury rates for a job or occupation are two such methods. To simplify the decision problem, I will assume that a worker can only undertake such information acquisition prior to beginning his employment career. The key question is how much money should a worker be willing to spend on such prior information, as opposed to relying on the information generated by on-the-job experience?

The answer depends, of course, on the likely accuracy of such information, the shape of one's prior assessments, the nature of the employment hazards, and similar features of the problem. For concreteness, consider the ten-period 2AB problem presented in Section 4.2, in which $p(0, 0)$ was given by $B(1, 2)$, w equaled 2, q was 0.8, and r was 0.4. A success on job II has a value of 1. Failures at either job receive a zero payoff. While the expected value of information observed prior to work on the job cannot be determined exactly without specifying the worker's assessment of its expected characteristics, it is considerably simpler to establish an upper bound on the value of such imperfect information by calculating the expected value of perfect information.

In general, the expected value of perfect information ($EVPI$) in the 2AB case is given by

$$EVPI = E \max_{a_1} v(0, 0, 0, 0, a_1) - \max_{a_1} E\, v(0, 0, 0, 0, a_1).$$

This value is always positive when there is any positive probability of switching jobs, since one incurs an irretrievable loss during the adaptation process.

To simplify the notation, let

$$x = \sum_{i=1}^{10} 1/(1 + r)^i = \sum_{i=1}^{10} 1/1.4^i = 2.41.$$

Keeping in mind that the value of the lifetime employment problem was 2.54 in the absence of prior information, we see that if P indicates probability,

$$EVPI = x[0.8P(p < 0.4) + wP(p \geq 0.4)E(p|p \geq 0.4)] - 2.54$$

$$= x\left[0.8 \int_0^{.4} 1dy + 2 \int_{0.4}^1 ydy\right] - 2.54$$

$$= 2.80 - 2.54 = 0.26.$$

The most that worker would be willing to pay for perfect information prior to beginning his employment career is 0.26, or 10 percent of the discounted expected value of employment in the absence of such information. The expected value of imperfect information is of course never more than this amount.[18]

The sensitivity of $EVPI$ to changes in the interest rate or the number of periods accords with one's intuition. Increasing the time horizon or decreasing the interest rate both increase the $EVPI$, since in uncertain situations such as this, the expected period payoff stream with perfect information always exceeds the expected period payoffs in the absence of such knowledge.

Somewhat more complicated is the effect of changes in w or q on $EVPI$. Consider the single period case in which job I is characterized by a wage w and a uniform probability distribution, that is, $B(d, e) = B(1, 2)$, while job II offers a wage equal to 1 and a probability of success equal to q. For the formulation below to be valid, job II cannot always dominate job I. In particular, I assume that $q \leq w$. Thus, the expected reward on job II cannot exceed the payoff for a certain success on job I.[19]

Following the same procedure as was employed above, one obtains

$$EVPI \equiv U = qP[dw/e < q] + wP[dw/e \geq q]E[d/e|dw/e \geq q]$$
$$- \max[dw/e, q]$$

$$= q \int_0^{q/w} 1\,dy + w \int_{q/w}^1 ydy - \max[0.5w, q]$$

$$= q^2/2w + 0.5w - \max[0.5w, q].$$

18. It may have the same expected value. The discounted expected value of learning whether p is greater than q is the same as for learning p exactly.

19. In situations in which this assumption is not satisfied, job II is necessarily preferred, and the bounds of of integration specified in the equation below are clearly incorrect.

I will distinguish two cases: (1) in which job I is preferred to job II in the absence of perfect information, that is, $0.5w \geq q$, and (2) job II is preferred, that is $0.5w < q$.[20]

CASE 1: If uncertain job I is preferred to job II in the absence of perfect information, EVPI is given by $q^2/2w$. As can be readily verified, $\partial U/\partial w < 0$. Further increases in the attractiveness of job I due to increases in w diminish the value of EVPI, since there is even less likelihood than before that the worker's selection of job I is not optimal. Somewhat analogously, the positive effect of increases of q on EVPI arises from the increase in the relative attractiveness of job II relative to the preferred, but uncertain, job I.

CASE 2: For situations in which job II is preferred in the absence of perfect information,

$$U = q^2/2w + 0.5w - q.$$

If q equals w, the worker will prefer job II irrespective of the true probability of success on job I. The value of EVPI and its derivatives with respect to w and q is necessarily zero. In nondegenerate cases, the effect of changes in w on EVPI is given by

$$\partial U/\partial w = -(q^2/2w^2) + .5.$$

In the Case 2 situations being considered $0.5w < q < w$, implying that $\partial U/\partial w$ is always positive. Increases in w raise the attractiveness of job I and increase the value of information in situations in which job II would otherwise be selected. Changes in the probability of success on job II can be analyzed similarly, since

$$\partial U/\partial q = (q/w) - 1,$$

which is always negative for the values of q and w being considered.

Although the signs in case 2 for $\partial U/\partial w$ and $\partial U/\partial q$ were opposite those found in case 1, all of the results reflect a common pattern of influence. Variations that increase the relative attractiveness of the preferred job reduce EVPI, while variations that narrow the disparities between the jobs make information acquisition more attractive.

More general results concerning information acquisition at various times requires more detailed specification of the worker's particular problem. The appropriate method of information acquisition hinges not only on the expected value of information, but also on the cost of obtaining it. Depending on the parameters of the problem, a worker might opt for information acquisition prior to work on the job, learning by experience, or some combination of the two. Except when perfect prior information is obtained or when the worker opts for a job with

---

20. For simplicity, the situation in which one is indifferent between the two jobs ($0.5w = q$) has been included in case 1.

known characteristics in the initial period, the optimal strategy calls for adaptive responses to the information generated by one's employment experience.

4.6 INDIRECT EXPERIENCE: THE THREE-ARMED BANDIT

Few employment decisions involve binary choices. Rather, workers are confronted with multi-armed bandit problems.[21] An important complication that is not a straightforward extension of the 2AB results is the possibility of indirect experience. A worker need not work at a job to learn about its characteristics. For example, most factory workers obtain fairly accurate information by observing the characteristics of the neighboring jobs on the assembly line. I will begin the analysis by considering the possibility of observing the job risk lottery outcomes on a prospective job. This framework will then be extended to consider the implications of job attributes and other indicators of likely job risks that may alter the worker's conditional probability judgments.

To analyze the indirect experience case, I will generalize the basic 2AB paradigm for the ten-period model to the case of a three-armed bandit (3AB). Job I is uncertain, as before, and is associated with a prior distribution function $B(1, 2)$. Job II continues to offer a certain probability of success—0.8. Suppose there is also a job III in the same enterprise as job I. In addition to offering a certain probability g of success each period, job III is also assumed to provide the worker with an opportunity to observe accurately all outcomes on job I without having to work on the uncertain job. The reward for a success on job I is w, while that on job II and III is 1.

Modification of equation (2) produces the recursive solution given by

$$E[v(m, n, y, k, a_k)]$$
$$= \max \begin{cases} G(m, n, y, k, \text{I}) \\ G(m, n, y, k, \text{II}) \\ g + p(m, n)bE[v(m + 1, n, y, k + 1, a_{k+1})] \\ \quad + b[1 - p(m, n)]E[v(m, n + 1, y, k + 1, a_{k+1})] \\ = G(m, n, y, k, \text{III}). \end{cases}$$

Let the probability g of success on III be given by .75. When the worker is now willing to accept an uncertain job provided that w is at least 1.18. The job he accepts is job III, which offers a lower expected immediate reward than does job II, but which also confers information

21. The solutions of multi-armed bandit problems differ little from those of the 2AB case. See Yakowitz (1969). Choices from a continuous range of jobs are analyzed in Section 4.7.

Table 4.3. Sequential Strategy for 3AB

	w = 1.18			w = 2.0		
	I	II	III	I	II	III
	Worst	Best		Worst	Best	
Period	(m, n)	(m, n)	(m, n)	(m, n)	(m, n)	(m, n)
10	7, 2	6, 3	—	4, 5	3, 6	—
9	6, 2	5, 3	—	3, 5	2, 6	—
8	5, 2	4, 3	—	3, 4	2, 5	—
7	5, 1	4, 2	—	3, 3	1, 5	2, 4
6	4, 1	3, 2	—	2, 3	1, 4	—
5	3, 1	2, 2	—	2, 2	0, 4	1, 3
4	3, 0	2, 1	—	1, 2	0, 3	—
3	2, 0	1, 1	—	1, 1	0, 2	—
2	1, 0	0, 1	—	1, 0	—	0, 1
1	—	—	0, 0	0, 0	—	—

about job I. This gain offsets the immediate loss, provided that w is large enough. As Table 4.3 indicates, the sequential strategy calls for a switch to job I or job II, depending on the first period outcome on job III. The sequential strategy after the first period looks remarkably similar to that of a 2AB problem. Once the worker leaves the uncertain job I, he never returns to it.

This result does not generalize to all 3AB problems of this type, however. As the results in Table 4.3 demonstrate, if w equals 2 it may be optimal to switch back and forth several times between jobs I and III. As before, once a worker accepts job II, he never leaves it. While the introduction of transactions costs of job switching would reduce the frequency of job changes, the typically lower costs for job changes within an enterprise as opposed to external shifts promotes the use of indirect experience as a method of gaining additional information about other employment prospects. If potential irreversibilities are involved, indirect experience offers the worker the opportunity to resolve the uncertainties without incurring the risk of permanent injury or death.

A common instance in which the worker learns through indirect experience is that in which he begins at an entry level job, which usually includes a large training component, from which he will later be promoted. Consider the two-period case in which job III is the entry level position and, if the worker does not quit, he will be promoted to job I in the second period. The payoff structure is the same as before. Job II offers an expected probability of success of q, job III offers an expected probability of success of g, and job I's properties are described by the Beta prior $B(d, e)$.

In the analysis below, I will reparameterize this prior, letting d equal γp and e equal γ. Consequently, the mean initial value of the prior is p, and γ is an index of its sharpness. While working on job III, there is a probability p that the worker will observe favorable information about job I and a probability $1 - p$ of observing unfavorable information. To include information acquisition other than observation of job risk outcomes, let s be a measure of the informational content of the worker's experiences. If s equals 1, the experience is equivalent to observation of the job outcome. Values of s less than 1 correspond to worker experiences that are less informative than observation of the job I lottery outcome, while values of s exceeding 1 represent more informative experiences.

The worker must choose between work at job II for both periods and work at job III in the initial period, with the option of working at job I or job II in the second period. In particular, he will

$$\max\{g + bp[(\gamma p + s)/(\gamma + s)]w$$
$$+ b(1 - p)\max[q, \gamma pw/(\gamma + s)], q + bq\}.$$

As in the earlier sections, the minimum job I wage sufficient to attract the worker initially to the entry level job III is not sufficient to retain the worker after an unfavorable work experience. The worker is indifferent in the initial period between work at the firm with the job III–job I sequence and work at job II if

$$g + bp[(\gamma p + s)/(\gamma + s)]w + b(1 - p)q = q + bq.$$

Solving for w, the minimal job I wage that will attract the worker to the firm with the potential for indirect experience satisfies

$$w = \frac{q(1 + bp) - g}{bp[(\gamma p + s)/(\gamma + s)]}.$$

Many of the properties of w are straightforward, since they parallel earlier results. For example, the value of $\partial w/\partial q$ is positive and $\partial w/\partial g$ is negative, since these changes enhance the attractiveness of job II and job III, respectively.

The two matters of greatest interest are the manner in which w is affected by initial worker uncertainty and by the potential for indirect experience. Partially differentiating w with respect to γ and simplifying, one obtains

$$\partial w/\partial \gamma = \frac{[q(1 + bp) - g]}{\{bp[(\gamma p + s)/(\gamma + s)]\}^2} bp \left[\frac{s(p - 1)}{(\gamma + s)^2}\right] > 0.$$

As in the direct experience case, greater precision of the worker's probabilistic judgments decreases the job's attractiveness. The effect of s on the required w is determined similarly and is given by

$$\partial w/\partial s = -\frac{[q(1 + bp) - g]}{\{bp[(\gamma p + s)/(\gamma + s)]\}^2}\, bp\, \left[\frac{\gamma(1 - p)}{(\gamma + s)^2}\right] < 0.$$

As one would expect, the required w for job I decreases as the extent of information acquisition about the job's properties is increased.

Although the structure of the indirect experience situations is quite different from the direct experience case, the spirit of the results is not. Workers prefer jobs whose implications are uncertain if there is the potential for learning and adaptive behavior. The findings in this section not only extend the circumstances under which this result is applicable, but also indicate that the attractiveness of the uncertain job is enhanced by the degree of informational content of the worker's experiences.

4.7 CHOICES FROM A CONTINUOUS SET OF JOB ALTERNATIVES

In a general multi-armed bandit context, workers can choose from broad ranges of jobs. Even when more than one of these jobs has uncertain characteristics, the recursive solution and the qualitative economic characteristics of the job choice problem do not diverge substantially from the cases already considered. The principal difference is that one may switch more than one time between two uncertain jobs—a result analogous to that produced by the indirect experience model in Section 4.6. While these complications pose few conceptual difficulties, they do complicate the description of the optimal strategy for the numerical examples.

To gain some insight into the optimal choice from a broad range of employment alternatives, I will restrict the analysis to a two-period choice problem in which all jobs are associated with a payoff of 1 for a success and 0 for a failure. The continuous set of job opportunities will consist of possible Beta distributions $B(d, e)$ for one's initial probability assessments.

I will consider three possible situations, illustrated in Figures 4.2 and 4.3, where d equals $f(e)$. First, d and e could be related linearly, as in the case of f_1. In this instance, all jobs offer an equal initial probability of success but differ in the sharpness of the prior. Second, d could be a concave function of e, as is f_2. As the sharpness of the prior increases, the expected probability of success declines. Finally, there could be a convex functional relationship between d and e, as is illustrated by f_3 up to the point e^*. In all of these situations, I exclude the certainty cases, that is, I restrict d and e such that

$$0 < d < e.$$

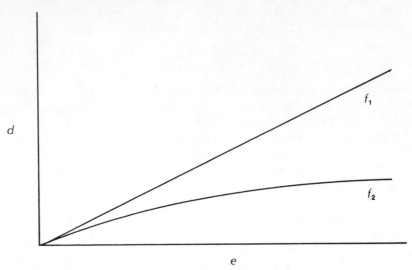

Figure 4.2   Linear and Concave Forms of f

For concreteness, it is helpful to think of these f functions as beginning at a specific lower position rather than simply being northeast of the origin.

In the linear case, one's prior assessments are given by $B(d, e)$ where

$$d = f_1(e) = p\gamma,$$

where p is some constant (between zero and one) corresponding to the mean probability assessment and γ is the parameter representing the value of e. Variations in the value of γ yield prior assessments of differing precision along f_1.

By substituting γp and γ for the earlier values of d and e, one can obtain the initial reservation wages for jobs along the f_1 curve. For the two-period job injury case, the expression for w in equation (4) becomes

$$w = \frac{q(1 + pb)}{p\{1 + [(\gamma p + 1)/(\gamma + 1)]b\}},$$

and equation (8) for w in the death risk situation is

$$w = \frac{q + q^2 b}{p + p[(\gamma p + 1)/(\gamma + 1)]b}.$$

Inspection of each of these expressions indicates that the lowest reservation wage rate is associated with the lowest available γ, since greater uncertainty increases the size of the denominator in these equations, owing to the greater updating of workers' probabilistic assessments. Similarly, for any given wage level and mean p's associated with the

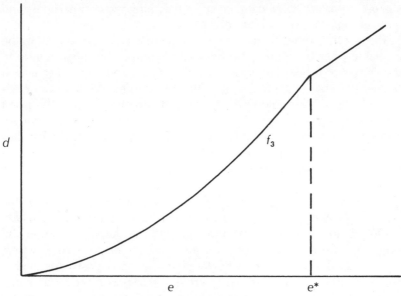

Figure 4.3 Convex Form of f

uncertain job, the worker will reap the greatest net reward at the minimal γ.

Other results from earlier sections also can be generalized to the continuous choice case by simply reparameterizing the Beta function as was done above. Consider, for example, the transactions costs situation. From the earlier results, it is apparent that if the uncertain job offers the same initial probability of success as job II, the worker would prefer the uncertain position if

$$t < d/e - d/(e + 1) = \frac{\gamma p}{\gamma} - \gamma p/(\gamma + 1) = p/(\gamma + 1),$$

for the generalized version of the problem. As the imprecision of the worker's probabilistic judgments is increased (that is, as γ is reduced), the maximum transactions cost level at which the worker will still prefer the uncertain job is raised.

The optimal choice for the concave function f_2 of alternative priors is straightforward. In the linear case, it was clear that a prior with a lower value of e was superior to priors with greater sharpness except in the transactions costs situations, when they are equal. Any point on f_2 is necessarily superior to priors with larger values of e, since they lie below the line passing through the origin and that point.[22] These

22. This statement obviously need not be true for all concave regions, but only for functions such as f_2. More generally, the region of available priors might mix linear, concave, and convex regions, presenting complicated tradeoff problems.

sharper priors are twice damned since they offer greater sharpness and a lower expected probability of success.

The results for the situation in which there is a convex region in the available prior function f_3 are more ambiguous. The linear region to the right of e* is not of interest, since the worker can do at least as well as these jobs by selecting the job with e equal to e*. What is not so evident is where he should end up along the domain (0, e*). The point offering the greatest initial probability of success is at the end of convex region. However, this point may be inferior to earlier points along f_3, since the gains from the higher initial probability of success may not offset the expected loss due to the increased sharpness of the prior.

Consider a concrete example. For the two-period case in which b equals 0.71 and the two possible priors are B(1, 2) and B(501, 1000), the former job is preferred even though p(0, 0) is larger for the second position. This result also holds for the transactions costs case, where t(1) equals 0.1. For sufficiently large transactions costs, the higher value of p(0, 0) for the second job makes that post more attractive.

An important implication of these results for the employer is that it will only be worthwhile to alter workers' probability assessments if the increase in the assessed probability of success is sufficient to offset the losses from increasing the sharpness of the prior as well as the costs of generating the information. I will return to this matter in Chapter 8.

4.8 THE POTENTIAL INEFFICIENCY OF ACCURATE BUT UNCERTAIN ASSESSMENTS

The results in the preceding sections indicate that in a wide variety of sequential choice situations workers will find uncertain jobs increasingly attractive as the precision of their prior assessments declines. An important economic issue is whether the choices determined in this manner are efficient. In terms of outcomes, the job may turn out to be better or worse than expected. A more meaningful basis of comparison is whether adaptive choices lead to nonoptimal behavior, assuming that the mean prior assessments are unbiased. Suppose a worker must choose between job 1, with uniform prior B(1, 2), and job 2, with a probability of success of 0.5. The unfavorable job outcome is death, which is valued at zero, while a successful outcome is accorded a value of one. There are two periods, and the interest rate used is 7 percent. Uncertain job 1 offers a discounted expected payoff of 0.812, as compared with 0.734 for job 2. The worker will prefer job 1 to known jobs offering slightly higher probabilities of success than the 0.5 mean value assumed.[23] If the mean of the prior assessment is the true probability distribution, selection of the uncertain job will lead to inef-

23. In particular, job 2 will not be preferable unless the value of q exceeds 0.54.

ficient outcomes, since the worker will always choose the uncertain job instead of an alternative position offering equivalent or somewhat lower risks that are known with precision. The difficulty is that workers update their priors after successful job outcomes, forming more favorable assessments than are warranted.

However, workers who follow optimal adaptive decision rules need not be making inefficient choices in all situations in which d/e is identical to the actual mean probability of success on the initial trial. Suppose there are two types of jobs in a firm. On the first, the probability of a successful job outcome is 1 for all trials. The second job leads to certain death. If a worker accepts a job in the firm, it is just as likely that his job will turn out to be the safe job as the unsafe one. The worker's discounted expected reward for this job lottery is

$$0.5(1 + 0.935) + 0.5(0) = 0.9675,$$

which exceeds the 0.812 payoff for job 2 with a known probability of success of 0.5.

Intuitively, this result reflects the fact that adaptive behavior will give the worker a higher expected reward (conditional on the true stochastic properties of jobs) only if the world turns out better than one's mean probability assessment. The possible existence of such a favorable situation is reflected in the shape of the worker's prior assessment and contributes to the advantages that adaptive behavior offers both to the individual and society at large.

To analyze the potential efficiency benefits for society, consider a situation in which there exists a job with a known probability of success of 0.51 and a continuum of other jobs with probabilities of success uniformly distributed from zero to one. The worker does not know which of these uncertain positions he is selecting. If there were more than a single period to the problem (and if r is not too high), the optimal individual job choice will involve some experimentation with the unknown jobs. In the latter stages of the worker's adaptive process, employment will be concentrated in the relatively better jobs. If job changes impose turnover costs on employers, one would expect a change in the job mix offered to workers as enterprises attempt to minimize the total costs of employment. This effect is explored in Chapter 10. An alternative mechanism by which future workers could benefit is that to the extent that the employment experiences of workers become known to future prospective employees, individuals will tend to select jobs with more favorable histories.[24]

24. Although information transfer is not perfect, much can be learned from others' experiences. The black lung risks of coal mining, the hazards posed by vinyl chloride in the rubber industry, and the dim prospects of success associated with being an alchemist are but a few examples of instances where learning from past experiences no doubt has occurred.

It should be emphasized that while some efficient sorting into more favorable occupations does occur, the job with the highest probability of a favorable outcome need not be the sole pursuit even in the long run due to limitations on the extent of information transfer, changes in the nature of occupations, the small size of samples for evaluating job risks, and other difficulties. From society's standpoint, the learning and switching to safer positions that does occur is beneficial. Indeed, there may be suboptimal experimentation to the extent that a worker is not compensated for the externality his employment experiences provide to future workers. A similar externality arises in adaptive contexts since the worker who has quit his job cannot recoup the benefits his turnover has had in leading the enterprise to improve working conditions.

4.9 GENERAL RAMIFICATIONS

The generalization of the employment choice model to adaptive contexts does not alter the role of the two widely discussed impediments to job changing. Workers are less likely to quit their jobs if their wages are high or if there are substantial transactions costs associated with changing jobs, such as foregone pension benefits and enterprise-specific skills and seniority rights.

The primary objective of the adaptive models was not to focus on these particular impediments to worker quitting but rather to structure the individual choice process that leads to these quit decisions. Workers typically are imperfectly informed about the job hazards they are incurring. If the individual is confronted with a sequence of job risk lotteries, he will not avoid jobs whose probabilistic implications are not fully understood. Instead, he will actually display a systematic preference for jobs with uncertain implications. This result was derived not only for adaptive contexts in which workers could quit if their direct or indirect experiences were unfavorable, but also for nonadaptive situations such as those involving death risks.

If individuals are making employment decisions based on imperfect information, one should be concerned not only with the wages required to lead the worker to accept the job initially, but also in another form of economic response to job risks through quitting. Direct job experiences and other sources of information can potentially alter the worker's conditional judgments of the risks he is incurring. If these experiences are sufficiently unfavorable given the wage level for the job, the worker will quit. The principal testable hypothesis is that there should be a positive relationship between job hazards and worker quit rates.

It should be emphasized that worker quitting after on-the-job experience does not require that workers originally underestimate the hazards involved. Since workers will display a systematic preference for jobs whose implications are dimly understood, experiences that do not alter the mean probability of success but simply increase the sharpness of the assessed probability distribution will diminish the job's attractiveness. Alternatively, workers may alter their judgments after adverse on-the-job experiences even though this information may lead them to overestimate the hazard involved and subsequently quit. The impact of worker experiences on their probabilistic judgments and their quit behavior will be investigated in Chapters 13 and 14.

The adaptive models also provide a new and different perspective on more general patterns of lifetime employment. In particular, an individual's initial period of experience at a firm or in the labor market will be a time of experimentation. If the worker's experiences are not sufficiently favorable, he will switch positions. Worker stability should increase with his experience at the firm, since additional information should not substantially alter his probabilistic judgments once he has acquired a substantial amount of information about the job. Older workers should be less prone to quitting, both because they will tend to have already sorted themselves into appropriate jobs and because the gains from additional experimentation are reduced if one has a shorter time horizon.

Whereas many analysts have viewed high youth turnover with alarm, the adaptive choice model suggests that much of this turnover may reflect optimal acquisition of job information. The analysis of Section 4.5 suggested that providing information to workers about jobs may be useful. However, the benefits from such policy efforts may not exceed the costs. Policy measures of this kind are likely to be particularly unsuccessful if the uncertainties vary with individuals, as do many employment hazards. A worker simply may not know whether he will be a successful welder or whether he will get ulcers working for a particular law firm until he obtains firsthand experience.

The stability of employment patterns of older workers is considerably less controversial. It has been argued, however, that this stability reflects habit-forming behavior that is inimical to the classical model of worker choice.[25] The adaptive models of job choice suggest that optimizing behavior leads to stability in one's employment pattern that may give the appearance of habitual behavior, but actually is adaptive behavior based on one's increased information.[26]

25. For bibliographic references, see the classic survey by Rottenberg (1956). More recent discussions of habit-forming behavior within the broader context of consumer choice have not been based on an adaptive choice model but, as in the work of Pollak (1970) and Gorman (1967), have been considerably more ad hoc.

26. There are of course other reasons for stable work patterns, most notably, the influence of specific training. A more elaborate adaptive model could include such influences, which have been treated here under the somewhat broader heading of transactions costs for job switching.

The implications of adaptive behavior for worker actions will be an important matter of concern to the enterprise, particularly if it has made a substantial hiring and training investment in the worker. By manipulating the wage structure and providing job risk information to workers, the firm can alter the mix of the workers it attracts and their subsequent quit decisions. The ramifications of adaptive behavior for enterprise decisions will be a principal focus of Part II of this volume.

5

Anxiety and the Temporal Resolution of Lotteries

5.1 Introduction

An important aspect of job hazards that cannot be readily incorporated in the analytic frameworks discussed thus far is the anxiety induced by hazardous jobs—that is, the effect on individual welfare of awaiting the outcome of a job hazard lottery. Interviews with workers reveal that the welfare of many workers is significantly affected by the expectation of unfavorable job effects.[1] The instances of worker anxiety range from an air traffic controller's fear of getting ulcers to a B. F. Goodrich worker's worry about whether he has contracted liver cancer through exposure to polyvinyl chloride.

A distinguishing economic feature of such phenomena is that the standard separability assumptions no longer hold. To analyze these influences, one can no longer assume that the future outcomes of job hazard lotteries do not impinge on a worker's present welfare. Consider the effect of anxiety on the dynamic programming methodology utilized in the preceding chapters. Traditional backward induction techniques optimize for the last period of the worker's choice problem, then optimize for the next-to-last period, assuming an optimal choice is made in the final period, and so on. Once anxiety is introduced, however, the optimal job hazard for the last period cannot be chosen in isolation, since the resulting anxiety from the choice has a backward influence on earlier welfare. This problem is especially great for career choices that represent long-term commitments, since the entire sequence of lotteries may affect one's anxiety. While a fully general

1. See, for example, the interviews by Terkel (1974) and Scott (1974).

analysis incorporating these temporal interdependencies tends to be unwieldy, it is somewhat easier to speak in general terms about how influences such as anxiety, anticipation, and suspense alter the earlier results.

This effort is facilitated by applying and extending the analytic contribution of Zeckhauser (1974), who has reconciled these formerly aberrant cases with conventional von Neumann–Morgenstern utility constructs. Much of the traditional difficulty with concepts such as anxiety arose from economists' failure to recognize that lotteries not resolved immediately are quite different entities from those resolved instantaneously. Thus, the cancer hazards posed by job A may be preferred to those posed by job B if the worker is informed of the health outcome immediately, whereas the preferences might be reversed if there were a five-year lag before the health effects would be known.[2]

The models in this chapter develop the economic conceptualization of anxiety, devoting particular attention to its relationship to employment hazards. For example, how might one reformulate the worker's choice problem to analyze the influence of anxiety on compensating wage differentials for jobs with temporally remote hazards? Is there any medical evidence that anxiety induced by job hazards alters the probability of health and safety hazards, and what are the economic implications of such feedback effects? It is to these types of questions that the next two sections are addressed.

5.2 ANXIETY CONCEPTS

The subsequent methodological arguments will focus on the negatively valued effects that I will refer to as anxiety. The analysis can be generalized with little difficulty to deal with positively valued temporal influences, such an anticipation, or influences whose desirability may be unclear, such as suspense.

Although the subsequent analysis will abstract from the diverse aspects of job risks, a multiplicity of job risk attributes actually contribute to the anxiety associated with a job. Why, for example, are the hazards facing a stock car racer or an astronaut considered exciting or perhaps glamorous, while the vibration-induced risks of spinal damage to a tractor driver viewed with less favor? Among the determinants of different worker attitudes toward anxiety effects are the perception of individual control over the risk, the desirability and familiarity of the possible outcomes, the probabilities attached to these outcomes, the

2. To assure that the only difference in these situations is the anxiety effect, I assume that the worker does not alter his actions if he learns the health outcome immediately instead of after five years.

imminence of the outcome of the job lottery, society's assessment of the job's importance, and the extent to which the hazard is viewed as being essential to the activity. Policy interventions in the job health and safety area seem to be motivated more by job risk attributes such as these rather than by more fundamental issues such as the severity of the outcomes involved or the extent of worker information about the hazard.

Appropriate consideration of the temporal resolution of lotteries provides an analytic motivation for job choices that otherwise would seem inconsistent with expected utility maximization. Suppose a worker must choose between two jobs that differ in the probability of injury, but otherwise are identical. Also assume that the worker prefers to remain uninjured when all other components of his utility function are unaltered. Static optimization would suggest that the worker always should pick the safer job. Yet, few analysts would deny that many workers may find some minimal risks enticing, if only to reduce life's monotony. Efforts to explain such behavior on the basis of worker risk loving (that is, willingness to accept some actuarially unfair monetary gambles) clearly are incorrect for the preferences I have delineated, since being healthy is assumed to be preferable to being injured. Even a risk lover will refuse to increase the probability of a less-preferred outcome if there is no additional compensation. If, however, one recognizes that job lotteries not resolved immediately entail anxiety or suspense effects in the time interval before the outcome is known, there need be no inconsistency with rational choice models.

A common feature of all of the temporal effects discussed above is that worker information is essential to any backward influence of lotteries resolved at some future time. The central role of information in producing an impact on individual welfare has been discussed extensively by Alfred Hitchcock in a series of interviews with Francois Truffaut (1967). Hitchcock observes: "In the usual form of suspense it is indispensable that the public be made perfectly aware of all of the facts involved. Otherwise there is no suspense." Hitchcock also provides examples that distinguish between suspense and surprise. If the audience is informed that a bomb may go off and kill several innocent people, there is suspense, whereas an explosion without any prior information involves only surprise.

These cinematic notions have direct parallels in the job risk situation and, more generally, in the economic analysis of anxiety effects. A coal miner who views the probability of contracting emphysema as being the same as that of getting hit by lightning will experience little anxiety. If, however, the miner observes signals of job characteristics, outcomes for other workers, or perhaps physical changes in himself, the probability of contracting lung disease may be revised upwards substantially, producing anxiety about his own health and about the effect of a possible loss of income on himself and his family.

It is this mingling of altruism and anxiety that no doubt is a principal contributor to the flourishing American life insurance industry. Somewhat curiously, economists have analyzed the desire for life insurance in terms of a bequest motive term appended to a conventional model maximizing the discounted sum of one's expected lifetime utility.[3] This formulation would be reasonable if the value of purchasing life insurance were reaped principally at the time of one's death. However, it seems that the purchaser of life insurance reaps virtually all of the benefits in terms of anxiety reduction throughout his life, since the policy does not even become payable until after his demise. This observation would not be particularly surprising to insurance companies, whose advertising campaigns are directed almost exclusively at generating anxiety and guilt among uninsured husbands.

A. The Basic Model. The analytic conceptualization of such temporal effects will be illustrated by incorporating in the worker's job choice analysis the influence of the negatively valued temporal component anxiety. The two alternative states of the world are the healthy state 1 and the injured state 2. Suppose that an individual accepts the job in the beginning of the period but does not work at the job and observe the lottery outcome until the end of the period. If p is the probability of being injured, the worker's anxiety, a, can be expressed by

$$a = f(p).$$

Figure 5.1 illustrates one plausible shape of the anxiety function. At very low probabilities, such as p below 10^{-5}, there may be no anxiety. Once the value of p reaches a critical level, anxiety may increase disproportionately, tapering off as p becomes very large. Anxiety is depicted as being greatest when the unfavorable outcome becomes a certainty, although it is not inconceivable that a worker might experience more anxiety at values of p less than 1.[4] Since virtually all job hazards involve probabilities of death and serious injury that are fairly low, the pertinent range of $f(p)$ is usually the steeply increasing initial portion.

The additional terminology needed to formulate the worker's optimization is the same as in Chapter 2. As before, let

---

3. The paper by Yaari (1965) is representative of this approach.

4. My format, which recognizes the possibility of anxiety at values of p equal to 1, differs from that of Zeckhauser (1974), who removes the anxiety term from the analysis in the certainty case. This difference is more one of mathematical format than one of substance.

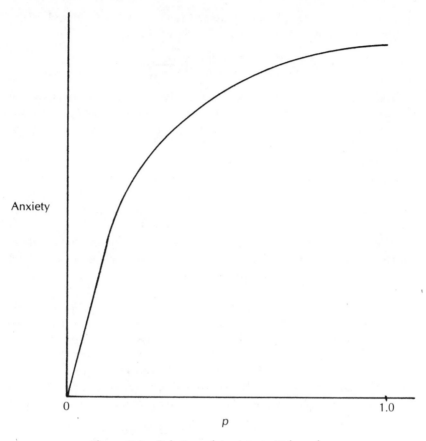

Figure 5.1 Relation of Anxiety to Value of p

u^i = the utility in state i
x = the composite consumption good, whose price equals 1
A = the worker's assets
$w(p)$ = the wage for the job offering a value p of injury
λ_1 = shadow price of the budget constraint
λ_2 = the shadow price of the anxiety constraint.

Suppose the worker must choose the optimal value of p from the market wage schedule and that anxiety during the period enters the period utility function for each state.

The Lagrangian for this optimization problem is given by

$$L = (1 - p)u^1(a, x) + pu^2(a, x) + \lambda_1[x - A - w(p)] + \lambda_2[a - f(p)].$$

Solving for the first-order conditions for an interior maximum yields the result that the marginal increase in the wage with an increase in the value of p is positive and is given by

$$(1) \qquad w_p = \frac{u^1 - u^2 - f_p[(1 - p)u_a^1 + pu_a^2]}{(1 - p)u_x^1 + pu_x^2}.$$

Since f_p is positive and the marginal utility of anxiety is negative, the compensating wage differential equation includes an additional positive term in the numerator once the influence of anxiety is incorporated in the analysis.

Equation (1) highlights the fact that, in the range where f_p is quite large, compensation for worker anxiety may become very costly. The principal dividends of enterprises' job health and safety efforts may be those of reassurance and anxiety reduction. The gains from reducing workers' perceived probability of death from 10^{-3} to 10^{-4} may be far greater in situations where lotteries are not resolved immediately, since anxiety rather than lottery outcomes per se may be of paramount importance to the worker's welfare.

B. *The Effect of Anxiety on Optimal Job Risks.* Workers experiencing anxiety effects need not receive higher wages than those who do not, however, since the optimal job risk also is affected by the anxiety influence. The impact of anxiety on individual job choice can be illustrated with the aid of a numerical example. Suppose that the variables and functions for the worker's optimization problem take on the following specific values. Let the utility function for state 1 equal

$$u^1 = \log \{[A + w(p)]/[1 + a]\},$$

and the value of u^2 equal $0.5u^1$. Initial worker assets equal 4, while the wage rate equals $1 + 10p$. The anxiety experienced by the worker will be set equal to kp, where the parameter k will be varied to illustrate the response of the worker to different levels of anxiety. The worker's expected utility U from selecting a job with associated probability p of injury is

$$U = (1 - p) \log [(5 + 10p)/(1 + kp)]$$
$$+ p(0.5) \log [(5 + 10p)/(1 + kp)],$$

or

$$U = (1 - 0.5p) \log [(5 + 10p)/(1 + kp)].$$

The optimal job risk for different values of k is illustrated in Figure 5.2. In the no-anxiety case for which k equals zero, the optimal job risk has an associated p value of 0.3. As k is increased, the optimal value of p declines, though at a diminishing rate. The worker's wage rate declines linearly with decreases in the value of p. For values of k greater

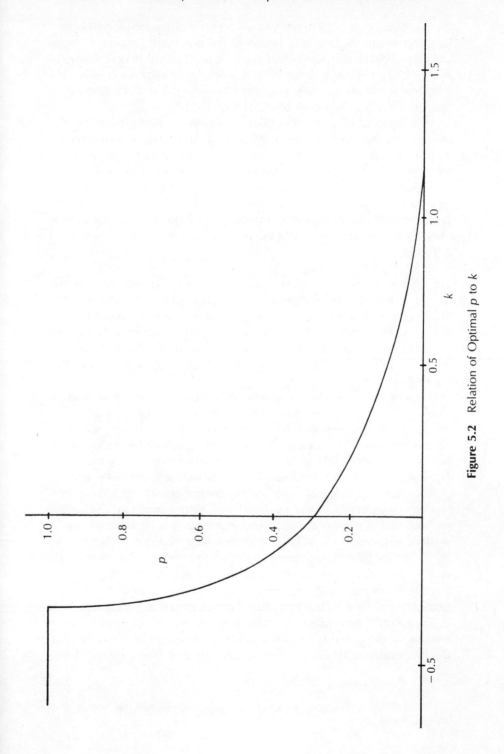

Figure 5.2 Relation of Optimal p to k

than or equal to 1.20, workers will select the riskless job since the anxiety impact for nonzero risks becomes the dominant influence. In the unlikely event that an individual places a positive value on anxiety or, in effect, sets k equal to a negative number, he will opt for greater risks than in the no-anxiety case and will choose a job with certain injury provided that k is less than or equal to -0.31.[5]

As is demonstrated in Appendix E, the patterns displayed in this numerical example hold under more general assumptions. The optimal value of p will be a decreasing function of k, provided that several reasonable restrictions on worker preferences are satisfied. This result implies that the anxiety influence will lead workers to select a less risky job than they would if there were no anxiety effect. Workers will require additional compensation to accept a job posing the higher risk, even though that risk was optimal in the situation in which anxiety did not enter.

C. *Multi-Period Considerations* The anxiety formulation in the one-period model generalizes to multi-period situations, although the analytics become more complicated. A pertinent conceptual issue is how anxiety is affected by the timing of lottery outcomes. Such concerns are raised particularly by the health hazards that have temporally remote implications for one's well-being, such as the risk of contracting cancer.

Suppose that a worker is accepting a hazardous job that is associated with some job outcome lottery L. In one situation, the lottery is resolved after one period, which I will label lottery $L(1)$. In another instance, the lottery is resolved after two periods, which I will indicate by $L(2)$. Clearly, one might argue that $L(2)$ creates more anxiety than does $L(1)$ since the worker must await the lottery outcome for twice as long.

However, suppose that a worker has the opportunity to acquire perfect information about the eventual job lottery outcome. Since the probabilities of unfavorable job outcomes tend to be quite small, information acquisition might be a desirable way to reduce anxiety. The worker might be willing to pay five dollars to know the outcome of $L(1)$ or five dollars in the next period to know the outcome of $L(2)$. Even though the worker might be willing to pay an additional 40 cents to know the outcome of $L(2)$ immediately instead of one period hence, at a 10 percent interest rate this would mean that the present value of learning about $L(2)$ is only \$4.95, while his willingness to pay to learn the properties of $L(1)$ is \$5. This result indicates that the rate of dis-

---

5. The magnitude of such negative values cannot be too large, however, since $1 + kp$ must be positive.

counting alone may make the anxiety induced by remote lotteries less important than the effect of nearer term lotteries.[6]

Other features of the worker's lifetime choice problem also may affect the anxiety produced by lotteries at different times. A worker who believes that his expected future lifetime is quite short will experience less anxiety from engaging in a life-endangering occupation than would a healthy young worker. If the major adverse effect of a possible health outcome is to reduce the individual's productivity, a worker nearing the mandatory retirement age probably will experience less anxiety than would a younger person who might be jeopardizing his future earnings. Examples such as these hark back to a major theme of Chapter 3—that one's attitude toward job outcome lotteries at various points in one's life is going to be influenced by many other features of the lifetime allocation process.

5.3 THE DYNAMIC INTERDEPENDENCE OF ANXIETY AND HEALTH HAZARDS

The discussion thus far has concentrated on the effect of job hazards on worker anxiety—a fairly well-established relationship.[7] However, there may also be a feedback effect of worker anxiety on various health hazards, giving rise to rather complicated interdependencies. While the discussion below will delve into some of these linkages, no attempt will be made to detail each of the causal connections. Rather, the term "anxiety" will be used to refer to undesirable worker experiences while awaiting future lottery outcomes.

Analysis of the effect of job-hazard-induced anxiety on the hazards themselves usually requires a discussion of multiple health risks, not just one. Fear of job hazards may give rise to such diverse ailments as backaches, skin rashes, asthma, ulcers, and heart attacks, where the typical intermediate causal linkage is physical or mental stress.[8]

Alternatively, anxiety stemming from a particular job risk may influence the probability of the unfavorable outcome directly. Psychological experiments have suggested that anxiety may interfere with or sometimes facilitate the functions of the organism, particularly cognitive processes.[9] In order to have such a feedback effect, the job risk must depend on the actions or mental processes of the individual. A cotton worker's anxiety about brown lung disease will not alter the

---

6. There must, however, be some time lapse before the nearer-term lottery is resolved or else there will be no anxiety.

7. See, for example, the survey by Kinnersly (1973). A sizable literature links fear of job hazards with worker stress.

8. See Kinnersly (1973) and Stellman and Daum (1973).

9. See the survey of anxiety of Mandler (1968) for a summary of this literature.

probability of his contracting byssinosis, but the onset of acrophobia for a construction worker in a high-rise building may be fatal.

Most of the discussions of the effects of anxiety emphasize their deleterious impacts on health and safety hazards. An important linkage is that fear or worry about job hazards may be a major cause of stress—a potentially important relationship since work injury rates are over twice as high in high-stress jobs as in low-stress jobs.[10] Anxiety-induced job hazards also may lead to worker injuries by increasing fatigue, thus diminishing the worker's ability to avoid accidents.[11]

An indirect effect of anxiety on job hazards is that anxiety induced by job risks may lead to behavior that avoids adverse stimuli, such as signals of the job's characteristics.[12] In some instances, auto workers have been found to forsake the use of safety glasses and hard hats in order to eliminate the constant reminder of the hazards they are facing.[13] A more general problem is that workers have resorted to the use of drugs and liquor in an effort to diminish anxiety caused by health and safety hazards.[14] Conventional analyses might label these actions, which increase the chance of an unfavorable job outcome, as being irrational, whereas a more general framework such as the one I am employing would suggest that such anxiety-reducing measures may be perfectly consistent with expected utility maximization.

Adaptive worker behavior becomes particularly important for repeated hazards. The anxiety faced by a fireman may decrease as he becomes more accustomed to encountering the risks of his profession. Much of the change in the anxiety effect may be attributable to learning about the properties of the job. As the worker revises his assessment of the job's characteristics after a series of favorable experiences, his anxiety also should be reduced.

If one abstracts from such learning effects, the analysis of the dynamic interdependence of anxiety and job hazards takes a fairly convenient form. The primary interest here is with the feedback effect of the anxiety induced by the job hazard on the job hazard itself. Since the principal matter of concern is not the change in anxiety per se, the probability of injury p_{t+1} in period $t + 1$ will be treated as a direct

10. The U.S. Dept. of Labor, *Job Safety and Health*, vol. 2, no. 4 (April 1974), reports that in a survey of 1,500 workers, work injury rates were 9.7 percent for those in high-stress jobs and 4.8 percent for those in low-stress jobs. The study did not ascertain the direction of causality.

11. See Stellman and Daum (1973).

12. B. F. Skinner (1953) was a principal contributor to the experimental verification of this phenomenon in a different context.

13. This example is based on the interviews by Scott (1974).

14. See Stellman and Daum (1973). A more recent exposition of the relation of drugs to job hazards can be found in the U.S. Dept. of Labor, *Job Safety and Health*, vol. 3, no. 2 (February 1975).

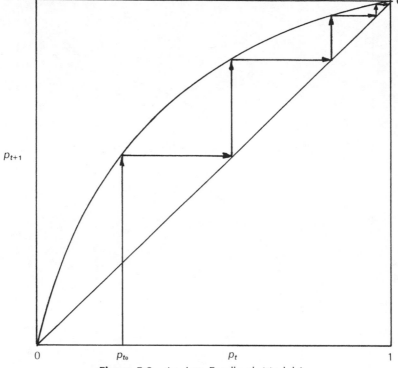

Figure 5.3 Anxiety Feedback Model I

function of the probability p_t of injury in period t, keeping in mind that it is anxiety induced by the risk that is responsible for the altering of the probability of an unfavorable outcome.

Figures 5.3 and 5.4 summarize two dynamic patterns of probability of injury.[15] Figure 5.3 depicts what might be termed anxiety neurosis. The arrows indicate how the probability is revised from its initial value of p_{t_0}. Any nonzero value of p_{t_0} eventually leads to an assessed value of p equal to 1. Point 0 is an unstable equilibrium, while point C is a stable equilibrium. Figure 5.4 indicates a more complicated feedback process in which the temporal effect of the job hazard reduces the job risk at very high and very low values of p. Assessed values of p_{t_0} between 0 and e result in equilibrium at 0, while assessed values of p_{t_0} between e and 1 lead to equilibrium at point B. Points 0 and B are stable equilibria, while points A and C are unstable equilibria. Individuals at unstable equilibria such as point A are in a particularly sensitive

---

15. Throughout this discussion, I assume that the updating of the probability can be described by a first-order nonlinear difference equation.

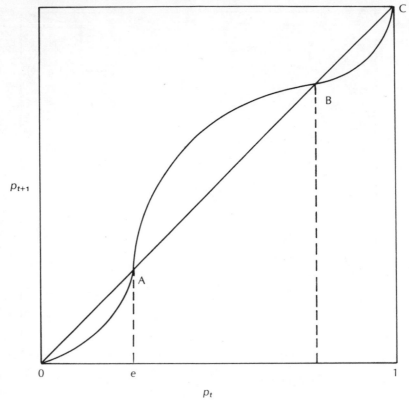

p_{t+1}

p_t

Figure 5.4 Anxiety Feedback Model II

situation, since any increase in the perceived value of p will affect the job hazard dramatically. The reassurance and anxiety-reducing value of health and safety programs consequently may affect not only worker anxiety but also may substantially alter the job hazards themselves.

5.4 CONCLUSIONS

Job hazard lotteries that are not resolved immediately may affect worker welfare quite differently than those resolved instantaneously. The welfare effects associated with this temporal feature of job risks were placed under the general heading of anxiety. Although anxiety effects of job hazards lie outside the economist's traditional bailiwick, their influence is amenable to economic analysis. The conceptualizations in this chapter generalized the compensating wage differential analysis to include the anxiety effect.

A principal implication for worker behavior is that individuals will select a lower risk position if there is a negative anxiety effect on worker welfare. The role of anxiety may be especially important when there is a significant feedback effect of anxiety on the job hazards themselves. In such instances, enterprise efforts to alter workers' perceptions of the job risks without directly influencing the job hazards themselves may have an indirect effect on the probabilities of various job outcomes.

PART TWO

Enterprise Decisions and Market Outcomes

6

SELF-SELECTION, GROUP EXTERNALITIES, AND JOB MATCHING

6.1 INTRODUCTION

In the standard competitive model, workers with different propensities toward accidents and illnesses will be matched to jobs appropriate to their capabilities and preferences. The heterogeneity of worker risk propensities is of clear-cut importance with respect to accidents that may injure the worker himself or his coworkers. One's alertness, agility, strength, and work habits all have an important effect on the safety of a particular job.

Health risks also vary on an individual basis, since the probability of illness involves the complicated and often not fully understood interaction of the characteristics of the individual and his job. An example of synergistic health effects is that of a cigarette smoker whose job exposes him to asbestos particles. This interaction will lead to a much higher death risk than the combined probabilities of death for a nonsmoker at that job and a smoker in a relatively safe occupation.

If employers and workers have perfect information regarding the implications of different match-ups of workers and jobs, an efficient allocation will result. In practice, however, employers may be unable to distinguish differences in worker riskiness, since many personal characteristics and activities that contribute to the probability of injury and illness are difficult to monitor. If workers are aware of these probabilities, there is the possibility that their own self-interest in the personal costs of accidents and illnesses will lead them to sort themselves among jobs in an optimal fashion.

In the subsequent sections, I will analyze the properties of this self-selection process. The implications of worker self-selection will depend on the severity of the risk, on whether the job risk has external effects on one's coworkers, on the extent of the heterogeneity of worker characteristics, and on other economic factors. The primary economic difficulty in these situations is that there are important informational externalities that affect individual actions and enterprise decisions, potentially undermining the efficiency and existence of an equilibrium allocation.

6.2 MARKET ALLOCATIONS WITH KNOWN RISKS

If the job risks are known, individuals will sort themselves among occupations in a systematic manner. Other things being equal, workers most likely to select hazardous positions are those for whom injuries are less undesirable, the probability of injury is less, or whose employment alternatives are relatively unattractive. These self-selection patterns are not controversial. Indeed, the principal function of competitive markets is to promote efficient sorting of this type.

Competitive allocations also serve another productive role. The probability of remaining uninjured can be viewed as a function of both individual and job characteristics. One such pertinent personal characteristic is the worker's age or, more accurately, the physical and mental capabilities correlated with age. As the empirical analysis in Chapter 14 indicates, these age-related productivity effects may be quite substantial. Optimal job allocations will link individuals and jobs to exploit this potential for producing health and safety.

The efficacy of market allocations in promoting efficient match-ups of workers and jobs can be illustrated with the aid of the following numerical example. Suppose that there are two firms and two types of workers engaged in a single-period choice problem. The output per man in a firm is the same for all workers, but is greater at the more hazardous enterprise. Let the value of the worker's marginal product be 1.2 at firm 2 and 1.0 at firm 1, as indicated in the top row of Table 6.1.

Table 6.1. Data for Job Allocation Problem

Category	Firm 1		Firm 2	
	Type 1 worker	Type 2 worker	Type 1 worker	Type 2 worker
Value of the marginal product	1.0	1.0	1.2	1.2
p_{ij} of no injury	0.9	0.6	0.8	0.3
Firm's expected injury costs	0.05	0.2	0.1	0.35
Wage rate	0.95	0.8	1.1	0.85
Worker's expected injury costs	0.1	0.2	0.2	0.35
Worker's expected net payoff	0.85	0.6	0.9	0.5

The second row of that table provides the probabilities p_{ij} of remaining uninjured for the j'th worker at the i'th firm. These probabilities are greater for both workers at firm 1. Work at the hazardous firm 2 involves a much greater incremental risk of injury for the hazard-prone type 2 worker.

Both firms and workers incur costs as a result of worker injuries. Costs to enterprises exclude ex post compensation costs (such as medical insurance benefits), temporary reductions in output, and the cost of hiring and training a replacement for the injured worker. Let these costs be 0.5 per injured worker. Multiplying this value by the probability of an injury $(1 - p_{ij})$ yields the expected injury cost of different types of workers to each firm. Since the only enterprise expenditures are worker wages and injury costs, the competitive wage rates will equal the value of the worker's marginal product minus the expected injury costs to the firm. These magnitudes are presented in the fourth line of Table 6.1.

Type 1 workers suffer a welfare loss of 1.0 unit if they are injured, while the more hazardous type 2 workers suffer a welfare loss of 0.5 unit per injury. The expected injury losses to these workers are given on the fifth line of the table. The bottom line presents the net expected value of the job to the worker. These figures were obtained by subtracting the workers' expected injury costs from their wage rates.

Given this wage structure and the expected utility loss because of injuries, type 1 workers will select the more hazardous firm 2, which offers an expected payoff of 0.9, as compared with 0.85 in firm 1. Type 2 workers will be employed in firm 1, reaping an expected reward of 0.6, which exceeds the expected payoff of 0.5 in their alternative place of employment. Type 1 workers exploit their comparative advantage at increasing health and safety by working in the unsafe firm, while the more hazard-prone workers opt for the safer enterprise. These competitive market allocations will serve as the standard of comparison in the next section for judging the implications of introducing imperfect information into the model.

6.3 Worker Sorting with Imperfect Monitoring of Riskiness

If job hazards are not known with precision by employers or workers, substantial misallocations may occur. If, for example, the likelihood of an injury for a type 2 worker at firm 2 is significantly underestimated by the worker or the firm, he will choose to work at firm 2 instead of firm 1. The fact that imperfect worker or employer information may lead to inappropriate match-ups of workers and jobs reflects the general principal that on an expected value basis (using the true stochastic properties of the jobs as probabilities), individual decisions in a world with inaccurate information will never be superior to those made in a situation of known risks. The observation that economic decisions are not improved by inaccurate information is neither surprising nor novel.

The analysis in this section will focus on a situation of greater analytic interest that will illustrate the difficulties facing an enterprise that cannot ascertain how risk-prone each individual worker is, but instead can only observe the average risk for the work force and adjust its wages accordingly. This situation is likely to arise when individual characteristics and actions that are difficult to monitor exert substantial impacts on the health and safety of the worker. In order to isolate the pertinent economic phenomena, workers are assumed to have perfect information about the risks they incur. This asymmetry in the possession of information about job risks will be reversed in later chapters.

Table 6.2 summarizes the data for this job allocation problem. The worker's marginal product and his perception of the probability p_{ij} of remaining uninjured have the same value as before. The enterprises can no longer monitor the riskiness of each individual but instead observe the average group risk, which depends on the proportion of each type of worker at the firm. Let the fraction of type 1 workers at firm 1 be g, and let their fraction at firm 2 be h. The enterprise's assessed probability $1 - p'_{ij}$ that a worker will be injured is a function of g and h and is given on the fourth line of Table 6.2. The value of p'_{ij} is the same for each type of worker, since the employer cannot distinguish them. Multiplying $1 - p'_{ij}$ by the cost per injury to the firm, which is 0.5, as before, yields the enterprise's expected injury cost, which is given on the next line of the table. The sixth line lists the resulting worker wage rates, which are obtained by subtracting the firm's expected injury costs from the value of the worker's marginal product.

Since the value of p_{ij} and the worker's injury costs remain unchanged, the expected injury costs to each worker are the same as in Table 6.1. However, because of the change in worker wage rates, the workers' expected payoffs net of these injury costs are now functions of the mix of the work force at each firm; these payoffs are given in the bottom line of Table 6.2. If, for example, a type 1 worker moves from firm 2 to firm 1, he will lower the value of h and raise the value of g, altering the relative attractiveness of work at the two firms.

The type 1 worker will choose employment at firm 2, as in the job matchups with perfect information, if

$$0.65 + 0.25h > 0.7 + 0.15g,$$

or

(1) $$h > 0.2 + 0.6g.$$

Table 6.2. Job Allocation Problem with Imperfect Monitoring of Worker Attributes

Category	Firm 1		Firm 2	
	Type 1 worker	Type 2 worker	Type 1 worker	Type 2 worker
Value of the marginal product	1.0	1.0	1.2	1.2
p_{ij} of no injury	0.9	0.6	0.8	0.3
Fraction of workers at firm	g	$1 - g$	h	$1 - h$
$1 - p_{ij}$	$0.1g + 0.4(1 - g)$	$0.1g + 0.4(1 - g)$	$0.2h + 0.7(1 - h)$	$0.2h + 0.7(1 - h)$
Firm's expected injury costs	$0.2 - 0.15g$	$0.2 - 0.15g$	$0.35 - 0.25h$	$0.35 - 0.25h$
Wage rate	$0.8 + 0.15g$	$0.8 + 0.15g$	$0.85 + 0.25h$	$0.85 + 0.25h$
Worker's expected injury costs	0.1	0.2	0.2	0.35
Worker's expected net payoff	$0.7 + 0.15g$	$0.6 + 0.15g$	$0.65 + 0.25h$	$0.5 + 0.25h$

Similarly, the type 2 worker will be appropriately matched to a job at firm 1 if

$$0.6 + 0.15g > 0.5 + 0.25h,$$

or

(2) $$h < 0.6g + 0.4.$$

Workers will be indifferent to which of the two jobs they take if the inequality signs are replaced by equals signs, and they will be inappropriately matched if the inequality signs are reversed.

The nature of the self-selection process can be illustrated with the aid of Figure 6.1. This diagram is particularly helpful for analyzing the incentives for actions that result in small changes in the composition in the workforce at different enterprises. To analyze situations in which g and h may change in stark fashion, such as when the distribution of workers lies on one of the two axes, equations (1) and (2) must be consulted to determine whether job switching is desirable.

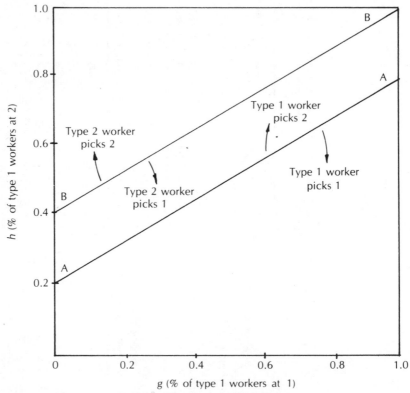

Figure 6.1 Sorting Determinants with Imperfect Monitoring of Worker Attributes

In the examples given below, the number of type 1 and type 2 workers in the population will be assumed to be equal. Since type 1 workers cannot outnumber type 2 workers at both firms or be outnumbered at both firms, the upper right quadrant ($g > 0.5$, $h > 0.5$) of Figure 6.1 and the lower left quadrant ($g < 0.5$, $h < 0.5$) of the figure do not represent feasible allocations and can be ignored.

Equations (1) and (2) are used to construct lines AA and BB, respectively, in Figure 6.1. The type 1 worker will select firm 1 for (g, h) pairs below AA, will select firm 2 for points above AA, and will be indifferent to work at the two firms for worker distributions along AA. The preferences of type 2 workers can be described analogously for the line BB and are indicated on the diagram. Type 1 workers will select firm 2, and type 2 workers will choose firm 1, as in the job allocation with perfect information, for all points between AA and BB. However, this region does not include the (g, h) pair (0, 1) which corresponds to the optimal allocation. Consequently, worker self-selection can never produce the desired match-ups of workers and jobs.

The process of worker mobility and the ultimate distribution of workers depends on the number of each type of worker, their initial distribution, and the order of worker movement. Let us assume there are ten workers of each type. These workers are distributed initially as in the optimal job allocation with perfect information. All type 1 workers are at firm 2, and all type 2 workers are at firm 1, producing an initial (g, h) pair (0, 1). Workers at firm 1 are permitted to switch jobs first, then those at firm 2, and so on. Within each firm, the opportunity for movement will alternate between type 1 and type 2 workers until no workers have an incentive to leave.

As the preferences sketched in Figure 6.1 indicate, each of the type 2 workers at firm 1 will have an incentive to switch from firm 1 to firm 2, moving the distribution of workers from (0, 1) downward along the vertical axis to (0, 0.5). The motivation for the preference of type 2 workers to join the type 1 workers at the more hazardous enterprise is that they will be pooled with the safer type 1 workers. The additional wages that they will receive because of this pooling are sufficient to offset their higher expected worker injury costs at firm 2.

This distribution is the beginning of a continuous cycling of workers that never settles down into a stable equilibrium. The presence of the type 2 workers at firm 2 sufficiently lowers the wages of the type 1 workers that these individuals will have an incentive to move to firm 1. Since such a movement will raise the value of g from zero to one, the incentives for job changing must be analyzed using equations (1) and (2) rather than Figure 6.1, which is only instructive for marginal changes in g and h. On alternating turns, each of the type 1 and type 2 workers will move to firm 1 until no workers remain at firm 2, producing a distribution of (0.5, 0).

This situation is unattractive to the type 1 workers, since not only are their wages reduced by the externalities generated by the type 2 workers, but they are also not matched to their appropriate enterprise. Once again, the type 1 workers will have an incentive to move to firm 2. After a succession of alternating opportunities to transfer to firm 2, the other workers all will eventually move to firm 2, so that the distribution will return to its value of (0, 0.5).

This sorting process is a bit slower than the movement from firm 2 to firm 1, since on three rounds the type 2 workers will forego movement to firm 2. Once h is increased sufficiently by additional job switching by the type 1 workers, the type 2 workers regain the incentive to move to firm 2. Graphically, the temporary absence of movement by type 2 workers is due to the occasional shifting of the distribution of workers below line BB in Figure 6.2. Additional movement of type 1 workers from firm 1 to firm 2 lowers g and raises h so that the worker distribution returns to the region above BB. All workers will eventually move to firm 2, starting a new round of exiting to firm 1.

The problems created by the presence of group externalities and the possible instability of the sorting process in this situation closely parallel the economic behavior in a related class of problems, such as adverse selection difficulties in insurance contexts.[1] An insurance company can monitor the overall risks of its policies, but cannot perfectly distinguish differences in individual riskiness. The bad risks will find it desirable to be pooled with the good risks, driving up the price of insurance and leading the good risks to switch companies or perhaps forgo insurance altogether. This exit will further increase the price of insurance to those remaining, producing additional exit of the good risks and perhaps the bad risks as well. If the good risks become concentrated at another insurance firm, resulting in a low price of insurance there, the bad risks once again will have an incentive to be pooled with them, continuing the sorting process.

Firms 1 and 2 are in a position analogous to that of the insurance company. Each firm monitors the average riskiness of its work force and subsequently adjusts the wage rate in much the same manner as the insurance company alters the price of insurance in response to changes in its mix of policies. The hazard-prone type 2 workers seek to benefit from pooling with the good risks, the type 1 workers, who in turn exit the firm—just as the good risks forgo insurance due to the increase in price deriving from adverse selection difficulties.

1. This general type of situation has been analyzed by Akerlof (1970). Schelling's (1972a, b) extensive analysis of residential segregation patterns and binary choice situations with group externalities also belong to the same general family of self-selection models. An early economic discussion of adverse selection problems can be found in Arrow (1969).

Despite the many close parallels between the two situations, there is an important difference. In the employment situation, the worker suffers additional injury costs if he accepts a more hazardous job in an effort to be pooled with the safer workers. For the example I presented, the economic benefits from the pooling offset the influence of the worker's self-interest in the cost of injuries. As a consequence, not only did workers not match themselves to jobs at the appropriate firms, but, even more fundamentally, no equilibrium distribution of workers was possible. Undesirable outcomes such as this need not occur, as the analysis in the following section will demonstrate.

6.4 WORKER SORTING WITH LARGE INJURY COSTS

The most fortuitous sorting result that one could hope for if employers cannot monitor individual riskiness would be that the expected injury costs would be so great that the high-risk individuals would not have an incentive to be pooled with the safer type 1 workers. Let the costs per injury costs to type 2 workers be increased from 0.5 to 1, producing the expected worker injury costs given on the second line of Table 6.3. This increase in the level of injury costs for the type 2 worker will not alter the optimal job match-ups for the perfect information model in Section 6.2, as can be readily verified. Subtracting these expected injury cost values from the wage rate, which remains unchanged, yields the expected net payoffs given on the bottom line of Table 6.3.

The type 2 worker is matched appropriately to firm 1 if

$$0.4 + 0.15g > 0.15 + 0.25h,$$

or

$$h < 1 + 0.15g.$$

Table 6.3. Modifications of Job Allocations Problem with Imperfect Monitoring of Worker Attributes

	Firm 1		Firm 2	
Category	Type 1 worker	Type 2 worker	Type 1 worker	Type 2 worker
Wage rate	$0.8 + 0.15g$	$0.8 + 0.15g$	$0.85 + 0.25h$	$0.85 + 0.25h$
Worker's expected injury costs	0.1	0.4	0.2	0.7
Worker's expected net payoff	$0.7 + 0.15g$	$0.4 + 0.15g$	$0.65 + 0.15h$	$0.15 + 0.25h$

This condition is satisfied by all possible (g, h) pairs except $(0, 1)$, where the worker is indifferent between work at the two firms. The type 2 worker would never switch to firm 2 in such a situation, since doing so would lower the value of h below 1, producing an incentive to return to firm 1, as can be seen by examining the above inequality. Graphically, the line BB in Figure 6.1 has shifted vertically upward, so that it shares only a single point $(0, 1)$ with the feasible region.

Equation (1) implied that the type 1 worker would be appropriately matched to a job at firm 2 if

$$h > 0.2 + 0.6g.$$

Since all type 2 workers will select firm 1, g will necessarily be less than 1, so that the right side of this inequality will always be less than 0.8. The movement of any or all type 1 workers to firm 2 will make the value of h equal to 1, providing an economic incentive for all type 1 workers to be matched to jobs at firm 1. The self-selection process consequently will produce the desired job allocation irrespective of the initial distribution of workers and jobs.

The implications of this result are quite general. If the injury costs to the worker are sufficiently large, the self-selection of workers will lead to optimal match-ups of workers and jobs. In effect, any wage gains arising from the group externalities will be swamped by the worker's interest in the injury costs.

This result can be derived more generally with a bit of additional notation. Let f_i be the value of the worker's marginal product at firm i, x be the injury costs to the enterprise, c be the costs per injury to the worker, and p_{ij} be the probability of no injury to the type j worker at firm i.[2] If the value of the p_{ij}'s are known to both classes of workers and firms, the wage rate will be given by

$$f_i - x(1 - p_{ij}) = f_i - x + p_{ij}x,$$

while expected injury costs to the worker are

$$-c(1 - p_{ij}) = -c + p_{ij}c,$$

producing a net expected value of

$$f_i - x + p_{ij}x - c + p_{ij}c.$$

Worker j will prefer work at firm 1 to work at firm 2 if

(3) $\quad f_1 - x + p_{1j}x - c + p_{1j}c > f_2 - x + p_{2j}x - c + p_{2j}c,$

or

(4) $\qquad\qquad f_1 + p_{1j}x + p_{1j}c > f_2 + p_{2j}x + p_{2j}c.$

2. The values of x and c could be made dependent on the type of firm and type of worker without altering the qualitative nature of the results in this section.

For very large values of c, the job choice hinges only on whether or not the job at firm 1 offers a greater probability of remaining uninjured, that is, or whether p_{1j} exceeds p_{2j}.

To analyze the situation of imperfect monitoring of worker characteristics, let g be the proportion of type 1 workers at firm 1 and h be their proportion at firm 2, as before. The wage at firm 1 is given by

$$f_1 - x[g(1 - p_{11}) + (1 - g)(1 - p_{12})],$$

where the bracketed expression is the average probability of a worker injury.

The wage at firm 2, which is derived similarly, is

$$f_2 - x[h(1 - p_{21}) + (1 - h)(1 - p_{22})].$$

The wage gains to the high-risk worker of being pooled with the low-risk workers increase with the value of x, the proportion of low-risk workers at the enterprise, and the disparity in the riskiness of the two groups.

The expected injury costs to worker j at firm i are

$$-c + p_{ij}c,$$

as before. Workers at firm 1 will prefer to work at firm 2 if

$$f_1 - x[g(1 - p_{11}) + (1 - g)(1 - p_{12})] - c + p_{1j}c$$
$$> f_2 - x[h(1 - p_{21}) + (1 - h)(1 - p_{22})] - c + p_{2j}c,$$

or

$$(5) \quad f_1 - x(1 - p_{11}) + (1 - g)(1 - p_{12})] + p_{1j}c$$
$$> f_2 - x[h(1 - p_{21}) + (1 - h)(1 - p_{22})] + p_{2j}c.$$

This expression differs from equation (4) above, in that the wage reductions due to the expected costs of injuries to the firm are based on the average characteristics of the workers at the enterprise. As in the earlier situation, for sufficiently large values of c, the worker will choose his place of employment based on the relative magnitude of p_{1j} and p_{2j}.[3]

These results suggest that for very severe health outcomes, such as those posing the risk of death, the self-interest of individual workers in being appropriately matched will offset any wage gains from being pooled with lower-risk workers. For minor injuries and illnesses, such as those that cause no serious or permanent welfare losses, the influence of group externalities on worker wages may lead to nonoptimal job allocations and may even threaten the existence of an equilibrium, as in the numerical example in Section 6.4.

---

3. It should be noted, however, that if both c and the probability of an injury are large, the individual may choose to forego employment altogether. The analysis here is restricted to instances in which the net expected values of the jobs are positive.

6.5 SELF-SELECTION WITH ACCIDENTS THAT AFFECT ONE'S COWORKERS

The most extreme instance in which the individual's self-interest will not produce an incentive for optimal match-ups is that in which the accidents caused by an individual injure or kill only his coworkers. The worker's own probability of causing an accident is not then a matter of consequence to him. The worker remains concerned with the expected accident costs that he must incur, but this value is independent of his own risk-proneness. It depends, instead, on the average probability of an accident due to his coworkers' actions.

For simplicity, reinterpret the p_{ij}'s as the average probability that an individual will not cause an accident that injures another worker. The average risks facing the worker at firm 1 and firm 2, respectively, are equal to the same expressions employed earlier—$[g(1 - p_{11}) + (1 - g)(1 - p_{12})]$ and $[h(1 - p_{21}) - (1 - h)(1 - p_{22})]$.

The worker will prefer employment at firm 1 to that at firm 2 if

$$(6) \quad f_1 - (x + c)[g(1 - p_{11}) + (1 - g)(1 - p_{12})]$$
$$> f_2 - (x + c)[h(1 - p_{21}) + (1 - h)(1 - p_{22})].[4]$$

Both enterprises and individuals are now concerned with the average riskiness of the work force rather than with person-specific probabilities.

If f_1 equals f_2, individuals will choose their jobs solely on the basis of the average riskiness of the firm's work force. No equilibrium can exist in this instance. If both enterprises have the same average risk, the low-risk workers will have an incentive to switch firms, lowering the average risk at their new place of employment.[5] The high-risk workers will also switch firms, equalizing the risk level and creating new incentives for the safer workers to switch firms.

Even if f_1 and f_2 differ, the group externalities may exert a dominant influence on worker decisions. As inspection of equation (6) indicates, higher values of personal injury costs make the group-externalities term the dominant influence in the case of accidents that have external effects on one's coworkers. This result is the opposite of the earlier finding for self-inflicted risks, since higher values of c diminish the importance of the group externalities in that instance.

In the usual employment situation, individual behavior affects the

---

4. This expression assumes that the work force is sufficiently large that the average accident risk facing a worker is the same as the average accident risk to the firm. This assumption is relaxed in footnote 5.

5. Even if movement by a low-risk worker will not alter his own expected injury costs in this situation, it will increase his wage level by lowering the expected injury costs to the enterprise.

risks both to oneself and to one's coworkers. In situations with mixed risks of this type, the role of differing magnitudes of c in affecting the influence of the external effects will depend on the relative importance of the external effects of worker actions. Suppose that p_{ij} represents the probability of not being involved in an accident, and that m and n represent the probability that an accident will injure another worker and oneself, respectively. The sum of m and n may exceed 1 since an accident that injures the worker responsible may also harm others. I assume that, at most, one other individual is affected by an accident, although this assumption is not essential to what follows.

Consider the accident costs at firm 1. The average injury costs to the firm consist both of costs from injuries due to coworker actions,

$$-xm[g(1 - p_{11}) + (1 - g)(1 - p_{12})],$$

plus the costs attributable to injuries for which the injured worker was responsible,

$$-xn[g(1 - p_{11}) + (1 - g)(1 - p_{12})].$$

Similarly, workers will incur injury costs from the actions of others, given by

$$-cm[g(1 - p_{11}) + (1 - g)(1 - p_{12})]$$

and injury costs due to their own actions equal to

$$-cn (1 - p_{ij}).$$

It is this final term that will lead individuals to allocate themselves optimally, since the worker's own accident probability is used in the calculation. As the relative importance of the costs reflecting these risks increases, the role of the group externalities will be diminished.

After calculating the injury costs at firm 2 in similar fashion, one obtains the result that worker j will prefer work at firm 1 if

$$f_1 - (xm + xn + cm)[g(1 - p_{11}) + (1 - g)(1 - p_{12})]$$
$$- cn(1 - p_{1j}) > f_2 - (xm + xn + cm)[h(1 - p_{21}) + (1 - h)(1 - p_{22})$$
$$- cn(1 - p_{2j}).$$

For a very large c (that is, as c approaches infinity), the worker's decision will be determined by which firm offers the lower probability of injury. Worker j will prefer firm 1 if the overall accident probability there is less, or

$$m[g(1 - p_{11}) + (1 - g)(1 - p_{12})] + n(1 - p_{1j})$$
$$< m[h(1 - p_{21}) + (1 - h)(1 - p_{22})] + n(1 - p_{2j}).$$

The critical magnitude is the average accident risk from all sources. Increasing c consequently does not necessarily increase the relative importance of either the external effects among workers or the person-specific risks, but instead makes the weighted average of these a central concern.

6.6 CONCLUSIONS

If the employer cannot monitor individual differences in the proneness to risk, but instead observes the average hazardousness of the work force and rewards workers accordingly, individual employment decisions will have external effects on other workers. The resulting job allocation may differ substantially from the optimal match-ups of workers and jobs and may even result in a continuous pattern of job switching, since no stable equilibrium may exist. Workers' decisions will produce efficient sorting if the costs of injuries are sufficiently great and if the worker causing the accident also bears the costs. However, even if the injury costs are very large, market outcomes may be significantly influenced by informational externalities if the accident affects the well-being of employees other than the person causing the accident.

Since individual self-selection patterns cannot be relied upon to produce optimal workplace health and safety, employers will have an incentive to invest in the acquisition of information about worker characteristics. At the time of hiring, workers should then be screened not only on the basis of their productivity, but also on their probabilities of illness or injury.

The use of physical examinations and personal characteristics requirements for jobs, such as those pertaining to height and age, are examples of such screening mechanisms. This monitoring continues after the period of employment has begun, as the employer may monitor the worker's accident record and signals of the individual's accident-proneness, such as the worker's punctuality and rate of absenteeism. In short, an enterprise will acquire information concerning the worker's risk propensity in much the same manner as it does for workers' productivity. I will not consider these enterprise actions in detail, since this process closely resembles the screening and monitoring of individuals on the basis of their productivity—a problem considered in detail by Arrow (1973), Spence (1974), and others.

It should be emphasized that even if employers make substantial investments in information acquisition of this type, they will seldom be able to acquire perfect information regarding the heterogeneity of workers' riskiness. Market outcomes may be improved, but group externalities among workers will still remain matters of economic consequence.

7

SELF-SELECTION, TURNOVER COSTS, AND THE OPTIMAL WAGE STRUCTURE

7.1 INTRODUCTION

Even if there is no heterogeneity in worker riskiness, worker self-selection patterns will be of substantial importance to an enterprise. The analysis in Chapter 4 indicated that in adaptive contexts the workers who are most attracted to the job will be those who have the least precise assessments of the risks involved. These individuals will have the most to gain from experimentation with a job with uncertain implications. Favorable job experiences will produce a substantial increase in their assessed probability of a successful job outcome, thus enhancing the job's attractiveness.

However, workers with the loosest probability assessments will also be most affected by adverse experiences, which, if sufficiently unfavorable, will lead them to quit. If worker turnover were costless, the employer would attempt to minimize the total wage bill, thus attracting many quit-prone workers to the enterprise. The analyses by Oi (1962), Becker (1964), and others indicate that the employer makes a hiring and training investment in its work force. The enterprise will have a twofold objective of keeping both the wage bill and turnover costs at a low level.

Since the employer does not possess information regarding the shape of the probability assessments of current and prospective employees, it cannot simply hire those workers with the probabilistic beliefs that will minimize its costs. The enterprise's role is restricted to designing a wage structure that will attract more stable employees.

The subsequent sections of this chapter will consider the use of three types of wage structures to induce desirable self-selection patterns. First, the company can alter the wage level. Increasing the wage will not discourage workers who found the job attractive at a lower wage rate, but it will increase the attractiveness of the job to other types of workers, thus altering the mix of the enterprise's work force. A second possibility is to manipulate the temporal structure of wages by increasing the wage level with the length of employment. A wage schedule that is positively related to worker experience will be more attractive to workers who expect to remain with the company for a long period of time. Finally, if the enterprise is able to monitor the outcomes of the job risk lotteries, it can make contingent wage payments depending on worker experiences. For example, the wages of injured workers could be increased to prevent them from quitting. As I indicate in the concluding section, although each of these types of wage structures can be used to influence the patterns of self-selection, none of the mechanisms is completely effective.

7.2 OPTIMAL WAGE POLICIES

A. *The Determinants of Employment Costs.* If an enterprise were concerned only with minimizing its total wage bill, the optimal wage policy would be to offer the lowest wage that would attract workers to the firm. The determinants of the minimal wage rate in adaptive contexts were analyzed in Chapter 4. Here I will introduce hiring and training costs into the enterprise's choice problem. The firm now is concerned with adopting a wage level that minimizes the discounted expected value of the combined wage and turnover costs. Worker self-selection patterns are critical determinants of the level of these costs, since the composition of the work force will determine the frequency of worker quitting.

Consider a modified version of the adaptive choice problem in Chapter 4. The uncertain job offers a probability of remaining uninjured equal to p in the first period and $p(m, n)$ after m successful outcomes and n unfavorable outcomes. As before, $p(m, n)$ will be updated on the assumption that it belongs to the Beta family of distributions. For concreteness, let this function be indicated by $B(\gamma p, \gamma)$, where p is the mean value of the prior, γ is a measure of its sharpness, and

(1) $$p(m, n) = (\gamma p + m)/(\gamma + m + n).$$

The enterprise pays a total wage of $w + c$ for the job, irrespective of whether the worker is injured. For simplicity, I will refer to w as the wage rate and c as the injury cost. If the worker incurs an injury, he suffers a cost equal to c, reducing his net payoff in that health state to w. Otherwise his net reward is $w + c$. The reward for the alternative job available is w_0. Worker rewards and enterprise costs are discounted using an interest rate of r, leading to a discount factor b equal to $1/(1 + r)$. There are two periods to the worker choice problem.

The worker selects the job that maximizes his discounted expected rewards or, more formally, his problem is to

$$\max\{w_0 + bw_0, w + pc + bp[w + p(1, 0)c] + b(1 - p)\max[w_0, w + p(0, 1)c]\}.$$

The first two terms give the value of the job alternative for the two periods, while the second set of terms indicates the value of the uncertain job. As formulated, the worker has the option of switching to the alternative job after an unfavorable outcome in period 1. Whether or not the worker will decide to do so depends on the relative magnitudes of w_0 and $w + p(0, 1)c$. Since the wage rate w is identical for the two periods, the worker will never switch after a favorable job outcome, since $w + p(1, 0)c$ will always exceed w_0 in all instances in which the worker is willing to accept the job in the initial period.[1]

The minimum wage required to attract the worker to the uncertain job will not be sufficient to retain him unless his work experiences are favorable. This minimum wage must satisfy the condition

$$w_0(1 + b) = w(1 + bp) + b(1 - p)w_0 + pc + bpp(1, 0)c,$$

which, if solved for w, implies that the lowest w the firm can offer to attract the worker in the first period is

$$(2) \qquad w = w_0 - \frac{pc + bpp(1, 0)c}{1 + bp}.$$

This w value will be indicated by w_1.

It should be noted that the value of w given by equation (2) satisfies the assumption on which this analysis was based—that the worker will quit the job after an unfavorable experience. More specifically,

$$w_0 > w + p(0, 1)c = w_0 - \frac{pc + bpp(1, 0)c}{1 + bp} + p(0, 1)c,$$

which necessarily holds, as one can readily verify.

The enterprise incurs the wage costs $w_1 + c$. It also incurs hiring and training cost h when it hires the worker in the first period and when it replaces the worker after he has quit. For simplicity, I will assume that the company must pay a wage equal to $w_1 + c$ in each period.[2] The

---

1. The proof of this assertion and a detailed motivation of the individual choice problem will be omitted, since it would overlap the discussion in Chapter 4.

2. In effect, I am abstracting from the complications arising from the shorter time horizon for employment decisions in period 2. This simplification does not affect the fundamental results of this section, but does facilitate the development of the model.

employment cost C_1 associated with a wage policy that is sufficient to attract workers but not retain them after an unfavorable outcome is given by

(3) $$C_1 = h + (w_1 + c)(1 + b) + bh(1 - p),$$

which consists of an initial hiring cost, the discounted wage bill, and the discounted expected hiring cost in period 2, which was calculated on the assumption that the worker does not misassess the probability of injury.

Alternatively, the employer could adopt a wage policy sufficient to retain the worker even after unfavorable experiences. The lowest w that satisfies this requirement is given by

(4) $$w = w_0 - p(0, 1)c.$$

This wage rate will be indicated by w_2. As before, the firm's total wage expenditure is the base wage rate w_2 plus c. The no turnover policy results in an employment cost C_2 where

(5) $$C_2 = h + (1 + b)(w_2 + c)$$

The only hiring and training cost is in the initial period.

For all adaptive contexts considered, the wage costs of the no-turnover policy are greater than those of the wage policy that permits turnover. This assertion, which accords with one's intuition, is easily formalized. To demonstrate that

$$w_1 < w_2$$

substitute for these wage values, yielding

$$w_0 - \frac{pc + bpp(1, 0)c}{1 + bp} < w_0 - p(0, 1)c,$$

which simplifies to

$$p(0, 1)[1 + bp] < p[1 + bp(1, 0)].$$

Since for all uncertain priors,

$$p(0, 1) < p < p(1, 0),$$

this inequality is always satisfied and the wage costs associated with C_1 are below those of C_2.

The advantage of the no-turnover policy associated with C_2 derives from the fact that if the hiring and training costs are sufficiently high, the reduced turnover costs may offset the added wage expenditures. Substituting for C_1 and C_2 from equations (2)–(5), produces the condition that

$$C_2 < C_1$$

if

$$h + (1 + b)(w_0 - p(0, 1)c + c) < h + bh(1 - p)$$
$$+ (1 + b)(w_0 - [pc + bpp(0, 1)c]/[1 - bp] + c).$$

Cancelling the h, $(1 + b)w_0$, and $(1 + b)c$ terms on each side and rearranging produces the condition that

$$bh(1 - p) > \frac{(1 + b)pc(1 + bp(1, 0))}{1 + bp} - (1 + b)p(0, 1)c.$$

For the Beta distribution of priors, $p(0, 1)$ equals $\gamma p/(\gamma + 1)$ so that this requirement can be written as

$$bh(1 - p) > (1 + bpc) \left[\frac{(1 + bp(1, 0))}{1 + bp} - \frac{\gamma}{\gamma + 1} \right].$$

The first term in brackets exceeds 1 since $p(1, 0) > p$, and the second term in brackets is less than 1, so that the bracketed term is positive. Dividing by $b(1 - p)$ produces the result that the no turnover cost policy is optimal if

$$h > \frac{(1 + bpc)}{b(1 - p)} \left[\frac{1 + bp(1, 0)}{1 + bp} - \frac{\gamma}{\gamma + 1} \right] > 0.$$

If there are positive and sufficiently large hiring and training costs, the optimal wage policy will be to eliminate turnover. Otherwise, employment costs will be minimized by not preventing worker quits after unfavorable experiences.

The enterprise decision problem discussed thus far has been formulated under the assumption that the firm is hiring a hypothetical worker whose probabilistic judgments are known. In reality, the firm is dealing with an entire population of individuals whose probabilistic beliefs cannot be ascertained. The most that the enterprise can do is to offer a wage structure that will attract the desired mix of workers. Although the analytic material developed in this section will be utilized in this analysis, the use of a wage policy as a self-selection device involves considerable new complexities.

B. Self-Selection and the Optimal Wage Rate. To analyze the properties of the optimal wage policy, suppose that the population of workers has the same mean value of their probability assessments p, but that they differ in the sharpness of their priors. Consideration of a population distributed along a single dimension facilitates the analysis but does not alter the qualitative nature of the optimal wage policy. Let the distribution of parameters γ that characterize the sharpness of the probability assessments be described by the density function $f(\gamma)$. The lowest value of γ in the population is $\underline{\gamma}$, while the highest value is $\bar{\gamma}$, where

$$0 < \underline{\gamma} \leq \bar{\gamma} < \infty$$

The company has a variety of wage policies that it could adopt. First, it could select a high turnover wage policy in which it would minimize its wage bill and incur turnover costs if the worker has an unfavorable job experience. The cost C_1 of this policy can be determined using equations (2) and (3), where the particular value of γ used is $\underline{\gamma}$, since the worker with the loosest prior will accept the lowest value of w_1.

A second possibility is to adopt a wage policy that will prevent turnover by all workers who might possibly accept the job in the initial period. The value of C_2 is calculated using equations (4) and (5) from the preceding section. The pertinent value of γ is $\underline{\gamma}$, since the probability assessments for these individuals will be altered the most by an unfavorable work experience. Any wage policy that prevents these workers from quitting will also prevent learning-induced quits by workers with sharper priors.

Finally, consider the intermediate and most interesting case, in which the company adopts a wage that is sufficient to retain some but not all workers. The individuals who require the lowest wage rate after an unfavorable job experience are those with the sharpest priors, since these values are lowered least by the job outcome. The analysis consequently is restricted to wage rates that satisfy a modified version of equation (4) for γ equal to $\bar{\gamma}$, or

(6) $$w \geq w_0 - \bar{\gamma}pc/(\bar{\gamma} + 1).$$

Let this wage rate be w_3.

If w_3 satisfies this condition, which workers from the population will be attracted to the job in the initial period? The reservation wage rate in the initial period is given by equation (2) for any hypothetical worker. This value is less than the offered w_3 if

$$w_0 - \frac{pc(1 + bp(1, 0))}{1 + bp} < w_0 - \frac{\bar{\gamma}pc}{\bar{\gamma} + 1} \leq w_3.$$

This inequality can be simplified by canceling the w_0's and dividing by $-pc$ to obtain

$$\frac{1 + bp(1, 0)}{1 + bp} > \frac{\bar{\gamma}}{\bar{\gamma} + 1}.$$

The left side of the inequality exceeds 1 for all workers, since $p(1, 0)$ is greater than p for all γ, while the right side is clearly always below 1. Consequently, any wage policy sufficient to prevent quitting by the worker with the sharpest $\bar{\gamma}$ will be attractive to all workers in the initial period. I will assume below that the hypothetical worker is drawn at random from the population of available workers.

The worker hired for the job will quit after an unfavorable experience if

$$w_3 + p(0, 1)c < w_0.$$

Substituting explicitly for the value of $p(0, 1)$ and rearranging terms implies that

$$\gamma p/(\gamma + 1) < (w_0 - w_3)/c.$$

Solving for γ produces the result that the group of workers who will quit after an unfavorable outcome consists of all individuals for whom

$$\gamma < (w_0 - w_3)/(pc - w_0 + w_3).$$

The value of γ that equals $(w_0 - w_3)/(pc - w_0 + w_3)$ will be indicated by γ_3.

The probability q that a randomly hired worker will quit after an unfavorable outcome consequently is

(7) $$q = \int_{\gamma}^{(w_0-w_3)/(pc-w_0-w_3)} f(e)de.$$

The cost C_3 of the wage policy that partially elimates turnover is

(8) $$C_3 = h + (w_3 + c)(1 + b) + (1 - p)bqh.$$

I assume that equation (6) is satisfied so that the wage rate is sufficient to attract workers to the firm.

The enterprise's decision problem is to select the value of w_3 that minimizes C_3. Partially differentiating equation (8) with respect to w_3 yields the requirement that

$$\partial C_3/\partial w_3 = 0 = (1 + b) + (1 - p)bh(\partial q/\partial w_3),$$

or

$$1 + b = -(1 - p)bh(\partial q/\partial w_3).$$

The left side of this equation is the increase in the discounted wage costs from a marginal increase in w_3. The right side of the equation is the discounted value of the turnover cost multiplied by the negative of the value of the marginal decrease in the quit rate owing to the increase in w_3. The critical tradeoff for the firm is to strike an appropriate balance between the higher wage costs and lower turnover costs associated with higher values of w_3.

The determinants of the effectiveness of wages in reducing turnover are also of economic interest. Differentiating equation (7) with respect to w_3 implies that

$$\partial q/\partial w_3 = f(\gamma_3)\partial\gamma_3/\partial w_3$$

$$= f(\gamma_3)\left[\frac{-1}{pc - w_0 + w_3} - \frac{(w_0 - w_3)}{(pc - w_0 + w_3)^2}\right].$$

This equation simplifies to

(9)
$$\partial q/\partial w_3 = f(\gamma_3) \left[\frac{-pc}{(pc - w_0 + w_3)^2} \right].$$

The magnitude of the marginal turnover reduction increases with the density of workers $f(\gamma_3)$ at the present value of γ_3. As one would expect, the wage increase is especially effective when the quit decisions of a large fraction of the potential workers are altered.

Increases in the magnitude of the bracketed term, which is $\partial \gamma_3/\partial w_3$, similarly boost the magnitude of $\partial q/\partial w_3$. The wage rates w and w_3 are two critical determinants of the extent of reduction in the critical value of γ_3, which is the γ value for which the worker is indifferent between whether to quit or not quit after an unfavorable experience. Since w_3 equals $w_0 - p(0, 1)c$ at γ_3 by the definition of γ_3, it follows that $pc - w_0 + w_3$ is positive, as one can verify by substituting $w_0 - p(0, 1)c$ for w_3 in this expression. Increases in the value of w_3 and decreases in w_0 consequently increase the magnitude of $(pc - w_0 + w_3)^2$, thus decreasing the (negative) magnitude of $\partial \gamma_3/\partial w_3$. The shift in the critical quit–no-quit parameter γ_3 is greatest at low levels of w_3 and at high values of the alternative wage w_0. Wage changes that increase the disparity between the two jobs enhance the turnover-reducing effects of higher wages.

After selecting the optimal wage rate w_3, the employer must then choose among the minimal C_1, C_2 and C_3 levels produced by the optimal strategy of each type. If C_3 is the least costly alternative, the enterprise will be making a critical trade-off between higher wage costs and reduced turnover costs. The need to make a trade-off of this type can be eliminated if the employer can design his wage structure to screen out all of the quit-prone workers. Although boosting the wage rate will be ineffective in promoting this objective, other wage policies may be useful, as the next two sections will demonstrate.

7.3 SELF-SELECTION AND THE WAGE STRUCTURE

Manipulation of the wage level is effective in attracting more stable employees, but is ineffective in screening out unstable workers. However, enterprises are not constrained to offering the same wage to a worker in each period. The analysis in this section will analyze the effectiveness of manipulating the structure of wages in a manner that will promote the desired worker stability.

The relation of the wage structure to worker turnover has been analyzed in a variety of contexts, including the pension benefit literature and Becker's (1964) analysis of general training. More recently, Salop and Salop (1976) have demonstrated that the wage structure can also be used as a self-selection device. The situation they considered was that in which workers were characterized by exogenous quit probabilities. By imposing a hiring fee on workers and raising their wage level in subsequent periods, workers with high quit propensities could be screened out and low quit workers could be attracted to the firm.

The situation I am considering is somewhat different, since the worker's decision to quit is not predetermined, but depends on his on-the-job experiences. Perhaps the most important difference is that in adaptive contexts the workers with the least precise initial judgments are those most attracted to the job. They are also the most likely to quit after unfavorable experiences. As the subsequent analysis will demonstrate, this complication has an important influence on the effectiveness of manipulations of the wage structure in producing the desired self-selection pattern.

A. Choice of the Wage Structure in a World without Turnover Costs. Instead of selecting a uniform wage rate, the enterprise can choose a wage structure characterized by $(w, w + x)$, where w is the first-period wage and $w + x$ is the second-period wage. The firm also incurs a fixed wage cost c in each period, in addition to w and x. I will follow my earlier convention of taking c as predetermined and defining the optimal w and x with respect to that level. The wage premium x may reflect not only wage payments but also pension benefits that the worker will receive if he does not quit after the initial period.

Even if turnover is not costly to the firm, altering the structure of wages conceivably could be desirable since workers have different probabilistic beliefs after the first period. Although an enterprise concerned with minimizing its wage bill would never raise the second-period wage rate to retain workers who had unfavorable experiences, it might wish to lower the wage rate of the workers whose experiences were favorable, since the minimal wage they require to continue on the job is below the value needed to attract them to the job initially. The firm consequently might choose some wage structure $(w, w + x)$, where x is negative.

Consider a hypothetical worker. The minimum value of x sufficient to retain him after a favorable outcome satisfies

$$w_0 = w + p(1, 0)c + x,$$

or

$$(10) \qquad x = w_0 - w - p(1, 0)c.$$

At the time of the initial employment decision the least costly wage structure must satisfy

$$w_0(1 + b) = w + pc + bp[w + x + p(1, 0)c] + b(1 - p)w_0.$$

Substituting for x from equation (10), one obtains

$$w_0 + bw_0 = w + pc + bpw + bp[w_0 - w - p(1, 0)c]$$
$$+ bpp(1, 0)c + b(1 - p)w_0,$$

which simplifies to

(11) $$w = w_0 - pc.$$

If this value is substituted into equation (10), one gets the result that

(12) $$x = w_0 - (w_0 - pc) - p(1, 0)c = pc - p(1, 0)c.$$

If the worker has not systematically misassessed the probability of being injured, the probability of a favorable work experience is p.[3] Using the values for w and x from equations (11) and (12), one can calculate the discounted expected cost of hiring a worker and retaining him if his experiences are favorable. This value is given by

$$C = (w + c)(1 + bp) + bpx = (w_0 - pc + c)(1 + bp)$$
$$+ bp[pc - p(1, 0)c],$$

which imples that

$$C = (w_0 + c)(1 + bp) - pc - bpp(1, 0)c.$$

However, the cost of similar expected labor services at a uniform wage level is $(1 + bp)(w + c)$, where w is the value given by equation (2). This wage strategy yields an identical discounted cost level, as can be readily verified.

We consequently get the result that if the enterprise's objective is to attract workers in period 1 and retain them in period 2 only after favorable on-the-job experiences, then the optimal wage structure and the optimal uniform wage policy are equally attractive to workers and impose the same discounted expected wage costs on the employer. There consequently is no advantage to altering the temporal structure of wages if the company is not concerned with worker turnover.

B. Turnover Costs and the Optimal Wage Structure. If the employer incurs turnover costs as a result of worker quitting, the properties of the optimal wage structure are quite different. Consider a situation in which there are two classes of individuals—type 1 workers characterized by the Beta distribution $B(\gamma_1 p_1, \gamma_1)$ and type 2 workers characterized by the Beta distribution $B(\gamma_2 p_2, \gamma_2)$, where $\gamma_1 < \gamma_2$. Type 1 workers have looser prior assessments, so that unfavorable information will lower their assessed probabilities of a successful outcome more than those of type 2 workers. If p_1 exceeds p_2 by a sufficient amount,

---

3. If workers systematically underestimate the likelihood of remaining uninjured, a wage structure such as the one above will reduce employment costs.

however, type 1 workers will be less likely to quit after an unfavorable outcome than type 2 workers. This situation will occur if

$$\gamma_1 p_1/(\gamma_1 + 1) \geq \gamma_2 p_2/(\gamma_2 + 1).$$

In that instance, type 1 workers can be attracted to the job at a lower wage and will also be at least as stable employees, so that the enterprise will never find it advantageous to adopt a self-selection mechanism to attract only type 2 workers. The analysis below focuses on nondegenerate instances in which such dominance does not prevail.

To find the least costly wage structure that will attract and retain the type 2 worker irrespective of the job outcome, I will first solve for the minimal value of x required in the second period and then substitute this function of w into the two-period optimization problem to ascertain the worker's reservation levels for w and x. The least costly $(w, w + x)$ choice that retains the type 2 worker after an unfavorable outcome satisfies

$$w_0 = w + p_2(0, 1)c + x,$$

or

(13) $$x = w_0 - w - p_2(0, 1)c.$$

This individual is just willing to accept the job in the initial period if

$$w_0(1 + b) = w(1 + b) + p_2c + bx + p_2bp(1, 0)c$$
$$+ (1 - p_2)bp_2(0, 1)c,$$

where the wage structure is sufficiently attractive to prevent quitting in period 2. Substituting for the value of x from equation (13) and solving for w, one obtains the result that

$$w = w_0 - p_2c - p_2bc[p_2(1, 0) - p_2(0, 1)].$$

If one substitutes for the Beta distribution values of $p_2(1, 0)$ and $p_2(0, 1)$, this equation becomes

(14) $$w = w_0 - p_2c - bp_2c/(\gamma_2 + 1).$$

To ascertain the value of x, substitute this expression for w in equation (13). If one also replaces $p_2(0, 1)$ by its specific Beta distribution value, one finds that x is given by

$$x = w_0 - w_0 + p_2c + [bp_2c/(\gamma_2 + 1)] - \gamma_2 p_2c/(\gamma_2 + 1),$$

or

(15) $$x = p_2c[1 + (b - \gamma_2)/(\gamma_2 + 1)].$$

Together, equations (14) and (15) define the wage structure $(w, w + x)$ that attracts and retains the Type 2 workers. The key issue to be investigated is whether $(w, w + x)$ will serve as an effective self-selection device. In particular, under what circumstances will type 1 workers not be willing to accept the job if the wage structure defined above is offered? Whether or not the employer will choose to use the wage structure as a self-selection device will not be considered, since the choice depends on the level of turnover costs and other economic factors already considered in Section 7.2.

Throughout the subsequent analysis I assume that the worker has no uncertainty regarding the value of x. In particular, the company cannot renege on the second-period wage premium by, for example, firing the workers. This assumption is reasonable if the company has established a reputation for providing the stated wage levels, if a labor union is present to enforce the $(w, w + x)$ structure specified in the contract, or if worker turnover costs are so large that it would not be in the firm's interest to discharge the workers after the initial period.

The situations to be analyzed can be divided into two general classes. The wage structure may or may not be sufficient to retain type 1 workers after an unfavorable job outcome. Neither of these situations presupposes that the wage structure is sufficiently attractive to lead the type 1 worker to accept the job in the initial period. Rather they are used to define the second period payoffs in the type 1 worker's dynamic programming problem.

The first case to be analyzed is that in which the wage structure would be sufficient to prevent type 1 worker quitting in period 2. The key issue is whether the optimal $(w, w + x)$ will serve as an effective self-selection device if this property holds. In particular, I will demonstrate that if the type 1 worker would remain after an unsuccessful job outcome, that worker would also choose to accept the job in the initial period, implying that the wage structure will not serve as an effective self-selection device.

The type 1 worker will remain on his job after an unfavorable experience if

$$(16) \qquad w + x + p_1(0, 1)c = w + x + \gamma_1 p_1 c/(\gamma_1 + 1) \geq w_0.$$

From equation (13), we know that

$$w + x = w_0 - \gamma_2 p_2 c/(\gamma_2 + 1).$$

Substituting this value of $w + x$ into equation (16) yields

$$w_0 - [\gamma_2 p_2 c/(\gamma_2 + 1)] + [\gamma_1 p_1 c/(\gamma_1 + 1)] \geq w_0,$$

or

$$\gamma_1 p_1/(\gamma_1 + 1) \geq \gamma_2 p_2/(\gamma_2 + 1).$$

However, this situation was ruled out earlier as being uninteresting, since type 1 workers could be attracted at a lower wage and would also be less likely to quit. Consequently, it would never be in the enterprise's interest to adopt a self-selection mechanism to attract only type 2 workers.

The type 1 worker consequently will not quit after an unfavorable outcome if

$$(17) \quad p_1 \geq [\gamma_2/\gamma_1][(\gamma_1 + 1)/(\gamma_2 + 1)]p_2$$
$$= [(\gamma_1\gamma_2 + \gamma_2)/(\gamma_1\gamma_2 + \gamma_1)]p_2 = zp_2,$$

where $z > 1$, since $\gamma_1 < \gamma_2$ by assumption. The first class of situations we are considering in which type 1 workers do not quit in period 2 excludes all instances in which $p_1 \leq p_2$. It can be shown that no $(w, w + x)$ structure can serve as an effective self-selection mechanism if both type 1 and type 2 workers would remain at their jobs after an unfavorable outcome, that is, if equation (17) is satisfied. This result is to be expected since type 1 workers in effect dominate type 2 workers, in that they are willing to accept and remain on the job at a lower cost to the firm if this condition is satisfied.[4]

Consider now the second and more interesting class of situations, in which the type 1 worker will quit after an unfavorable outcome. The restrictions on worker preferences are the opposite of those specified in equation (17), that is, $p_1 < zp_2$. The value of p_1 can be less than, equal to, or greater than p_2 provided that it does not exceed p_2 by a factor the size of z or greater. If the type 1 worker quits after an unfavorable outcome, his expected second-period payoff will be w_0. The wage structure will be an effective self-selection device if

$$w_0 + bw_0 + > w + p_1c + bp_1[w + x + p_1(1, 0)c] + b(1 - p_1)w_0.$$

Substituting for w and x from equations (14) and (15), and inserting the explicit form of $p_1(1, 0)$ produces

$$w_0 + bw_0 > w_0 - p_2c - [bp_2c/(\gamma_2 + 1)] + p_1c$$
$$+ bp_1\{w_0 - p_2c - [bp_2c/(\gamma_2 + 1)] + p_2c + bp_2c/(\gamma_2 + 1)$$
$$- p_2c\gamma_2/(\gamma_2 + 1) + [(\gamma_1p_1 + 1)/(\gamma_1 + 1)]c\} + bw_0 - bp_1w_0.$$

This requirement can be rewritten as

$$p_2 \left[1 + b\frac{(\gamma_2p_1 + 1)}{(\gamma_2 + 1)}\right] > p_1 \left[1 + b\frac{(\gamma_1p_1 + 1)}{(\gamma_1 + 1)}\right].$$

To make the denominators comparable, one multiplies each side by appropriate terms so that

$$p_2 \frac{(\gamma_2 + 1 + bp_1\gamma_2 + b)}{(\gamma_2 + 1)} \frac{(\gamma_1 + 1)}{(\gamma_1 + 1)}$$

$$> p_1 \frac{(\gamma_1 + 1 + b\gamma_1p_1 + b)}{(\gamma_1 + 1)} \frac{(\gamma_2 + 1)}{(\gamma_2 + 1)}.$$

4. If workers had no incentive to quit, the enterprise would have no interest in designing a self-selection mechanism, so this result is not of great practical consequence.

After canceling the common denominators and expanding, one obtains

(10) p_2

$$> p_1 \frac{[(\gamma_1\gamma_2 + bp_1\gamma_1\gamma_2 + 1 + b + \gamma_1 + \gamma_2) + b(\gamma_2 + \gamma_1 p_1)]}{[(\gamma_1\gamma_2 + bp_1\gamma_1\gamma_2 + 1 + b + \gamma_1 + \gamma_2) + b(\gamma_1 + \gamma_2 p_1)]}$$

$$\equiv p_1 y.$$

To ascertain the magnitude of y, one must determine whether the final term in parentheses in the numerator is greater than its corresponding term in the denominator, that is, if

$$\gamma_2 + \gamma_1 p_1 > \gamma_1 + \gamma_2 p_1,$$

which reduces to

$$1 > p_1,$$

which we have assumed. Thus, $(w, w + x)$ will be an effective self-selection device if p_2 exceeds p_1 by a sufficient amount (that is, $p_2 > p_1 y$, where $y > 1$). Although it must necessarily be the case that $zp_2 > p_1$ (where $z > 1$) for those situations being considered in which the type 1 worker would remain on the job only if his experiences are favorable, there is no guarantee that the stronger requirement on p_2 is satisfied. If this requirement is indeed met, the type 1 worker would necessarily quit after an unfavorable outcome, since equation (17) would be violated. Consequently, this condition assures that type 1 workers' preferences will be of the type assumed for this portion of the analysis.

A wage structure $(w, w + x)$ will screen out the quit-prone workers with the looser prior assessments only if the mean values of their assessed probabilities of a successful job outcome are sufficiently below those of workers with more precise initial judgments. While manipulations of the wage structure may be partially effective, for the usual situation in which there is substantial heterogeneity in workers' priors, the enterprise will be forced to make the kinds of tradeoffs analyzed in Section 7.2B. In particular, the firm's increases in the values of w and x above the levels needed to attract workers to the firm will increase wage costs but also will reduce the likelihood of worker turnover by altering the mix of workers at the firm and influencing their quit decisions.

7.4 CONTINGENT WAGE PAYMENTS

The final form of wage structure to be considered involves contingent wage payments. If the enterprise knows which workers are injured, it can pay them an amount that will mitigate their loss and reduce their incentive to quit. The economic properties of insurance schemes for a hypothetical worker have already been analyzed. Here I will consider the impact of contingent wage payments on worker self-selection patterns in the types of simple models used in this chapter.

Suppose that the enterprise pays each worker an amount c after he is injured. This contingent payment will make the net payoff to the worker equal to $w + c$, whether or not he is injured. Workers will not quit jobs they accepted in the first period, and their prior probability assessments will not affect their job choices, since the lottery involved is a degenerate situation that offers the same reward irrespective of the worker's health status. The company's total wage expenditures $(w + c)$ will be reduced to w_0 plus the contingent wage payments.

The primary difficulty with contingent wage payments is that individuals have no incentive to sort themselves in an optimal fashion. All individuals in the population will be equally attracted to the job, since the risk is totally borne by the enterprise. If the average probability of remaining uninjured is $\bar{p}$ and if the enterprise hires at random from the population of individuals willing to accept the job, the expected cost of the contingent wage payments will be a $(1 - \bar{p})c$. If this value exceeds the reduced wage and turnover costs, it will not be in the enterprise's interest to offer a contingent wage.

Although the analysis must be modified somewhat for state-dependent utility functions and partial insurance coverage, the essential point remains. Contingent wage contracts suffer from the same types of adverse selection difficulties that affect insurance contracts in general. If the enterprise provides contingent wage payments, its role becomes that of insurer for the job risks. As this insurance function is increased, individuals have a reduced self-interest in being matched to a low-risk job, boosting the cost of the insurance to the company. If these adverse selection difficulties are especially great, it will not be in the enterprise's interests to perform this insurance function.

The analysis in Chapter 2 indicated that from the standpoint of maximizing a hypothetical worker's expected utility, the optimal insurance scheme would not involve full compensation for the losses from injury or death. This result is reinforced by the results in this section for insuring a population of workers with heterogeneous risks, since full insurance will eliminate the benefits of worker self-selection.

7.5 Conclusions

If the employer cannot ascertain the nature of workers' probability assessments, the wage structure selected will have an important effect on the population of workers who accept employment. The resulting mix of workers will have an important impact on enterprise expenditures, especially those funds allocated for worker hiring and training.

The self-selection properties of three types of wage mechanisms were considered. First, the firm could raise the wage rate. This policy would not discourage workers who found the job attractive at lower wage rates, but could alter the mix of workers and their quit decisions so that turnover costs might be reduced sufficiently to offset the higher wage costs. Second, the firm could manipulate the temporal structure of wages by offering a wage rate that was positively related to the worker's experience at the enterprise. A wage structure of this type would screen out quit-prone workers with loose priors, provided that the mean values of their assessed probabilities of a successful job outcome were sufficiently below those of workers with sharper priors. Policies that alter the structure of wages consequently can only serve, at best, as a partial self-selection device.

The third possibility is that the enterprise can offer an additional wage payment contingent upon a worker injury. If this payment fully insures the worker, enterprise turnover costs and wages will be reduced. However, the resulting adverse selection problems may result in sufficiently large costs that this policy will not be desirable.

These findings suggest that while self-selection patterns will be an important concern in designing a wage structure, it will not ordinarily be economical to adopt a wage policy that eliminates learning-induced quits. Enterprise decisions consequently will not prevent the type of learning-induced quits generated by the adaptive model of worker behavior.

8

INFORMATION TRANSFER BY EMPLOYERS

8.1 INTRODUCTION

The uncertainty of job hazards and the inequality of the information held by different market participants creates a potential market for information. Workers sometimes provide job information directly to employers, although this activity is usually limited to complaints made in the hope of altering or switching jobs. Information provision of this type may be verbal, may involve disruptive activity such as slowdowns or wildcat strikes, or may be expressed through quitting behavior. Except for worker quitting, such behavior occurs most frequently in unionized situations. The most important manner in which employers learn about job outcomes from workers is through medical services and ex post compensation schemes, since reporting the injury is typically a precondition for receipt of benefits.

The discussion in this chapter will focus exclusively on information provision by firms and other organizations. In particular, I will be concerned with their economic motivations for providing information to workers as well as reasons for their failure to disclose all of the job hazard information in their possession. For example, one does not observe firms informing their employees that they face an annual risk of 10^{-6} of being killed, 10^{-3} of being temporarily injured, and 10^{-4} of suffering a permanent physical impairment. However, firms do engage in some other diverse forms of information provision.

Detailed information on the frequency with which such job-hazard information is provided is available for unionized firms. Table 8.1 summarizes various types of information transfer provisions included

Table 8.1.   Information Transfer Provisions in Collective Bargaining
Agreements, 1974–75

Type of information transfer	Agreements with such provisions	Workers covered (thousands)
Dissemination of safety information to employees	273	2130.1
Safety rules and procedures	186	991.5
Possible job hazards	73	1,121.8
Warning signs or labels	74	682.8
Dissemination of safety information to union	335	2,164.7
Safety rules and changes	58	405.3
Reports, minutes of safety meetings	158	1,477.4
Accident, mortality, morbidity data	213	1,209.7
Safety Education and Training	132	1,497.0
Safety inspections	335	2,356.9
Union-Management cooperation on safety	757	3,946.3
Sample size of all agreements studied	1,724	7,868.0

Source: U.S. Dept. of Labor, Bureau of Labor Statistics, *Major Collective Bargaining Agreements: Safety and Health Provisions,* Bulletin 1425–16 (Washington: U.S. Government Printing Office, 1976), pp. 4–55.

in collective bargaining agreements. Only 27 percent of all workers are covered by agreements in which the employer disseminates safety information directly to workers, such as information on possible job hazards. Unions themselves are somewhat more likely to be recipients of such information, although even they are not widely informed. Only 15 percent of the workers in the sample were covered by agreements that stipulated procedures for formal provision of accident, mortality, and morbidity data to the union. Provisions pertaining to safety training, safety inspections, and union-management cooperation on safety also reflect different modes of information transfer.

There is of course a substantial degree of informal information dissemination with or without unions. During training workers are invariably shown some safety procedures. If the enterprise is a particularly safe firm, the company will inform the worker of the excellence of the firm's record at the job interview and later during the worker's tenure at the firm. Nevertheless, Table 8.1 correctly conveys the general impression that information provision is only partial.

These data also suggest that worker uncertainty about job characteristics may influence enterprise policies other than the design of the wage structure. This chapter analyzes the circumstances under which an employer will provide health and safety information, the type and extent of the information it will provide, and the economic implications of the information transfer process. The interdependence of enterprises within an industry in this information transfer process will be discussed in the next chapter.

As an economic good, information has long been noted to have deviant properties associated with its nonexcludability aspects, that is, the company cannot prevent the information from being conveyed to others. These difficulties are enhanced in the job hazard situation by the fact that the employer has a direct economic interest in workers' use of this information, and this self-interest may not be conducive to the promotion of social welfare. Many of these fundamental economic issues are introduced in Section 8.2 within the context of single-period models.

In multi-period contexts in which there is adaptive worker behavior, worker preference for jobs with uncertain implications will diminish the economic incentive for information provision, as the analysis in Section 8.3 demonstrates. If, however, worker turnover costs are substantial, the provision of information will reduce the influence the workers' on-the-job experiences have on their probability assessments, thus diminishing the magnitude of learning-induced quits and subsequently enhancing the attractiveness of providing information to workers. This matter is considered in Section 8.4.

The preceding two chapters have indicated the impact of worker self-selection patterns on the costs of employment. The optimal information provision policy must reflect not simply the wage and turnover costs associated with hiring a new worker, but also should induce the desired pattern of worker self-selection from an entire population of potential workers, as is indicated in Section 8.5.

8.2 Information Transfer: The Single-Period Case

A. Incentives for Information Provision. In simple static models there are two health states—being healthy or being injured. In such models only the worker's mean probability assessment is of import. If an enterprise can lower the assessed probability of an injury, it will provide information so long as the costs of doing so do not exceed the gains to the enterprise in terms of reduced wages and efficiency gains from reallocating workers to different activities.[1]

Alternatively, an enterprise might not attempt to raise the assessed value of p, where p is the probability of remaining uninjured, but may

1. Throughout the discussion, I will consider the impact of information on a hypothetical worker. If the impact of information differs for individuals, one must also analyze the distribution of worker probability assessments, preferences, and information acquisition and learning. Consideration of the distribution of worker characteristics is the subject of Section 8.5.

attempt to convince workers that the job hazards are no greater than the risks posed by his other activities—that is, reduce the assessed probabilities of remaining uninjured for all alternative pursuits, including leisure time. The ubiquitous reference to the National Safety Council's claim that workers are safer on the job than at home seems directed more at reducing the assessed incremental risks of the occupation than at raising the level of the assessed probability of remaining uninjured. For analytic simplicity, the discussion below is restricted to efforts to raise the value of p.

Redistributive Interests and Information Provision. Additional information may increase economic efficiency by leading workers to choose jobs that they formerly considered too dangerous or by convincing workers that they should switch to safer job alternatives. These efficiency gains need not exceed the costs of providing the information, since the enterprise may be motivated principally by redistributive interests, that is, the possibility of lowering the wage bill. There is no guarantee that any efficiency gains that might accrue will exceed the costs the company is willing to incur to provide the information.

Consider a particularly inefficient case in which workers' initial assessments correspond to the true stochastic properties of their jobs and, as a result, individual match-ups with jobs are optimal. A company with a particularly good record might wish to convey this information to workers, boosting the assessed probability of success above its actual value. The motivation for doing so is to reduce wage costs and hence increase profits. This activity will occur provided that the redistributive gain exceeds the costs of information provision and any other efficiency losses it might generate. In terms of economic efficiency, all impacts are negative. The enterprise has incurred the cost of providing the information, while workers who have switched jobs are allocated less efficiently than before. The role of enterprises' self-interest in the use of information will be a central theme throughout the remainder of this chapter. Adverse job outcomes will be treated as equivalent to monetary losses. Although this assumption facilitates analysis of shifts in the probability of an accident, health risks also involve an additional complication deriving from the shape of workers' utility functions. In particular, if the underlying implications of the job are completely deterministic rather than stochastic, the job lottery can be eliminated altogether by the provision of information. The incentives for information provision in the health lottery case are quite different from the monetary lottery situation.

To establish a basis of comparison, consider first the monetary gamble situation. Suppose that the piecework system at a firm is designed so that each job offers a base income of y, but that a fraction

$1 - p$ of the workers will earn only $y - z$ using this piecework system, where z is some positive number. Each worker has a reservation wage equal to y.

The company has two options. First, it could inform the workers on the less productive jobs of their positions' characteristics, giving them an additional payment of z so that they will accept the position. This perfect information policy has an average cost per worker above the piecework remuneration of $(1 - p)z$.

Alternatively, the company could let each worker incur the lottery in which their output would earn them an expected piecework income of $y - (1 - p)z$. If workers are risk averse, their certainty equivalent CE for this lottery will be

$$CE = y - (1 - p)z - R,$$

where R is a positive risk premium. The CE value will be less than the reservation wage y by an amount $(1 - p)z + R$. Since all workers incur this lottery, the average cost per worker above the piecework pay of this policy will be $(1 - p)z + R$. This value exceeds the per worker cost in the certainty case by the value of this risk premium. Perfect information provision always involves a lower cost than accurately perceived job lotteries, so that information provision will always be attractive to the firm.

This result does not generalize to lotteries on health states. It will be shown for a very wide class of utility functions that it is not in an enterprise's interest to inform workers of their jobs' implications. This result holds irrespective of whether workers are risk-loving, risk-neutral, or risk-averse.

Suppose Type 1 jobs offer a certain probability of remaining uninjured and an equal number of Type 2 jobs offer certain injury. The employer's choice problem is whether to let the workers assess the chances of being on either job as being 0.5 or whether to reveal the true job properties. It is assumed that the workers have identical preferences.

Using a subset of the general class of utility functions introduced in Chapter 2, let u^1 be the utility function in the healthy state 1 and u^2 be the utility function in the injured state 2. For any given level of wealth x, a person reaps more utility if he is healthy than if he is not ($u^1[x] > u^2[x]$); he has a higher marginal utility of wealth when healthy ($u^1_x > u^2_x$); and the ratio of these marginal utilities u^1_x/u^2_x does not decline as x increases. This formulation imposes no stipulation on the individual's attitude toward risk.

To analyze the effect of uncertainty on compensation, consider the risk-neutral utility functions in Figure 8.1. Let u^0 be the expected utility

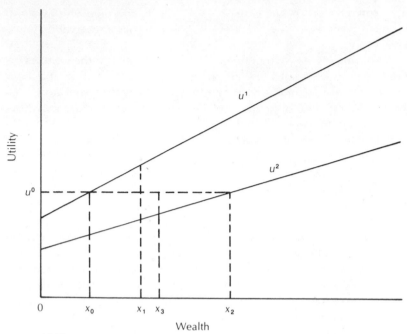

Figure 8.1 Utility Functions for the Job Choice Problem

of the job alternative. If there is no chance that the worker might be injured, the required wage is x_0.[2] If the worker's job leads to certain injury, the required wage is x_2. The average wage paid by the firm is $x_0 + (x_2 - x_0)/2$, or x_3 in the diagram. Alternatively, if the worker faces a (0.5, 0.5) lottery on the two health states, a wage of only x_1 is required. Even if workers' mean assessments correspond to the average properties of jobs in an enterprise, the employer may incur substantial wage costs if the properties of each job are revealed.

In a very broad class of situations it will be in the employer's self-interest to withhold the information from the workers. The company may have to pay substantially greater wages if workers are employed at jobs involving certain death or injury, rather than in the imperfect, but unbiased, information situation in which workers are engaged in job hazard lotteries, where the assessed probabilities are accurate reflections of the average risk at the firm.

There may be situations in which the company will provide workers with such information, in particular, if u_x^1/u_x^2 declines sufficiently as the

---

2. For expositional simplicity, I treat initial wealth as zero, although the graphical results are consistent with nonzero wealth holdings.

value of x is increased. However, what is most important for the analysis in this chapter is that the company's incentive to provide such information may be diminished when dealing with health risks rather than monetary gambles.

Impacts of Information Provision on the Production of Workplace Safety. The information transfer choice becomes more complicated if the actual risk of an adverse outcome is altered by the information as, for example, information pertaining to safety regulations and procedures.[3] To analyze the impact of information on safety, consider a simple, single-firm example. The two critical magnitudes altered by information are the assessed probability of success p and the actual probability of a successful job outcome p'. Increasing the value of p lowers the wage costs to the firm and increasing p' reduces actual expected injury losses, such as forgone output or ex post compensation costs.

If both p and p' are raised, the enterprise will convey information if the reduced wage and injury costs exceed the costs of information transfer. The choice problem becomes more complicated if the directions of change in p and p' differ, since the overall desirability depends on whether the net effect of these changes reduces costs to the firm and, if so, whether this amount offsets the cost of information transfer.

With none of the four possible combination of changes in p and p' is there the guarantee that the enterprise's choice will lead to efficiency. For example, consider the most favorable case, in which information transfer boosts p and p'. Expected injuries on the particular job are reduced. However, the assessed value of p after information transfer may be much higher than before and much greater than its true value. Workers who correctly refused to work at this hazardous job before updating their probability assessments may now find the job attractive. In general, there is no assurance that the benefits from increasing safety for this position will exceed the possible efficiency loss caused by the misallocation of workers and the costs of providing the information.

Group Characteristics and Signaling Activity. If worker information is imperfect, there may be group externalities among enterprises that may affect the safety levels in different firms in a nonoptimal fashion. Consider the typical situation in which individuals do not know the injury rates for each firm in the industry but may be aware of the industry's average injury rate.[4] The industry consists of two firms, each of which must select its own level of safety. On an individual basis, each will select a suboptimal level of safety, since it cannot recoup the ex-

3. A closely related impact is the reassurance value of information, which has been examined earlier in Chapter 5.

4. Indeed, this is the most any investigator can ascertain using data published by the Bureau of Labor Statistics.

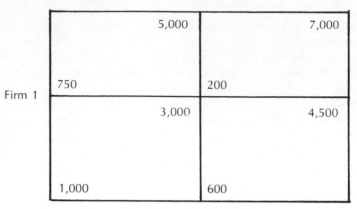

Figure 8.2 Safety Choice Problem

ternality it confers to the industry as a whole by favorably affecting workers' perceptions of safety at these firms.

This strategic situation is analogous to the conventional prisoner's dilemma problem summarized in Figure 8.2.[5] Payoffs to firm 1 are in the lower left-hand corners, while those for firm 2 are in the upper right-hand corners. Higher-valued payoffs are preferred. Each firm will select its dominant strategy—selecting unsafe working conditions. This choice results in the Pareto-inferior equilibrium of unsafe employment in all enterprises.

Each firm could be made better off if both provided safe environments. This situation would be unstable, however, since each enterprise would have an incentive to let working conditions deteriorate. Enforcing agreements to promote safety may be both costly and difficult, since an increase in the injury rate might be attributed to bad luck rather than deliberate actions. Moreover, coordination problems become especially difficult when the number of firms in the industry is large. This enforcement problem creates a potential role for union or government action. By bargaining on an industry-wide basis for improved working conditions and by enforcing the contract provisions, unions can assist firms in reaping the benefits of coordinated actions. Government safety standards can serve a similar function if the efficient safety levels at different firms are not too dissimilar.

5. This may be a very common occurrence in situations in which information is imperfect and group characteristics are pertinent. Spence's (1974) job market signaling case possesses a similar strategic structure. The choice for individuals in that instance is whether or not to signal. Signaling may be the dominant strategy for each individual, but may result in a Pareto-inferior equilibrium.

Two forms of information provision are of interest in the group externalities situation. First, if the employer can provide information that will enable workers to ascertain the firm's specific risks, safety investments may become desirable if the reduction in wages exceeds the cost of information provision and the safety investment cost. This type of information transfer situation is considered in detail in the next chapter. Some enterprises may not find information provision attractive in this situation. Moreover, even if they do choose to provide workers with information, the resulting outcome may not be economically efficient.

The group externalities would function somewhat differently if workers treated information provided by a particular firm as being characteristic of the entire industry or of all firms in a particular region. The principal effect of providing favorable safety information in this instance would be to confer an external benefit on other firms, while doing little to alter the relative attractiveness of employment at the enterprise providing the information. There would be severe impediments to enterprise provision of information in this instance.

B. General Considerations Pertaining to the Nature of Information as a Commodity. Situations involving information acquisition and dissemination are renowned for being associated with properties, such as increasing returns and public goods aspects, that are inimical to economic efficiency.[6] In this section, I will examine the deviant characteristics that seem most important to the specific context of job hazards.

Perhaps the principal feature of information is that it is a public good. If, for example, a firm reveals the job characteristics to the current work force at a plant, it will be difficult to deny prospective workers access to this knowledge. Even if the employer could charge workers for information and extract from current workers their total willingness to pay for it, unfavorable information may damage the general reputation of the enterprise and boost the wage rates required to attract future workers—an externality whose value is difficult to recoup.

Even within an enterprise, problems of limiting access to information may impose costs on the firm that offset the possible efficiency benefits. A firm, for example, might wish to convey information only to those workers who are not matched to appropriate jobs, perhaps because they have overestimated the safety of their positions. While revelation of the true job characteristics may increase the safety of the workplace by promoting better job allocations, such disclosure may also increase the wage costs required to retain the appropriately as-

6. More general discussion of many of these issues can be found in Arrow (1971).

signed workers for whom the information was not intended.[7] Since the information cannot be selectively provided, the firm will not be able to avoid the increased wage costs associated with the lower assessed probabilities of success of present and prospective workers, and thus it has a powerful incentive for nondisclosure.

Another intrinsic problem undermining the possibility of a market for information is that the employer has an economic interest in subsequent worker actions, since worker quitting may impose substantial hiring and training costs.[8] Since an enterprise may not be willing to sell extremely unfavorable information, the information that is sold will be provided on a discretionary basis. Workers will place a value on the expected worth of information conditional on the fact that the employer is willing to sell it for a specific price. Very unfavorable information would have a high price due to the higher wage and turnover costs it would generate. Once the worker knows that he can learn the true stochastic properties of his job for a dollar, he may already have learned what he wants to know about the job without having to incur any information acquisition costs. This difficulty stems from the fact that the seller of the information has a financial stake in its use.

A somewhat different but equally important problem is that the seller of information may not be able to reap its true value since he has to reveal his product before purchasers are aware of its worth. This familiar problem may arise frequently in employment contexts. The B. F. Goodrich Company might have been willing to disclose the polyvinyl chloride hazard at its plants if it could have collected the total value that, in retrospect, workers would have placed on this information. However, the prior assessed probabilities for this extremely adverse possibility would be so low that workers would have offered little for this knowledge. The preponderance of deviant properties associated with a market for information no doubt is responsible for the failure of such an arrangement to exist.

8.3 Information Transfer: The Multi-Period Case

In multi-period contexts, the incentives of enterprises to provide information may be diminished. To be favorable, it is no longer sufficient for information to raise the worker's mean probability of success. As the adaptive job choice models in Chapter 4 demonstrated, the possi-

---

7. Consider a concrete example. Suppose in the job allocation model in Section 6.2 that workers had perfect knowledge of the properties of jobs in firm 1 but that they incorrectly assessed the probability of remaining uninjured at firm 2 as 1. Firm 2 could reduce its injury rate and assure efficient job allocations for society if it revealed the actual job characteristics to type 2 workers, who would then move to firm 1. The higher wage costs would offset the efficiency gains, however.

8. Additional ramifications of turnover costs are explored in Sections 8.4 and 8.5.

bility of information acquisition and job switching makes workers willing to sacrifice some additional probability of success in return for greater looseness in the prior. A similar pattern occurred in nonadaptive situations, such as those involving death risks or unfavorable job outcomes that require the worker to leave his job.

Suppose, for example, that workers' prior assessments are given by the Beta prior $B(d, e)$, where d/e is the mean initial probability of success. Let the information provided by the firm be described by the parameters (d', e') resulting in a posterior probability assessment of $B(d + d', e + e')$. This information is equivalent to the worker observing d' successes in e' trials. If d'/e' does not exceed d/e, the information is necessarily unfavorable in multi-period contexts. Moreover, it may be unfavorable if $(d + d')/(e + e')$ does not exceed d/e by enough to offset the increased sharpness of the probability assessment. This result is a straightforward application of the findings in Chapter 4.

Consider a few specific examples. Let the worker's probability assessment be given by a uniform prior—the Beta distribution $B(1, 2)$. The unfavorable job outcome is death. The attractiveness of the information depends on its effect on both the mean initial probability of staying alive and on the precision of one's probability assessment. For different values of e', what value of d' is required for the information provided not to be unfavorable? For higher values of d', information transfer becomes desirable. The critical level depends both on the interest rate and the number of periods in the problem.[9]

Table 8.2 summarizes results for three different interest rates and three different time horizons. As the last column indicates, any value of d' that is not at least half the size of e' will never be favorable. If the interest rate is infinite, all that matters is the worker's initial probability of success, since only initial period payoffs are considered. For the finite interest rate cases, the required value of d'/e' ranges from 0.53 to 0.65.

There are three other patterns in Table 8.2 that are of interest. First, for any particular time horizon and value of e', the required value of d' declines with the value of the interest rate. As one's present orientation increases, the role of information in sharpening the probability assessment is of less consequence, thus reducing the extent to which information must increase the mean probability assessment for it to be favorable.

A second effect reflected in the results is that the required value of d'/e' increases with e', since the information must be increasingly favorable to offset the loss imposed by the sharpening of the worker's

9. The exposition below focuses on numerical examples, since the problems posed cannot be solved in their general form. In particular, the equations involve d, d', e, and e' terms raised to the third power, as well as complicated interaction effects.

Table 8.2. Minimum Characteristics of Favorable
Job Information

Number of periods	e'	Minimum value of d'		
		r = 0.07	r = 0.5	r = ∞
2	0.1	0.053	0.053	0.05
2	1	0.54	0.53	0.5
2	10	5.4	5.4	5.0
2	100	54.0	54.0	50.0
6	0.1	0.059	0.056	0.05
6	1	0.59	0.57	0.5
6	10	6.2	5.8	5.0
6	100	62.0	58.0	50.0
10	0.1	0.06	0.056	0.05
10	1	0.62	0.57	0.5
10	10	6.4	5.9	5.0
10	100	65.0	59.0	50.0

probability assessment. The required d'/e' does approach a limiting value—the known probability of success that yields a discounted expected reward equal to the amount the worker can obtain with his initial prior assessment. In the two-period case for which r equals 7 percent, the discounted expected payoffs equal

$$0.5[1 + 0.67(1.07)^{-1}] = 0.813.$$

An equivalent situation in which the probability of success takes on a known value q arises if

$$q[1 + q(1.07)^{-1}] = 0.813.$$

Solving this quadratic equation for q yields a value of 0.54, which inspection of Table 8.2 indicates is the limiting ratio d'/e'.

An increase in the number of periods in the worker choice problem increases the opportunities for information acquisition and adaptive response. In the death lotteries case, the impact is to increase the extent to which the probability assessment will diverge from its initial value after a streak of successful outcomes. The attractiveness of this updating increases with the worker's time horizon—a result reflected in Table 8.2. As the number of periods increases, the minimal d'/e' also rises, though at a diminishing rate.

The disincentives for providing all but the most favorable information no doubt contribute to the widespread reluctance of enterprises to make their safety records public. Unions similarly might be reticent about the level of job risks at an enterprise. Contract agreements that call for the promotion of workplace safety would be superior to those that imposed a maximum average worker fatality rate of 10^{-4}, because of workers' preference for loose probability assessments. Increasing this penchant of the enterprise to withhold information is the lower level of average compensation costs when workers use average injury rates as their probability assessments rather than the actual probabilities for each job.

Precedent-setting implications may also enter the revelation decision. If a firm discloses the accident rate in 1979, unions and workers may expect this practice to continue. If the 1980 injury level is unusually high, the firm must decide whether or not to reveal this result. The latter option will be quite unattractive if workers' probability assessments conditional upon this nondisclosure decision are extremely low. Particularly when there are substantial fluctuations in the injury rate, the optimal long-run policy may be to maintain the confidentiality of job outcomes.

A similar result may arise with respect to partial information provision in static contexts. Consider a multi-plant firm that publicizes a favorable injury record at a single location. Even if the employment bill is reduced at that plant, workers in other locations may revise downwards their assessed probability of success after taking into account both the publicized injury rate and the fact that no similar disclosure was made for their own job situation. Seemingly favorable information provided on a selective basis in either static or multi-period contexts need not further the enterprise's interests.

Finally, in dynamic situations the beneficial effects of reducing injuries through job safety information includes not only direct injury costs but also the altered injury record of the enterprise. More favorable worker experiences will tend to reduce the turnover of present employees and enhance the enterprise's reputation as a safe place to work, reducing hiring costs.

8.4 TURNOVER COSTS AND INFORMATION PROVISION

The hiring and training investment of an enterprise in its workers makes worker turnover costly to the enterprise. Whereas the only matter of concern in the previous sections was the minimization of the wage level, the introduction of turnover costs into the model makes the stability of employment a matter of potential significance in determining the optimal wage level and the information provided to workers.

To introduce the basic features of the choice problem and to provide a standard of comparison for subsequent results, consider the following two-period model in which turnover is costless. The objective of the employer is to minimize discounted expected wages. The value of the wage is the wage level that will lead the worker with a two-period employment choice problem to accept the job in the initial period. If the worker quits after an unfavorable job outcome, a new worker will be hired at the same wage as was paid in period 1. The enterprise's task thus reduces to choosing the level of information provision that will minimize this wage level.

For concreteness, assume that worker probability assessments $p(0, 0)$ for job I in the enterprise is described by the Beta function $B(d, 2)$, that a successful job outcome is valued at the wage w and a failure is valued at 0.[10] Somewhat analogously, the alternative job II offers a known probability of success of 0.5, with a success being valued at 1 and a failure being valued at 0. The discount factor b, or $1/(1 + r)$, is 0.9.

The enterprise is able to alter the desirability of job I by providing information to influence the worker's prior assessment. Suppose that the true value of p is 0.5 and that the employer can provide only accurate information, that is, $d'/e' = 0.5$. The worker's posterior distribution is thus $B(d + 0.5e', e + e')$, where the employer selects the optimal value of e', thus determining the sharpness and perhaps the level of the worker's prior assessment. The employer must pay the worker his wage irrespective of the job outcome.[11]

The wage level w is the minimum amount that will make job I at least as desirable as job II to the worker or, more specifically, would satisfy

(1) $[(d + 0.5e')/(2 + e')]w + 0.9[(d + 0.5e')/(2 + e')]$
$[(1 + d + 0.5e')/(3 + e')]w + 0.9\{1 - [(d + 0.5e')/(2 + e')]\}$
$\times \max\{[(d + 5e')/(3 + e')]w, 0.5\} \geq 0.5 + 0.9(0.5).$

The terms on the left side of equation (1) represent the discounted expected value to the worker of starting job I in the initial period of this two-period adaptive choice problem. The first term represents the expected first period reward. The second term is the discounted value of

10. The model in Section 8.5 treats injuries somewhat differently, viewing them as a fixed monetary loss c. The analytic results are not significantly affected by which format is employed.

11. This assumption clearly represents a great simplification when coupled with our earlier assumption that the worker values an unfavorable outcome at zero, irrespective of the wage. The justification for this approach is analytic simplicity and a desire to make the results comparable to the earlier adaptive models. None of the analytic results of interest would be affected by the use of a more general model.

the expected second period payoff after a success in period 1, multiplied by the probability of an initial period success. The final term on the left side is the discounted value of the maximum reward the worker can obtain after an initial period failure either by remaining at job I or by switching to job II, multiplied by the probability of an initial period failure. The terms on the right side of the equation represent the rewards associated with job II.

In the first situation that I will consider, the employer is interested only in minimizing the value of w.[12] Except in instances of perfect worker information where e' is infinite, the minimal wage will be sufficient to attract workers but not to retain them after an unfavorable job outcome, or

$$0.5 > [(d + 0.5e')/(3 + e')]w.$$

The analytic motivation for this result is that workers will necessarily require a greater wage in period 2 after a job injury in period 1, since they have lowered the mean value of their probability assessments.[13] This result, which was derived for the general adaptive choice situation in Chapter 4, can be readily verified.

The minimum value of w required to attract, but not retain, workers can be obtained from equation (1) and is given by

$$(3) \quad w = \frac{0.5 + 0.45[(d + 0.5e')/(2 + e')]}{[(d + 0.5e')/(2 + e')]\{1 + 0.9[(1 + d + 0.5e')/(3 + e')]\}}.$$

The appropriate information provision procedure for this situation is for the firm to withhold all information from the worker (that is, set e' at zero) if d is greater than or equal to 0.93, and to provide perfect information to the worker (that is, set e' at infinity) if d is less than 0.93. This result is quite general. The enterprise provides perfect information if the worker underestimates the probability of success sufficiently and it provides no information otherwise.

If turnover is costly to the enterprise, the hiring and training costs associated with each new worker enter the cost minimization procedure. Let the features of the choice problem be the same as before, except that the firm incurs a hiring cost h both in the initial period and in the second period if the worker quits after an unfavorable job outcome.

The firm has two options. First, it can provide the minimal wage as before and incur the turnover cost if there is an unfavorable job outcome, which has an associated probability of 0.5. The discounted expected cost C_1 of this procedure is

$$C_1 = 1.9w_1 + h + 0.9(0.5)h = 1.9w_1 + 1.45h,$$

12. We exclude, of course, Beta priors for which d and e are infinite or zero.
13. Their time horizon is also shorter, raising the required wage level.

where w_1 is identical to the value of w determined (by equation (2) above). Alternatively, the firm can choose the wage and information mix that will retain the worker irrespective of the job outcome. The associated cost C_2 is given by

(4) $$C_2 = h + 1.9w_2,$$

where

$$w_2 = \min_{e'} [0.5(3 + e')/(d + 0.5e')].^{14}$$

If the value of d is less than 1.5, the firm will provide perfect information; otherwise it will provide no information in its effort to minimize w_2.

The choice between the two procedures hinges on the value of d and the level of the firm's investment in workers h. If h equals 1, the first high turnover option will be desirable unless d is less than 1.22. Below that level of d, it will be desirable to provide perfect information to workers, thus eliminating job switching in the second period. If the value of h is increased to 2, the second procedure is preferable for all values of d. The least costly method of eliminating turnover is to provide perfect information if d is less than 1.5 and no information for higher values of d. The wage policy for this no-information decision, however, is higher than with the high-turnover option. In particular, the wage determined by equation (4) is sufficient to keep the worker at the enterprise even after an unfavorable job outcome. Information provision results in a tradeoff between higher wage costs and lower turnover costs.

The principal ramification of turnover costs is that enterprises' concern with worker mobility may make it worthwhile to increase the wage rate or provide perfect information to the workers in an effort to reduce quitting. As in the no-turnover-cost case, it is never optimal to provide imperfect information (that is, e' always equals 0 or ∞). Below a critical value of d, no information is provided; above that value, full information is provided.

An important difference in the no-turnover-cost case is that information provision may be attractive even if workers do not underestimate the mean probability of success. Full and accurate information provision may be desirable even if the assessed probability of success is substantially higher than its true value, provided that the decrease in turnover costs offsets the added wage costs that this procedure entails.

The analytic results become altered somewhat if the expected dura-

___

14. The expression for w_2 can be derived in straightforward fashion from the third term in equation (1). It is simply the requirement that 0.5 not exceed the expected reward that job I offers in period 2 after an initial period failure.

tion of employment of prospective employees differs. The influence of different worker time horizons can be captured with a simple variation of the earlier model. Let the employer's choice situation be the same as before except that if the worker quits after the first period, the worker hired in period 2 considers the job to be a single-period position only. The minimum wage that this worker will accept is

$$w_3 = 0.5[(2 + e')/(d + 0.5e')].$$

Information provision lowers w_3, provided that d is less than 1.

The overall discounted expected costs C_1 associated with the high-turnover choice are now given by

$$C_1 = 0.45w_3 + 1.45w_1 + 1.45h.$$

This expression is the same as C_1 was before, except that $0.45w_1$ has been replaced by $0.45w_3$, which is the discount factor 0.9 multiplied by the wage w_3 and the probability 0.5 of an unfavorable job outcome in the initial period. The costs C_2 associated with the no-turnover situation remain unaltered.

Table 8.3 summarizes the results associated with this enterprise choice problem. Column 1 lists different values of d, while column 2 presents the values of e' that minimize C_1. The introduction of different worker time horizons has altered the optimal information-provision

Table 8.3. Data for Information Provision Problem

d	e' to min C_1	$C_1 - 1.45h$	e' to min C_2	$C_2 - h$	$h*$
0.2	∞	1.9	∞	1.0	0
0.4	∞	1.9	∞	1.9	0
0.6	∞	1.9	∞	1.9	0
0.8	∞	1.9	∞	1.9	0
0.89	25	1.90	∞	1.9	0.00
0.9	9	1.90	∞	1.9	0.00
0.91	4.9	1.89	∞	1.9	0.02
0.92	2.7	1.89	∞	1.9	0.02
0.93	1.4	1.88	∞	1.9	0.04
0.94	0.55	1.86	∞	1.9	0.09
0.95	0	1.85	∞	1.9	0.11
1.0	0	1.76	∞	1.9	0.31
1.2	0	1.50	∞	1.9	0.89
1.4	0	1.30	∞	1.9	1.33
1.6	0	1.16	0	1.78	1.38
1.8	0	1.04	0	1.58	1.20

policy. The enterprise no longer switches from full information provision to a no-information policy as d is increased, but instead provides imperfect information (that is, finite nonzero values of e' are optimal) in the intermediate range.

The reason for this change in policy is that when worker time horizons differ, the critical value of d is not identical for different workers.[15] In such instances, there may be trade-offs between the benefits that increased information offers in reducing the wage costs of one worker and the costs it imposes in terms of the increased wages required by another employee. In striking a balance between these competing concerns, the optimal policy may call for information provision that is less than perfect. The discounted expected wage costs associated with the optimal values of e' are presented in column 3.[16]

The fourth column presents the optimal e' that minimizes C_2. As I remarked earlier, full information provision minimizes C_2 for values of d below 1.5, and no information is provided above that value. The discounted expected wage costs associated with the optimal C_2's are in the fifth column. The last two values in the column are less than 1.9, since the value of d for these entries is so high that w_2 (see equation [3]) is minimized with no information provision.

The final column of the table presents the critical value of turnover costs h^* above which the no turnover option becomes preferable. The region of finite information transfer in column 2 will be associated with the optimal enterprise decision, provided that the actual value of h is not too high. The level of turnover costs required to make it worthwhile to eliminate mobility steadily increases with the assessed probability of success (that is, with the value of d) until d becomes very large. The wage costs associated with C_2 then decline, since the wage required to eliminate mobility is less than in the full information case once d exceeds 1.5. The value of h^* rises and then falls as d is increased.

The introduction of differences in workers' time horizons does not disrupt the general result that it may be worthwhile for firms to pay higher wages or convey information to workers when turnover is costly. What did change was the nature of information provision. The optimal level of e' no longer switches from 0 to ∞ at the critical value of d, but instead may take on a finite, nonzero value as the firm attempts to strike a balance between the differential impacts of information provision across the members of the work force.[17] As the next

15. A similar result arises when the prior assessments of workers are not identical, but the time horizons are the same.

16. The value of these costs when d is equal to 0.89 and 0.9 is less than 1.9, but the difference between 1.9 and these amounts is less than 0.01.

17. This result remains true even if turnover costs equal zero.

section will demonstrate, trade-offs of this type are present in other situations in which the employer is dealing with a heterogeneous population of workers rather than a single hypothetical individual.

8.5 Self-Selection, Turnover Costs, and the Optimal Provision of Information

Minor modification of the self-selection model in Section 7.2B permits one to analyze the optimal provision of information in situations in which there are worker turnover costs. In particular, workers' prior assessments will be described not by $B(\gamma p, \gamma)$, but by $B(\gamma sp, \gamma s)$, where s reflects the extent of information provision. The analysis here is restricted to interior solutions with partial information provision so that[18]

$$1 < s < \infty.$$

The model is the same as in Chapter 7, except that γ is replaced by γs. The sharpness of the worker's prior assessment can be increased by the firm. As before, the distribution of γ's ranges from $\underline{\gamma}$ to $\bar{\gamma}$ and is described by the density function $f(\gamma)$. Individuals in the population differ in the sharpness of the prior assessments but not in their mean value.[19]

The cost of a wage policy that eliminates turnover is given by equation (8) of Chapter 7, with the following modifications obtained by replacing γ by γs in the earlier analysis. First, the wage rate w_3 that eliminates the turnover of the workers with the sharpest probability assessments must satisfy

$$(5) \qquad w_3 \geq w_0 - (\bar{\gamma} spc)/(\bar{\gamma} s + 1).$$

Second, the lowest value of γ for which the worker will not quit after an unfavorable outcome in the initial period satisfies

$$\gamma s < (w_0 - w_3)/(pc - w_0 + w_3),$$

or

$$(6) \qquad \gamma < (w_0 - w_3)/s(pc - w_0 + w_3).$$

The value of γ that equals the right side of equation (6) will be indicated by γ_3. The analysis in Chapter 7 considered the special case in which s equaled 1.

---

18. The generalization to corner solutions is straightforward.

19. Differences in the mean values will require one to employ double integrals rather than a simple integral in equation (7) and will also alter some of the other equations a bit. The trade-off discussed in the context of the model in the text will still be present, but in a slightly different form.

The probability q that a random employee will quit is given by a modified version of equation (7) in that chapter, or

$$(7) \qquad q = \int_{\underline{\gamma}}^{(w_0-w_3)/s(pc-w_0+w_3)} f(e)de,$$

where the upper bound on the interval of integration follows from equation (6).

The earlier sections have assumed that enterprises could provide information costlessly. While this assumption facilitated the analysis, it abstracted from the perhaps substantial costs of altering workers' probabilistic judgments. To reflect these costs, let $g(s)$ represent the cost of providing the level s of information, where

$$g'(s) \geq 0.$$

Incorporation of the preceding changes into equation (8) of the preceding chapter yields an enterprise cost function of the form

$$(8) \quad C_3 = g(s) + h + (w_3 + c)(1 + b) + (1 - p)bqh$$
$$+ \lambda[w_3 - w_0 + (\bar{\gamma}spc)/(\bar{\gamma}s + 1)].$$

where λ equals zero if the strict inequality in equation (5) is satisfied. The enterprise's decision problem is to pick the wage level w_3 and level of information provision s that minimize its discounted expected costs per worker for the two periods, which is given by C_3.

Since the differentiation of equation (8) with respect to w_3 yields a result similar to that in the previous chapter, I will focus only on the other first-order condition. At an interior solution, the value of s satisfies

$$(9) \qquad \partial C_3/\partial s = 0 = g'(s) + (1 - p)bh(\partial q/\partial s) + \lambda[\bar{\gamma}pc/(\bar{\gamma}s + 1)^2].$$

Increasing the value of s involves a critical trade-off, since it generates a marginal cost $g'(s)$, decreases the expected turnover costs, and increases the wage costs. The third term on the right side of equation (9) represents the increased wage costs due to the greater precision of the worker's probability assessments after information provision. It consists of the shadow price λ of the wage constraint multiplied by the increase in w_3 caused by the increased sharpness of the worker's prior assessment from a marginal increase in s. The second term on the right side of equation (9) is the marginal turnover cost effect, which is the product of the probability $(1 - p)$ of an injury, the discount factor b, the hiring and training cost h, and the marginal decrease in the quit rate from increased provision of information, which is given by $\partial q/\partial s$.

The determinants of the magnitude of $\partial q/\partial s$ can be ascertained by differentiating equation (7) with respect to s, implying that

$$\partial q/\partial s = [(w_0 - w_3)/(pc - w_0 + w_3)][-1/s^2]f(\gamma_3).$$

The effect of increasing s on the quit rate is increased if there is a large concentration of workers at the γ_3 value at the quit–no-quit margin given by $(w_0 - w_3)/s(pc - w_0 + w_3)$. Increases in s also have sizable impact on q if they lower this critical γ_3 value substantially, where the value of $\partial\gamma_3/\partial s$ is

$$\partial\gamma_3/\partial s = [(w_0 - w_3)/(pc - w_0 + w_3)][-1/s^2].$$

The presence of the s^2 term in the denominator indicates that marginal increases in the provision of information will have rapidly diminishing effects on worker turnover.

8.6 CONCLUSIONS

If enterprises possess superior information concerning the nature of job hazards, provision of this information to workers could ameliorate the individual misallocations arising from worker uncertainty. Because of the many deviant properties of information as an economic good, most notably its nonexcludability aspects, a market arrangement in which the enterprise charges for the information is not viable. These well-known difficulties are compounded by the fact that the potential provider of the information has a direct interest in its effect on individual behavior, further diminishing the incentives for information transfer.

Previous analyses of information provision have focused on single-period situations in which individual learning and adaptive behavior do not enter. The analysis presented here indicates that incorporation of the adaptive structure of the individual choice problem has two competing effects on the desirability of information provision. Worker preferences for jobs with dimly understood properties diminishes the attractiveness of information provision. However, the introduction of adaptive behavior also introduces learning-induced quits as a potential matter of concern. If worker turnover is sufficiently costly, information provision may be attractive.

The optimal degree of information transfer depends not only on the cost of information provision and the relative strength of these effects, but also on the underlying characteristics of the population. Due to the substantial economic barriers to full information provision, worker observations and judgments will remain important determinants of their assessments of the likely implications of employment.

9

INFORMATION PROVISION AND UNRAVELING PHENOMENA

9.1 INTRODUCTION

On January 24, 1976, President Ford made his medical records public. Within the next four days all major presidential candidates except Eugene McCarthy opened their medical files to public scrutiny and subsequent publication in *Medical World News*. This group included Governor George Wallace—the candidate whose physical condition was least suited to the duties of the presidency.

Unraveling effects, in which a sequence of actions may be generated by one such action, have been observed in a variety of contexts. Schelling (1972b), for example, has analyzed the importance of these interactive effects in influencing patterns of residential segregation. A slight change in a neighborhood's racial mix may lead to dramatic movements generating a pattern of total segregation. Analyses of adverse selection by Arrow (1970) and market signaling by Spence (1974a and b) likewise are concerned with the impact of group externalities on individual decisions. A broad class of such situations with unraveling effects and qualitative uncertainty has been considered by Akerlof (1970), whose principal paradigm is the market for used cars or, more specifically, the lemons' market.

The analysis in this chapter is concerned with unraveling effects in enterprises' provision of information about the firm's hazards. If workers judge the firm's riskiness by the average risk at firms that have not disclosed their level of risk, the incentives of other market participants to reveal this information will be altered once one enterprise has done so. The subsequent unraveling process may continue until full disclosure by all enterprises in the industry has been achieved. Alternatively, there may be stable equilibria with some participants withholding information.

Section 9.2 presents the basic model for structuring these situations and analyzes the most salient properties of the market outcomes. In Section 9.3, I analyze the influence that variations in information-transfer costs have on the equilibrium outcome. Section 9.4 considers some of the additional ramifications arising when the analysis involves more than a single period. Although the analysis focuses on enterprises' provision of safety information to employers, the analytic implications are applicable to a variety of market contexts in which quality certification occurs. Throughout this section I make the simplifying assumption that the firms in an industry and the job mix at these firms remain unchanged after information provision. The potential efficiency gains that I neglect need not offset the efficiency losses involved in the information transfer process.

9.2 THE BASIC MODEL

The nature of the interdependence in market contexts where information is imperfect can be illustrated using the following simple model. Suppose there are nine firms in an industry, each with a single job for workers. Each job offers a wage w_i and a probability p_i of a successful job outcome, such as remaining uninjured. The values of p_i are given by $i/10$, and only each firm i knows its true p_i. Workers and firms know the overall distribution of these probabilities, however, and assess the probability of success for all firms as being the average for the industry, where $\bar{p}$ equals 0.5 for the case being considered. To complete the model, assume that workers place a value of -1 on an unfavorable job outcome and that they maximize expected payoffs, where the wage is paid irrespective of the job outcome. Alternative employment with a reward of 0.2 is available, and the wages are set competitively.

In the absence of any information transfer, workers will be employed in the industry at a wage w for each firm, provided that

$$w + (\bar{p} - 1) \geqq 0.2,$$

or

$$w \geqq 0.7.$$

All firms with above average probabilities of job success can lower the wage required by altering the worker's assessments in the direction of the true probability involved. For simplicity, assume that each firm can convey the true probability p_i to the worker or, alternatively, alter the

Table 9.1. Data for the
Basic Model

Firm	p_i	w_i	c_i
9	0.9	0.3	0.4
8	0.8	0.4	0.35
7	0.7	0.5	0.3
6	0.6	0.6	0.25
5	0.5	0.7	0.2
4	0.4	0.8	0.15
3	0.3	0.9	0.1
2	0.2	1.0	0.05
1	0.1	1.1	0

individual's probability distribution so that its mean is equal to p_i.[1] The firm with the most to gain from such information transfer is firm 9, which can lower the wage it must pay to 0.3. As a result, firm 9 would convey such information provided that doing so doesn't cost more than 0.4.

After the characteristics of firm 9 are made known, workers' assessments of the average probability $\bar{p}$ for the remaining eight firms in the industry will drop to 0.45, increasing the incentive of all firms with $p_i > 0.45$ to indicate the true job characteristics. Firm 8 will have the greatest incentive to do so and will be willing to incur a cost of up to 0.35 to transfer this information. For the parameters of this example, the unraveling process will continue until workers have perfect information about all of the jobs in the industry.

Table 9.1 summarizes the market outcome. The equilibrium wage w_i is paid by firm i with a probability p_i of a successful outcome. Assuming that no lower-numbered firms have revealed the true job characteristics and that all higher numbered firms have done so, each firm will be willing to incur a cost up to c_i (see the last column of Table 9.1) to provide accurate information about the job. This amount decreases linearly as the unraveling process occurs. For a uniform information transfer cost across firms that exceeds 0.05, an equilibrium with partial information will result. Although the figures in Table 9.1 assume that complete unraveling occurs, the extent of information transfer in any instance in which information transfer costs are uniform across firms can be identified in straightforward fashion using the data in Table 9.1.

1. The process of enterprises learning their relative hazards and investing in credible forms of information transfer raises nontrivial market signaling problems. I will neglect these issues in order to concentrate on the unraveling effects.

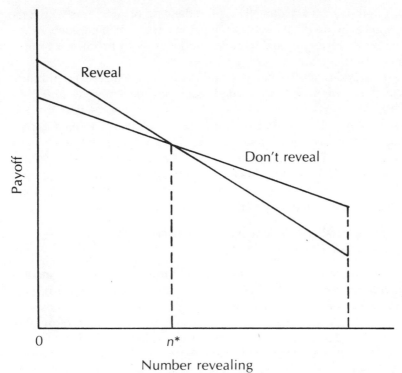

Figure 9.1 Payoffs for Information Transfer Decision

The process of reaching an equilibrium outcome is depicted diagrammatically in Figure 9.1. The payoff for revealing or not revealing the true job characteristics depends on the number of firms that have already revealed. For simplicity, I assume that the unraveling procedure follows its natural ordering (from highest p_i to lowest p_i). For the payoff curves drawn, the information transfer process stops after n^* firms have indicated the true job characteristics. It is easy to devise other payoff structures resulting in no information provision, full information provision, or multiple equilibria. Moreover, one can generalize the behavior pattern so that firms take into account the likely actions of their competitors in making the decision whether to reveal information or not.

The unraveling process in quality certification closely resembles group behavior in lemons-type models of qualitative uncertainty and asymmetrical provision of information. In each instance, enterprises or individuals at the above-average end of the quality spectrum successively distinguish themselves from the group in a process that unravels from the top down. The major difference is that instead of exiting from the market altogether, as in the case of good risks who forgo insurance or used-car owners who don't trade in high-quality cars, enterprises invest in quality certification so as to practice a form of price discrimination.

Finally, consider the efficiency properties of the market equilibrium. When no information is provided, each firm pays a wage of 0.7, resulting in a total wage bill of 6.3. With complete information, the total wage bill remains at 6.3. The difference is that there has been a redistribution from workers in less hazardous jobs to those in more hazardous positions. The wages paid by firms change similarly. More importantly, firms are willing to incur an information transfer cost of up to 1.8 during the unraveling process. This amount is a total efficiency loss to society and is the only efficiency effect in the model.[2]

9.3 Equilibria and Variations in Information Transfer Costs

In the basic model, the amount c_i that firms are willing to incur to provide information declines linearly to zero as the number of firms conveying information increases. If information provision costs are nontrivial, one will observe interior solutions with partial information provision. Other market situations create substantially different patterns for c_i, with obvious implications for equilibrium.

Let the parameters of the problem be the same as before, except that the job lotteries in the industry are lotteries on life and death. Assume that death receives a value of zero, and that workers maximize expected payoffs, as before. If workers judge jobs in the industry by the average probability of success $\bar{p}$, the required wage w for all firms must satisfy

$$\bar{p}w = 0.5w \geq .2,$$

or

$$w \geq 0.4.$$

The information transfer process occurs as before, with the resulting values of w_i and c_i summarized in Table 9.2.

Two results are of interest. First, the amount c_i that firms are willing to incur no longer declines as i decreases. Instead, it increases throughout until leveling off at 0.333 for the last two firms with an incentive to convey information. If actual information-transfer costs were uniform across firms, the revelation process would necessarily proceed

---

2. If an enterprise pays a certifying agent to verify and publicize its work quality level, the information transfer cost might best be viewed as a transfer payment rather than a net loss to society.

Table 9.2.   Data for the
Death Risk Model

Firm	p_i	w_i	c_i
9	0.9	0.22	0.178
8	0.8	0.25	0.194
7	0.7	0.29	0.214
6	0.6	0.33	0.238
5	0.5	0.4	0.267
4	0.4	0.5	0.3
3	0.3	0.67	0.333
2	0.2	1.0	0.333
1	0.1	2.0	0

to the perfect information equilibrium once it had begun. Even in instances in which signaling costs varied, there would be a much stronger tendency toward disclosure than in the basic model in Section 9.2.

The second important result is that even though workers are risk-neutral (that is, they maximize expected monetary payoffs), they require greater total pay when each of the firm-specific risks is known than they do when they choose randomly from the nine jobs. The total pay package for workers is 5.7, as compared with 3.6 in the situation where information is not revealed. This redistribution of 2.1 to workers equals the potential efficiency loss, which is also 2.1 if all firms incur their maximum c_i.[3]

Thus far, the distribution of job types has been assumed to be uniform in the industry. A nonuniform distribution may contribute to substantial changes in c_i as the unraveling process proceeds. Consider a six-firm industry with p_i's given in Table 9.3. Firm 6 is much safer than the rest, firms 3–5 are in the mid-range, and firms 1 and 2 are considerably more hazardous. Assume that the unfavorable job outcome is an injury valued at -1. The pattern of c_i's is no longer monotonic in this instance. The value of c_i first declines, then increases, and subsequently declines. Variations of this type are likely to be especially important in influencing equilibrium outcomes when signaling costs or the number of employees varies from firm to firm.

Complications such as these may give rise to more complicated

3. This equalization of the potential efficiency loss and the redistribution amount is not a phenomenon that is generalizable to situations involving other wage distributions or utility functions. For example, if there were three firms in the industry with p_i's of 0.9, 0.8, and 0.1, the potential efficiency loss would be 0.306—far less than the 1.47 redistribution to workers.

Table 9.3. Data for the
Nonuniform Case

Firm	p_i	w_i	c_i
6	0.9	0.3	0.46
5	0.5	0.7	0.15
4	0.49	0.71	0.17
3	0.48	0.72	0.22
2	0.2	1.0	0.05
1	0.1	1.1	0

behavior patterns. For example, firms with high p_i's will not provide information until their group mean has been made very unattractive by
the information transfer activity of firms with lower p_i's. Alternatively,
the model can be generalized to include the provision of imperfect information that alters workers' probability assessments in an imperfect
manner. In such instances, the assessed value of p_i after information
transfer may change as additional information is acquired. The next section considers an analytically similar problem in which worker
learning occurs.

9.4 THE MULTI-PERIOD CASE

The information transfer process becomes somewhat more complicated if the model includes more than a single period. The first principal difference is that information transfer affects an enterprise's reputation and hence its future wage costs. Consider a simple example in
which workers have a work life of only one period, but the information
provided in the first period remains public for an additional period.
The total population and employment are the same in each period.
Thus, the amount a firm will be willing to pay to provide information
will increase from its former value of c_i to $(1 + b)c_i$, where b equals
$(1 + r)^{-1}$ and r is the interest rate. The information transfer process
would be substantially more likely to unravel since firms would be
willing to incur signaling costs almost double those in the single-
period case. This tendency will be increased to the extent that firms
anticipate additional unraveling in the second period and wish to reap
the gains of information transfer for both periods.

An influence in the opposite direction is that in multi-period contexts loose probability assessments are more attractive to workers than
are tighter distributions with identical mean probabilities of success.
To analyze the implications of this result, modify the death lottery example summarized in Table 9.2 to include a second period of work for
those workers who survive. Assume that workers maximize discounted

Table 9.4. Data for the Two-Period
Death Case

Firm	p_i	d_i	w_i	c_i
9	0.9	1.8	0.143	0.175
8	0.8	1.6	0.170	0.194
7	0.7	1.4	0.205	0.216
6	0.6	1.2	0.253	0.240
5	0.5	1.0	0.324	0.266
4	0.4	0.8	0.432	0.271
3	0.3	0.6	0.618	0.300
2	0.2	0.4	1.000	0.218
1	0.1	0.2	2.171	0

wages and use a discount factor of 0.935 (or an interest rate of 7 percent) in obtaining the present value of rewards in the second period. The alternative occupation offers a known probability of survival of 0.2 in each period and an associated reward of 1 for a successful outcome.

I will assume that workers have the same mean probability assessments for jobs as in the single-period case. The principal difference is that the shape of the distributions is now of import, since learning occurs after initial period successes. As in the earlier chapters, these priors will be treated as Beta functions $B(d, e)$. For concreteness, I assume that workers assess the nine jobs available as being characterized by a value of e equal to 2 and a value d equal to that given in the third column in Table 9.4. The problem is that workers do not know which of the nine jobs is associated with each firm so that they initially employ an aggregative assessment of $B(9, 18)$.

For simplicity, assume that the mean probability that would be assessed if d_i were known (that is, $d_i/2$) is in fact the true p_i for that job. When firms provide information to workers, they provide the true value of p_i, which is not altered by subsequent information. As firms reveal job properties to workers, those d_i's in Table 9.4 corresponding to the actual p_i's already involved are eliminated from consideration so that the new worker assessment for the uncertain jobs is given by $B(\Sigma d_i, \Sigma e_i)$, where the summation refers to all jobs whose true properties are not known.

If a firm indicates the actual value of p_i, its wages must satisfy the property that

$$p_i w_i + p_i^2 w_i(0.935) \geq 0.2 + (0.2)(0.2)(0.935),$$

or

$$w_i \geq 0.2374/(p_i + 0.935 p_i^2)$$

For firms in the group with uncertain jobs,

$$w \geqq \frac{0.2374}{\dfrac{\Sigma d_i}{\Sigma e_i} + 0.935 \dfrac{\Sigma d_i}{\Sigma e_i} \left(\dfrac{1 + \Sigma d_i}{1 + \Sigma e_i}\right)},$$

where the summation is for the group of remaining uncertain positions. The objective of the firm is to minimize the wage rate and information transfer costs for workers facing the two-period job choice problem.

The results for the two-period death lottery case are summarized in Table 9.4. In the absence of information transfer, the prevailing wage would be 0.318, as compared with 0.4 in the single-period case. This difference reflects in part the attractiveness of loose prior assessments in multi-period contexts. Though one might have expected substantial increases in the value of c_i as a result of the doubling of the number of periods, the actual values are similar to those found in the static model. As a comparison of the results in Tables 9.2 and 9.4 indicates, the value of c_i is now less for firms at the two extremes and greater for firms with intermediate risks. Whereas c_i steadily increased in the single-period case as the unraveling process occurred, in the two-period model c_i rises and then declines. This pattern is less conducive to a full-information equilibrium following an initial information transfer than is the corresponding pattern in the static model.

The principal impacts of information transfer on efficiency and equity are, in this case as in the static case, to redistribute income to workers on more hazardous jobs, to increase the total wage bill, and to impose efficiency losses equal to the information transfer costs. However, the increase in wages to workers (that is, 2.45) exceeds the maximum possible signaling costs (that is, 1.88) once the time horizon is extended to two periods.

Perhaps the principal implication of these results is that one should avoid generalizations as to whether information transfer is more or less likely as the number of periods is increased. While information provision becomes more attractive in a society with a memory because it establishes a reputation, the predilection of individuals in multi-period contexts to prefer an uncertain alternative to one with a known probability of success serves as a countervailing influence. The impact of discounting and the manner in which workers update their prior assessments as a result of experience complicate further any efforts to derive a straightforward relationship in the provision of information between the number of periods involved and unraveling phenomena.

9.5 CONCLUSION

The models in this chapter suggest that there may be important interdependencies in information transfer. In particular, the provision of job hazard information by one firm may alter the incentives of other firms to do likewise. The unraveling process resulting from these externalities affects the extent of worker information about different firms, the distribution of wages for jobs posing different risks, the total wage bill of workers, and the efficiency of market outcomes.

An indirect implication of the analysis is that a governmental or private investigation of the hazards in a particular firm may generate a subsequent unraveling process that might not have occurred otherwise. Phenomena of this type are most likely to unravel from the top down, that is, the safest firms in an industry are first identified, and subsequently workers lower their assessments of the average safety levels for firms that have not revealed. However, actual publicity relating to job hazards invariably focuses attention on the most hazardous enterprises. Straightforward application of the models in this chapter to this behavior would suggest that such revelations will impede rather than accelerate the unraveling process. These efforts may, however, be productive in altering the job conditions in the particular firm under scrutiny. Moreover, publicizing job conditions in the most hazardous enterprises may lower the assessed mean safety level for the industry, which in turn may lead to information transfer from the relatively safe firms and to a subsequent unraveling pattern.

10

PROBABILISTIC LABOR SUPPLY, THE PRODUCTION FUNCTION, AND ENTERPRISE DECISIONS

10.1 INTRODUCTION

There are always uncertain elements about an enterprise's labor supply. Stochastic elements influencing both the acquisition of new workers and the retention of present employees make the process of securing a work force fundamentally different from the neoclassical norm of instantaneously clearing markets. The retention of present workers involves substantial uncertainties, since the enterprise typically can assess only the average rate at which workers will quit or be forced to leave on account of job-related injuries or other influences that are not totally subject to the firm's discretion. The hiring process can be described in similar terms, since imperfections in worker information and search costs limit the size of the applicant pool at any one time, while screening costs and the time-consuming nature of hiring procedures introduce additional delays in the hiring process. The accession of new workers to a firm and the departure of present workers both occur at finite, probabilistic rates.[1]

This chapter will explore the implications that various types of labor supply uncertainties have for a firm's production function and will investigate some of the more salient economic ramifications of this structure. The economic influences considered include the impact of job risks and other stochastic elements on the degree of returns-to-scale, as

---

1. A third element—the output of a given supply of workers—also is important but will not be incorporated in the models in this chapter. Moreover, I will assume that the quit and hiring rates are known with precision, thus abstracting from learning effects.

well as an analysis of the interrelationship among the firm's allocations for wages, training, hiring, screening, and improvements in the quality of the workplace. These types of concerns have never been articulated within the context of a production function for which the associated supply of labor is probabilistic. Although Mortensen's (1970) insightful examination of wage and employment dynamics incorporated the stochastic nature of quits and accessions, he did not investigate the impact of these probabilistic influences on the form of microeconomic production functions since his analysis was directed at more aggregative concerns, such as the Phillips' curve relation.

As the analysis will indicate, the probabilistic aspects of labor supply have other important ramifications, both for the form of the production function and the nature of enterprise decisions. Many of these implications can be illustrated using a simple static model, which is introduced in Section 10.2. In Section 10.3, I investigate the ramifications of probabilistic labor supply for the dynamic optimization model that will be employed throughout the remainder of this chapter. The first-order conditions for optimal enterprise decisions are presented in Section 10.4, while Section 10.5 is devoted more specifically to the impact of worker turnover on optimal training investments. In Section 10.6 I consider the role of scale effects within the context of enterprise choice and, in particular, the likely variations of safety investments with enterprise size.

10.2 PROBABILISTIC LABOR SUPPLY AND THE FORM OF THE PRODUCTION FUNCTION: THE STATIC CASE

A. The Fixed-Coefficients Model. Although the impact of labor supply uncertainties on the production function has never been scrutinized, existing economic analyses do provide some insight into the nature of the problem. The analytic structure implied by probabilistic labor supply bears a strong resemblance to the classic repairman problem, originally formulated by the Swedish engineer Palm.[2] The principal economic features of this machine breakdown problem can be summarized using a simple single-period example, which will be

---

2. See Feller (1971) for a description of Palm's work. Arrow first examined the economic implications of this problem in his 1951 essay "Alternative Approaches to the Theory of Choice in Risk-Taking Situations" and in an appendix to his 1953 essay "The Role of Securities in the Optimal Allocation of Risk-Bearing," both of which are reprinted in Arrow (1971). The asymptotic properties of the production function associated with the repairman problem have been examined by Levhari and Sheshinski (1970) and by Arrow, Levhari, and Sheshinski (1972). A seminal economic analysis of the implications of variability in both inputs to the production process is provided by Walters (1960).

described in terms of stochastic labor supply rather than stochastic machine availability.[3]

Consider an enterprise with n machines and M workers. Each worker faces a 0.5 probability of injury. This lottery is independent of the number of machines or the lottery outcomes for other workers. Each uninjured worker produces a single unit of output if he alone is assigned to a mchine, and he produces zero units of output otherwise—in other words, total output equals min $[n, m]$, where m is the number of uninjured workers. The values of M and n that will be considered are the integral amounts from 1 to 10. Using binomial distribution formulas, one can calculate for different initial workforce levels the probabilities associated with the different possible work force levels after the lotteries have occurred.

Utilizing these probabilities and data on the number of machines, one can determine expected output levels in straightforward fashion. For example, if p represents probability, the expected output EV from one machine and three workers is given by

$$EV = p(m = 0) \cdot 0 + p(m = 1) \cdot 1 + p(m = 2) \cdot 1 + p(m = 3) \cdot 1,$$

or

$$EV = 0 + [1 - p(m = 0)] \cdot 1 = 1 - 0.125 = 0.875$$

Table 10.1 summarizes the expected output levels for different combinations of workers and machines. Several patterns are of interest. Despite the fixed-coefficients nature of the technology, the isoquants implied by the results no longer exhibit the usual kinked shape, but rather display some curvature in the region where the number of workers exceeds the number of machines. One can analyze the expected marginal product EMP of workers by inspecting the columns of the table. If the number of workers does not exceed the number of machines, EMP equals 0.5. However, once workers outnumber machines, EMP declines but does not drop to zero as in the deterministic analogue of this example. Provided that the wage is not too high, it will be worthwhile for enterprises to hire a precautionary labor reserve when the availability of workers is subject to stochastic influences.

The EMP of the workers in this buffer group increases with the scale of operation. For the one worker–one machine situation, an additional worker has an EMP of 0.25. This value is a little more than half of the 0.49 EMP of an extra employee for an eight worker–eight machine enterprise, since in this latter case the likelihood of worker injuries is so

---

3. This example is an elaboration of the discussion in the aforementioned 1953 article by Arrow (1971). He considered the machine breakdown case involving two machines and one worker and the case involving four machines and two workers.

Table 10.1. Expected Output as a Function of the Number of Workers and the Number of Machines

| Workers | Expected Output | | | | | | | | | |
| | Machines | | | | | | | | | |
	1	2	3	4	5	6	7	8	9	10
10	1.00	1.99	2.93	3.76	4.37	4.76	4.93	4.99	4.99	5.00
9	1.00	1.98	2.89	3.63	4.13	4.39	4.48	4.50	4.50	4.50
8	1.00	1.96	2.81	3.45	3.81	3.96	3.99	4.00	4.00	4.00
7	0.99	1.93	2.70	3.20	3.43	3.49	3.50	3.50	3.50	3.50
6	0.98	1.87	2.53	2.86	2.97	3.00	3.00	3.00	3.00	3.00
5	0.97	1.78	2.27	2.44	2.50	2.50	2.50	2.50	2.50	2.50
4	0.94	1.62	1.94	2.00	2.00	2.00	2.00	2.00	2.00	2.00
3	0.88	1.38	1.50	1.50	1.50	1.50	1.50	1.50	1.50	1.50
2	0.75	1.00	1.00	1.00	1.00	1.00	1.00	1.00	1.00	1.00
1	0.50	0.50	0.50	0.50	0.50	0.50	0.50	0.50	0.50	0.50

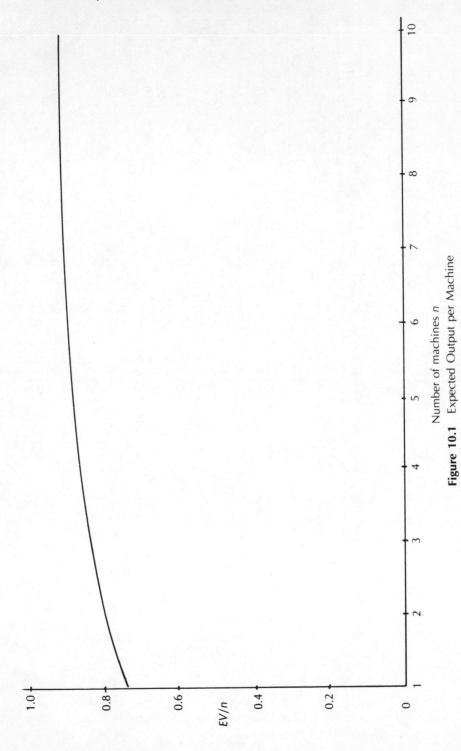

Figure 10.1 Expected Output per Machine

great that the first worker in the reserve group has an EMP only 0.01 less than that of the core labor force.

The most important pattern related to the scale of operation is that the production process exhibits increasing returns to scale if the number of workers exceeds the number of machines, as can be seen from inspection of expected output levels along rays from the bottom left corner of Table 10.1. The expected output level per machine when there are twice as many workers as machines are graphed in Figure 10.1.[4] The number of machines is represented by the horizontal axis, with the per machine expected output levels along the vertical axis. While there is evidence of increasing returns to scale, the importance of this effect diminishes quite rapidly as the results approach a situation of constant returns. The increasing returns phenomena nevertheless may be an important economic consideration even for very large enterprises if there is a great deal of heterogeneity of worker skills.

B. The Cobb-Douglas Model.   Although subsequent sections will also focus on the fixed-coefficents production function, the analytic implications of the stochastic aspects of labor supply generalize to other forms of production functions. Consider two Cobb-Douglas situations. First, if the labor supply is uncertain, then using the earlier notation, total output Q_1 equals

$$Q_1 = \sum_{i=1}^{M} p(m = i)(n)^\alpha (i)^{1-\alpha}.$$

Alternatively, let the firm's labor supply be invariable, with its value equal to the mean labor supply for the probabilistic case. The total output Q_2 for this situation is

$$Q_2 = (n)^\alpha \left[\sum_{i=1}^{M} p(m = i)(i) \right]^{1-\alpha}.$$

For concreteness, the parameter α will be set at 0.25.

The results for the Cobb-Douglas situations are presented in Tables 10.2 and 10.3. Consider the first columns in the tables, which pertain to the one-machine case. Although Q_2 is never less than Q_1, the difference in total output narrows as the number of workers is increased. The marginal product of labor in the mean labor supply case initially exceeds that for the probabilistic labor supply situation by 0.09. However, with a greater number of workers, labor's marginal product is never greater in the mean labor supply situation. With two workers

---

4. A curve has been drawn through these points to assist in the interpretation of the results. Due to the indivisibility of men and machines, only the points associated with integral numbers of machines are pertinent.

Table 10.2. Output Q_2 with the Mean Value of Labor Supply

Output Q_2

Workers	Machines									
	1	2	3	4	5	6	7	8	9	10
10	3.34	3.98	4.40	4.73	5.00	5.23	5.43	5.62	5.79	5.95
9	3.09	3.67	4.07	4.37	4.62	4.84	5.03	5.20	5.35	5.49
8	2.83	3.36	3.72	4.00	4.23	4.43	4.60	4.76	4.90	5.03
7	2.56	3.04	3.37	3.62	3.83	4.00	4.16	4.30	4.43	4.55
6	2.28	2.71	3.00	3.22	3.41	3.57	3.71	3.83	3.95	4.05
5	1.99	2.36	2.62	2.81	2.97	3.11	3.23	3.34	3.44	3.54
4	1.68	2.00	2.21	2.38	2.51	2.63	2.74	2.83	2.91	2.99
3	1.36	1.61	1.78	1.92	2.03	2.12	2.20	2.28	2.35	2.41
2	1.00	1.19	1.32	1.41	1.50	1.57	1.63	1.68	1.73	1.78
1	0.59	0.71	0.78	0.84	0.89	0.93	0.97	1.00	1.03	1.06

Table 10.3. Output Q_1 with Probabilistic Labor Supply

| | Output Q_1 | | | | | | | | | |
| | Machines | | | | | | | | | |
Workers	1	2	3	4	5	6	7	8	9	10
10	3.31	3.94	4.36	4.68	4.95	5.18	5.38	5.57	5.73	5.89
9	3.05	3.63	4.02	4.32	4.57	4.78	4.97	5.14	5.29	5.43
8	2.79	3.32	3.67	3.95	4.17	4.37	4.54	4.69	4.83	4.96
7	2.52	3.00	3.32	3.56	3.77	3.94	4.10	4.24	4.36	4.48
6	2.24	2.66	2.94	3.16	3.34	3.50	3.64	3.76	3.87	3.98
5	1.94	2.31	2.55	2.74	2.90	3.04	3.16	3.26	3.36	3.45
4	1.63	1.94	2.14	2.30	2.43	2.55	2.65	2.74	2.82	2.89
3	1.29	1.53	1.70	1.83	1.93	2.02	2.10	2.17	2.24	2.30
2	0.92	1.09	1.21	1.30	1.38	1.44	1.50	1.55	1.59	1.64
1	0.50	0.59	0.66	0.71	0.75	0.78	0.81	0.84	0.87	0.89

and one machine, for example, labor's marginal product is 0.42 in the probabilistic situation and 0.41 in the mean value instance. This pattern reflects the general applicability of the precautionary labor surplus concept introduced in the fixed-coefficients case.[5]

The degree of returns to scale also is influenced by uncertainty in the supply of labor. In the mean value Cobb-Douglas case in Table 10.2 returns to scale are, of course, constant. However, with the introduction of stochastic fluctuations in the labor supply, as shown in Table 10.3, returns to scale increase. Unlike the fixed-coefficients case, there are increasing returns even in the situation in which the number of workers does not exceed the number of machines. The results for the Cobb-Douglas example share with the earlier fixed-coefficient results the property that the degree of returns to scale declines as the ratio of workers to machines is increased.

The economic patterns associated with these simple static models also arise in multi-period contexts through stochastic accession and turnover rates. Subsequent portions of this chapter will consider the as yet unexplored issues of the impact of stochastic input supplies on enterprise decisions. The analysis will be restricted to fixed-coefficient production functions because of their general manipulability and the greater clarity they offer in illuminating pertinent analytic phenomena.

10.3 PROBABILISTIC LABOR SUPPLY AND THE STRUCTURE OF FIRM DECISIONS: AN INTRODUCTION TO THE DYNAMIC MODEL

The probabilistic dependence of the size of the work force on rates of accession and turnover can be structured most appropriately as a continuous-time stochastic birth and death process.[6] Consider the one worker–one machine case. There are two states—state 1 in which there is a worker for the machine and state 2 in which there is not. The objective of the firm is to select its different kinds of expenditures—wages, hiring and screening costs, workplace quality investments, and

---

5. The surplus aspect is less clear-cut in the Cobb-Douglas case, since all workers always have nonzero marginal products. The central property common to the fixed-coefficients and Cobb-Douglas production functions is that in probabilistic contexts the enterprise's demand for labor is motivated in part by the flexibility additional workers provide. The superiority of the fixed-coefficients model in illuminating this and other results is responsible for my emphasis on that type of production function.

6. This probabilistic structure is identical to the variant of the repairman problem for which the number of repairmen equals the number of machines. My analysis differs from that of Arrow, Levhari, and Sheshinski (1972) since they were concerned exclusively with the asymptotic properties of the differential matrix, whereas I focus on the Markovian decision framework and its economic implications. For a more formal motivation of the analytic structure employed, see Wagner (1969) and Howard (1971).

training expenditures—to maximize the discounted expected rewards associated with residency in each of the two states.

If the system is now in state 1, it will remain there if the worker does not leave the enterprise, or it will move to state 2 if the worker quits, is injured or killed, or terminates employment for some other reason. Let λ be the rate at which a worker will leave the enterprise—in other words, the duration of a worker's tenure at the enterprise is exponentially distributed with mean $1/\lambda$.

If there is no worker currently employed, the enterprise will attempt to hire a replacement. This process is not instantaneous, since the nature of the worker search process limits the applicant pool, while the inherent features of the screening and hiring process introduce delays on the employer side of the market. A worker will be hired at an exponential rate μ, implying a mean time of $1/\mu$ to fill the job opening.[7]

The parameters λ and μ are the transition rates a_{12} and a_{21}, respectively, where the transition rates from state i to state j in this continuous time process are given by $a_{ij}(i \neq j)$. The stochastic nature of these rates produces random time intervals between transitions. In any short time interval dt, $a_{ij}dt$ is the transition probability from state i to state j. The probability of two or more transitions is of the order of dt^2 or higher and is negligible in the limit as $dt \rightarrow 0$. The remaining elements of the transition rate matrix A are the diagonal elements a_{ii}, which are given by

$$a_{ii} = - \sum_{j \neq i} a_{ij},$$

since the rows of such a differential matrix sum to zero. For the one worker–one machine case,

$$A = \begin{bmatrix} -\lambda & \lambda \\ \mu & -\mu \end{bmatrix}.$$

A similar procedure is used to construct transition rate matrices of greater size, where M is the peak work-force size and k is the number of job openings. The total number of states in this more general system is $M + 1$. If there are k job vacancies, the current state of the system is $k + 1$. The rows of the transition matrix A and other matrices and vectors are indexed according to these states.

For simplicity, I will refer to departures from the workforce as quits and accessions as hires.[8] The quit rate q_{k+1} for this situation is simply λ

7. In a more general model, this parameter μ also could include the rate at which injured workers recuperate and return to the firm.

8. The chance of simultaneous quits or simultaneous hires is assumed to be negligible compared to the chance of a single quit or hire.

times the current workforce size m, or

$$q_{k+1} = m\lambda = (M - k)\lambda.$$

Somewhat analogously, the hiring rate h_{k+1} for an additional worker is given by

$$h_{k+1} = k\mu.$$

The overall quit and hiring rates are proportional to the number of individuals now at work and the number of job openings, respectively. This format is not especially restrictive since the exponential rates λ and μ will be dependent on enterprise decisions.[9]

Since the chance of multiple quits or hires is negligible compared to the likelihood of a single quit or hire, only single-state transition effects enter, producing a differential matrix of the form

$$\begin{bmatrix}
-q_1 & q_1 & 0 & 0 & 0 & 0 \\
h_2 & -(h_2 + q_2) & q_2 & 0 & 0 & 0 \\
0 & h_3 & -(h_3 + q_3) & q_3 & 0 & 0 \\
0 & 0 & h_4 & -(h_4 + q_4) & q_4 & 0 \\
0 & 0 & 0 & h_M & -(h_M + q_M) & q_M \\
0 & 0 & 0 & 0 & h_{M+1} & -h_{M+1}
\end{bmatrix}.$$

Excluding the special cases of the top and bottom rows, the only non-zero elements of the matrix are the diagonal elements ($a_{ii} = -q_i - h_i$) and the two terms in each row bordering the diagonal ($a_{di} = q_i$ and $a_{ei} = h_i$, where d equals $i + 1$ and e equals $i - 1$).

The optimal policy for an enterprise depends not only on the transition rates, but also on the associated payoffs. In its general form, the earnings rate v_i for any state i is given by

$$v_i = s_{ii} + \sum_{j \neq i} a_{ij} s_{ij},$$

where s_{ii} is the reward rate per unit time for remaining in state i and s_{ij} is the reward for a transition from state i to j.

To derive the particular earnings rate formula for the firm's labor choice problem, some additional notation is required. The firm can

---

9. The mathematical structure of this problem also is sufficiently flexible to incorporate variations in λ and μ for different states. Such variations are quite plausible, since, for example, a firm may wish to increase the hiring rate parameter μ as the size of the work force declines. Since my focus will be on the one machine–one worker case and the rate of returns to scale in the production process, this additional complication would not be central to the analysis and would only serve to complicate further the analytics of the problem.

alter four types of costs, where

c_1 = costs incurred to alter working conditions
c_2 = wage costs
c_3 = hiring and screening costs
c_4 = the costs of the firm's investment in the workers it hires.

I will assume that c_1 and c_2 are proportional to the number of workers, that c_3 is proportional to the number of vacancies, and that c_4 is incurred with each new hire. Output per worker $f(c_4)$ increases at a diminishing rate with the company's investment in worker skills, that is, $f' > 0$ and $f'' < 0$. For a firm with n machines, a peak work-force of M workers, and k job openings, the earnings rate for state i is

$$v_i = \min[n, m] \cdot f(c_4) - mc_1 - mc_2 - k\mu c_4 - kc_3,$$

where i equals $k + 1$ and m equals $M - k$. The earnings rate vector $\mathbf{v}$ consists of the $m + 1$ v_i's.

The motivation for incurring costs other than the training investment c_4 is that these expenses are the mechanisms by which the firm influences the turnover and accession rates. The rate at which workers quit is dependent both on the wage level c_2 and the working conditions.[10] It is also assumed that working conditions improve with increases in the c_1 allocation. If the working conditions pertain to health and safety aspects of the job, the influence of c_1 on turnover may not be restricted to quits but may also encompass the role of on-the-job injuries and deaths in prompting exit from the firm. The exponential quit rate parameter λ consequently is given by

$$\lambda = \lambda(c_1, c_2),$$

where $\partial\lambda/\partial c_1$ and $\partial\lambda/\partial c_2$ are both negative.

The functional dependence of the hiring rate on firm expenditures consists of three types of influences. Higher wages c_2 increase the hiring rate, implying that the firm faces a rising supply curve and in effects acts as a dynamic monopsonist.[11] Nonwage hiring costs c_3 also can increase the likelihood of acquiring additional workers. Advertising, changes in screening procedures, and increases in the number of interviewers are among the most important areas of choice. Finally, the hiring rate may depend on λ to the extent that this parameter serves as an observable measure of working conditions for prospective workers. The components of λ include injuries, deaths, and

10. The importance of working conditions and wages to workers' quit decisions has been articulated in the earlier treatment of adaptive behavior in Chapter 4.
11. This term was coined by Mortensen (1970).

discharges—each of which may be pertinent to a worker's employment decision. The hiring rate μ consequently is given by

$$\mu = \mu(\lambda, c_2, c_3),$$

where $\partial\mu/\partial\lambda$ is less than zero, while $\partial\mu/\partial c_2$ and $\partial\mu/\partial c_3$ are positive.[12]

The $(M + 1) \times (M + 1)$ transition rate matrix A takes on the same general form as introduced earlier except than λ and μ are functions, not fixed parameters. To determine the optimal levels of λ and μ, I will formulate the firm's choice problem as an infinite time horizon, Markovian decision model. Let I be an $(M + 1) \times (M + 1)$ identity matrix. Rewards are discounted using an interest rate r, and the discounted expected value of starting in state i is u_i. Recalling that $\mathbf{v}$ is the previously described $(M + 1) \times 1$ earnings rate vector, one can solve for the $(M + 1) \times 1$ vector $\mathbf{u}$ of discounted expected payoffs to the firm, which is given by

(1) $$\mathbf{u} = (rI - A)^{-1}\mathbf{v}.[13]$$

The objective of a firm starting in state i is to select c_1, c_2, c_3, and c_4 to maximize discounted payoffs u_i.[14]

An important feature of the model is that it highlights the enterprise's concern with two critical margins—the hiring rate and the turnover rate. The investment in the workplace that alters working conditions and the flow of workers has been treated in terms of overall outlays c_1. The aggregative treatment of these expenditures reflects in part the nonexcludability aspect of the work environment, as enterprises typically select an overall quality level instead of attempting to vary working conditions on an individual basis.[15]

To investigate the use of the optimization model, consider the following discrete choice example. A one man–one machine firm currently in state 1 and facing an interest rate of 12 percent must select the optimal expenditure mix. In particular, it must choose between high and low levels of working conditions expenditures (c_1 equal to 0 or 0.1), wages (c_2 equal to 0.2 or 0.3), hiring and screening expenditures (c_3 equal to 0.05 or 0.1), and training investments (c_4 equal to 0.1 or

12. The working conditions variable c_1 could have been included in μ but was not, since workers cannot monitor its value. The impact of c_1 is indirect, through the observable variable λ.

13. For derivation of this formula, see chapter 8 of Howard (1960).

14. More generally, the firm also selects the number of machines and the peak work-force size. However, we will for the most part abstract from the choice of the production process in order to isolate the analytic phenomena of particular interest.

15. Employers can, however, alter the assignment of workers to jobs of differing risk. This aspect of enterprise decisions is not considered in this analysis.

0.2). The exponential quit rate is given by

$$\lambda = y - 10c_1c_2;$$

the hiring rate is

$$\mu = 1 + 10c_1c_2 - .1\lambda;$$

and worker output level is

$$f(c_4) = \ln(1 + xc_4),$$

where the values of x and y are varied in the example to illustrate the effect of changes in worker productivity and turnover on firm decisions.

Table 10.4 summarizes the optimal cost allocations under different circumstances. Initially, let x equal 400 and y equal 2. In this situation of highly productive labor, u_1 is maximized by incurring high levels of training costs and other expenditures designed to secure and retain the work force. If worker productivity is reduced, as in case 2 ($x = 50$), extensive hiring and screening procedures no longer are worthwhile, and it becomes optimal to select a lower level of c_3 and hence a longer mean worker replacement time. Further reduction of worker productivity resulting from a drop of x to a value of 15 makes all types of high expenditure levels unattractive except for the training investment, which remains sufficiently productive despite the high turnover rate and low hiring rate. However, even this expenditure level will be reduced to a low level if worker productivity declines further, as in case 4, or if there is an increase in worker quit rates, as in case 5.

The types of patterns reflected in these examples seem to be of general importance. The level of training investment is likely to be positively correlated with other allocations to secure and retain workers. However, particularly for the intermediate worker productivity cases, the appropriate mix and level of expenditures hinges on more complex interdependencies than can be formalized with the use of illustrative examples. The derivation in the next section of the first-order condi-

Table 10.4. Data for the Discrete Choice Problem

Case	x	y	c_1 (working conditions)	c_2 (wages)	c_3 (hiring and screening)	c_4 (training)
1	400	2	High	High	High	High
2	50	2	High	High	Low	High
3	15	2	Low	Low	Low	High
4	10	2	Low	Low	Low	Low
5	15	3	Low	Low	Low	Low

tions for optimal enterprise decisions should clarify these types of relationships.

10.4 FIRST-ORDER CONDITIONS FOR OPTIMAL MULTI-PERIOD DECISIONS

To analyze the optimality conditions for situations in which continuous variations in expenditure levels are permitted, consider the general one worker–one machine example.[16] The value determination equation (1) takes on the specific form

$$(2) \qquad \mathbf{u} = \left\{ r \begin{bmatrix} 1 & 0 \\ 0 & 1 \end{bmatrix} - \begin{bmatrix} -\lambda & \lambda \\ \mu & -\mu \end{bmatrix} \right\}^{-1} \begin{bmatrix} f - c_1 - c_2 \\ -\mu c_4 - c_3 \end{bmatrix},$$

'where the functional dependencies of λ, μ, and f have been omitted in the interest of notational simplicity. For concreteness, assume that the initial position is state 2 — no workers have been hired. Solving equation (2) for u_2 produces the result that

$$u_2 = [\mu(f - c_1 - c_2) + (r + \lambda)(-\mu c_4 - c_3)][r^2 + r\mu + r\lambda]^{-1}.$$

The first-order conditions for optimal enterprise allocations are obtained by partially differentiating u_2 with respect to the four types of expenditures and setting these partials equal to zero, yielding

$$(3a) \quad \frac{\partial u_2}{\partial c_1} = 0 = [r^2 + r\mu + r\lambda]^{-1} \left[(f - c_1 - c_2) \frac{\partial \mu}{\partial \lambda} \frac{\partial \lambda}{\partial c_1} - \mu \right.$$

$$+ \frac{\partial \mu}{\partial c_1}(-c_4 - c_3) + (r + \lambda)\left(-c_4 \frac{\partial \mu}{\partial \lambda} \frac{\partial \lambda}{\partial c_1} \right) \Bigg]$$

$$- [r^2 + r\mu + r\lambda]^{-2}[\mu(f - c_1 - c_2)$$

$$+ (r + \lambda)(-\mu c_4 - c_3)] \left[r \frac{\partial \mu}{\partial \lambda} \frac{\partial \lambda}{\partial c_1} + r \frac{\partial \lambda}{\partial c_1} \right];$$

$$(4a) \quad \frac{\partial u_2}{\partial c_2} = 0 = [r^2 + r\mu + r\lambda]^{-1} \left[\left(\frac{\partial \mu}{\partial \lambda} \frac{\partial \lambda}{\partial c_2} + \frac{\partial \mu}{\partial c_2} \right)(f - c_1 - c_2) \right.$$

$$- \mu + \frac{\partial \lambda}{\partial c_2}(-\mu c_4 - c_3)$$

$$+ (r + \lambda)\left(-c_4 \frac{\partial \mu}{\partial c_2} - c_4 \frac{\partial \mu}{\partial \lambda} \frac{\partial \lambda}{\partial c_2} \right) \Bigg]$$

$$- [r^2 + r\mu + r\lambda]^{-2}[\mu(f - c_1 - c_2)$$

$$+ (r + \lambda)(-\mu c_4 - c_3)] \left[r \frac{\partial \mu}{\partial c_2} + r \frac{\partial \mu}{\partial \lambda} \frac{\partial \lambda}{\partial c_2} \right.$$

$$+ r \frac{\partial \lambda}{\partial c_2} \Bigg];$$

16. Throughout this section I will analyze only interior solutions.

(5a) $\quad \dfrac{\partial u_2}{\partial c_3} = 0 = [r^2 + r\mu + r\lambda]^{-1} \left[\dfrac{\partial \mu}{\partial c_3}(f - c_1 - c_2) \right.$

$$- (r + \lambda)\left(1 + c_4\dfrac{\partial \mu}{\partial c_3}\right)\bigg]$$

$$- [r^2 + r\mu + r\lambda]^{-2}[\mu(f - c_1 - c_2)$$

$$+ (r + \lambda)(-\mu c_4 - c_3)]\left[r\dfrac{\partial \mu}{\partial c_3}\right];$$

and

(6a) $\quad \dfrac{\partial u_2}{\partial c_4} = 0 = [r^2 + r\mu + r\lambda]^{-1}\left[\mu\dfrac{\partial f}{\partial c_4} - (r + \lambda)\mu\right].$

After some simplification, these equations become

(3b) $\quad c_1 = \left\{\dfrac{\partial \mu}{\partial \lambda}\dfrac{\partial \lambda}{\partial c_1}(r + \lambda)[f - c_2 + c_3 - (r + \lambda)c_4]\right.$

$$- \mu\dfrac{\partial \lambda}{\partial c_1}(f - c_2 + c_3 + rc_4)$$

$$\left. - \mu(r + \mu + \lambda)\right\}\left\{\dfrac{\partial \mu}{\partial \lambda}\dfrac{\partial \lambda}{\partial c_1}(r + \lambda) - \mu\dfrac{\partial \lambda}{\partial c_1}\right\}^{-1};$$

(4b) $\quad c_2 = \left\{\dfrac{\partial \mu}{\partial c_2} + \dfrac{\partial \mu}{\partial \lambda}\dfrac{\partial \lambda}{\partial c_2}[(r + \lambda)(f - c_1 + c_3 - (r + \lambda)c_4)]\right.$

$$\left. \mu\dfrac{\partial \lambda}{\partial c_2}\cdot[f - c_1 + c_3 + \mu c_4 + r + \lambda + \mu]\right\}$$

$$\left\{(r + 2\mu + \lambda)\left(\dfrac{\partial \mu}{\partial \lambda}\dfrac{\partial \lambda}{\partial c_2} + \dfrac{\partial \mu}{\partial c_2} + \dfrac{\partial \lambda}{\partial c_2}\right)\right.$$

$$\left. - \dfrac{\partial \lambda}{\partial c_2}(r + \mu + \lambda)\right\}^{-1};$$

(5b) $\quad c_3 = \dfrac{(r + \mu + \lambda) - \dfrac{\partial \mu}{\partial c_3}[f - c_1 - c_2 - (r + \lambda)c_4]}{\dfrac{\partial \mu}{\partial c_3}};$

and

(6b) $\quad\quad\quad\quad\quad\quad\quad f' = r + \lambda.$

What is particularly striking about these results is that the four types of enterprise allocations—investments in working conditions, wage payments, hiring and screening costs, and training investments—are interlinked through a series of complicated feedback loops. The optimal expenditure levels can be ascertained by solving this simultaneous equation system for the optimal expenditure levels. The enterprise invests in each of the four areas until expected marginal benefits no longer exceed expected marginal costs appropriately discounted.[17]

Investments in workplace conditions are productive for two reasons. First, they decrease turnover directly, as the terms in equation (3b) involving $\partial\lambda/\partial c_1$ indicate. Second, they exert an indirect effect on the hiring rate through the quit rate impact, reflected in the $(\partial\mu/\partial\lambda)$ $(\partial\lambda/\partial c_1)$ terms. The appropriate level of expenditures to improve the work environment depends on the amount of other expenditures, worker productivity, the levels of the hiring and quit rates, and the interest rate. Similar interdependencies can be observed for equations (4b) and (5b) as well.

The reasons for these interdependencies are illuminated in part by the numerical examples presented in the previous section. If, for example, training investments are unproductive or the quit rate is very high, a firm may find the possible allocation mixes involving sizeable expenditures to improve the job environment unattractive. Alternatively, the optimal c_1 may be low if wages are a much more effective mechanism for altering λ of if μ can be increased so efficiently that the enterprise finds a high turnover, low training, and quick worker replacement policy optimal.

Equation (4b) identifies the three types of wage impacts that are of import. Higher wages may reduce quit rates (the $\partial\lambda/\partial c_2$ terms), may increase the hiring rate directly (the $\partial\mu/\partial c_2$ terms), and may increase the hiring rate indirectly (the $(\partial\mu/\partial\lambda)(\partial\lambda/\partial c_2)$ terms). The principal implication for wage determination is that wages are not equalized with the worker's marginal product as it is conventionally defined.

As is well-known, the training investment by an enterprise drives a wedge between the wage and the worker's marginal product. Even abstracting from this impact, however, the relationship between wages and marginal productivity is no longer direct. First, firms are willing to incur a higher wage in order to decrease worker turnover. This wage should not, however, be viewed as a windfall gain for labor but rather as the economic inducement workers require to provide continued labor services to the enterprise rather than switching to alternative economic activities, such as another job. Second, higher wages increase the rate at which workers will be hired. This latter influence alone is sufficient to disrupt the conventional equilization of wages and marginal productivity, since the enterprise no longer purchases labor services but instead incurs costs to manipulate the likelihood that it will receive such services.

17. It should be noted that for equations (3b), (4b), and (5b), terms involving λ and μ are often functions of the cost terms on the left side of the equation.

The standard economic result in which wage premiums for turnover reduction are viewed as being less directly linked to marginal output than the base wage rate is simply the consequence of an asymmetric analytic approach. The relation of wages to the stochastic flows into and out of the work force suggest that one should broaden the correspondence between wages and marginal productivity to include not only worker output per se, but also the marginal impacts of wages on turnover and quit rates. Marginal benefits and marginal wage allocations remain equated, but simply in a more general form.

The hiring and screening cost equation (5b) is much simpler, involving only one marginal benefit term—$\partial \mu / \partial c_3$. Perhaps the most important feature of this result is that it provides an analytic motivation for the emphasis of many enterprises on nonwage recruitment measures—policies which are usually attributed to institutional factors and a desire to avoid disruptions in the community wage structure.[18] The probabilistic labor supply model suggests that more traditional optimizing forces may be at work. Hiring and screening expenditures, c_3, enter only during the hiring process and are proportional to the number of vacancies, whereas higher wages are paid to the entire work force and, unless there is a change in the remuneration policy, will continue to impose additional costs in future periods. Moreover, the effectiveness of wages, c_2, and nonwage hiring expenditures, c_3, in altering the hiring rate μ may be different. The appropriate mix of nonwage expenditures will be determined on the basis of their relative effectiveness and the types of cost patterns they impose or, in short, on the basis of the structure of the firm's optimization problem.

Finally, the marginal condition that can be interpreted most readily is equation (6b) for enterprise training investments. Since this result is quite pertinent to the mainstream of the labor economics literature, the entire next section will be devoted to an exploration of its implications.

10.5 TURNOVER AND TRAINING INVESTMENT

The expected dividends an enterprise reaps from its investments in worker productivity increase with the payoff period, that is, with the duration of the employee's tenure with the enterprise. Although this observation is not new, the relationship between the optimal training investment and worker turnover has never been formalized.[19] In the one worker–one machine model, the firm incurs a training investment

18. See Doeringer and Piore (1971) for this alternative approach.

19. Pathbreaking analyses by Becker (1964) and Oi (1962) discuss the impact of labor turnover, but do not develop a detailed analysis of the enterprise's optimization problem, such as that presented here.

of c_4 for each new worker. The appropriate investment level must satisfy equation (6b), which equates the marginal product of training investment f' with the sum of the interest rate r and the quit rate λ.

Although the discussion below will treat λ as a fixed parameter, it is actually endogenous to the model. If the firm has a large training investment, it will be worthwhile for it to incur wage and work environment improvement costs to reduce its value. Indeed, such efforts must necessarily accompany large values of c_4, since the marginal value of training investment diminishes with c_4 (that is, if $f'' < 0$) and equation (6b) must be satisfied at the optimum. With a fixed interest rate, high levels of c_4 and the corresponding low values of f' must be associated with low quit rates.

The dependence of the training investment on the quit rate accords with one's intuitions. As the duration of employment becomes very long (that is, as λ goes to zero), the marginal product of training investment is reduced and perhaps eliminated altogether.[20]

The relationship between training and quit rates generalizes to different employment contexts. Consider the two worker–two machine case. Solution of the version of equation (1) that applies to this situation produces the result that the discounted expected rewards starting in the no-worker state are given by

$$(7) \quad u_3 = \{2\mu^2(2f - 2c_1 - 2c_2) + 2\mu(r + 2\lambda)(f - c_1 - c_2 - c_3 - \mu c_4) \\ + [(r + 2\lambda)(r + \mu + \lambda) + 2\lambda\mu][-2\mu c_4 - 2c_3]\} \\ \{(r + 2\lambda)[(r + \mu + \lambda)(r + 2\mu) - 2\lambda\mu] \\ + 2\mu(r + 2\mu)\}^{-1}.$$

After setting the partial derivative $\partial u_3/\partial c_4$ equal to zero, the relationship simplifies to

$$f' = r + \lambda,$$

which is identical to equation (6b) for the one worker–one machine case. Indeed, due to the constant returns nature of the n worker–n machine problem, this marginal condition holds for all such situations.

If there is a precautionary labor reserve, the optimal investment in each worker is slightly different. Consider the two worker–one machine situation. The reward rate for state 1 is reduced from $2f - 2c_1 - 2c_2$ to $f - 2c_1 - 2c_2$, resulting in a change of one term in equation (7). Solving for the optimal training investment produces the result that

$$f' = r + \lambda + (r + \lambda)/(\mu + r + 2\lambda).$$

For fixed parameter values, the marginal product of training invest-

---

20. A corner solution results if f' is less than $r + \lambda$ at a zero level of investment.

ment is less than in the two-machine case by the amount given by the last term in this equation. This result implies that the firm invests less per worker in training when it has a buffer stock of labor, since the investment in the reserve worker is only productive when there is an employment vacancy.

Finally, consider the importance of utilizing a decision framework in which expected payoffs are discounted. If one considers only the asymptotic properties of the production function, the optimal training investment is somewhat different. The limiting state probability vector π for the one worker–one machine problem is given by

$$\pi = [\mu/(\lambda + \mu), \lambda/(\lambda + \mu)].$$

Multiplying the earnings rate vector $\mathbf{v}$ by these asymptotic probabilities yields the average gain g for the process, which is

$$g = [\mu/(\lambda + \mu)][f - c_1 - c_2] + [\lambda/(\lambda + \mu)][-\mu c_4 - c_3].$$

Setting the partial derivative with respect to c_4 equal to zero and solving produces the result that

$$f' = \lambda.$$

Consideration of the asymptotic properties alone will lead to an overinvestment in training, since it neglects the role of the interest rate, which plays a pivotal role in this intertemporal trade-off situation. The asymptotic formulation of the model will be examined further in the next section.

10.6 SCALE EFFECTS

A potentially important determinant of an enterprise's decisions is the scale of the enterprise. The static examples provided in Section 10.1 illustrated the increasing returns phenomenon in instances in which there is a buffer stock of workers. A similar result has been formalized for asymptotic production functions for stochastic processes similar to those considered here.[21] The analysis in this section assesses the importance of such scale effects within a Markovian decision framework.

The first issue is the impact of enterprise size and other problem features on the discounted value of expected output. For purposes of this analysis, all enterprise expenditures will be ignored. This problem is a simpler variant of our earlier examples; all c_i's now equal zero and λ and μ are fixed parameters. Table 10.5 summarizes the discounted expected value of output for the infinite time horizon case in which the interest rate takes on values of 1 percent, 12 percent, and 100 percent;

21. See Arrow, Levhari, and Sheshinski (1972) and Levhari and Sheshinski (1970).

Table 10.5.   Discounted Expected Output for Different
Optimization Problems

λ, μ	$r = 0.01$	$r = 0.12$	$r = 1$	$r = 0.01$	$r = 0.12$	$r = 1$
	one worker–one machine			*two workers–one machine*		
1, 2	66.777	5.662	0.75	88.944	7.460	0.929
2, 4	66.722	5.610	0.714	88.917	7.435	0.912
0.1, 0.2	67.742	6.349	0.923	89.424	7.782	0.990
2, 10	83.347	6.958	0.846	97.226	8.105	0.975
2, 1	33.555	2.992	0.5	55.777	4.842	0.714
	two workers–two machines			*four workers–two machines*		
1, 2	133.555	11.325	1.5	187.728	15.708	1.927
2, 4	133.444	11.22	1.429	187.691	15.674	1.907
0.1, 0.2	135.484	12.698	1.846	188.358	16.117	1.994
2, 10	166.695	13.916	1.692	198.306	16.528	1.985
2, 1	67.110	5.983	1.0	121.436	10.511	1.525
	four workers–four machines			*six workers–three machines*		
1, 2	267.11	22.650	3.0	288.145	24.080	2.934
2, 4	266.889	22.440	2.857	288.106	24.044	2.913
0.1, 0.2	270.968	25.397	3.692	288.821	24.508	2.997
2, 10	333.39	27.833	3.385	299.065	24.923	2.992
2, 1	134.219	11.966	2.0	188.747	16.323	2.355
	six workers–six machines			*ten workers–five machines*		
1, 2	400.665	33.974	4.5	490.076	40.905	4.950
2, 4	400.333	33.660	4.286	490.039	40.870	4.930
0.1, 0.2	406.452	38.095	5.538	490.722	41.298	4.999
2, 10	500.087	41.749	5.077	499.757	41.648	4.998
2, 1	201.329	17.949	3.0	324.591	28.138	4.077
	ten workers–ten machines					
1, 2	667.776	56.624	7.5			
2, 4	667.224	56.100	7.143			
0.1, 0.2	667.419	63.492	9.231			
2, 10	856.667	71.548	8.722			
2, 1	335.913	30.252	5.240			

the (λ, μ) pairs consist of (1, 2), (2, 4), (0.1, 0.2), (2, 10), and (2, 1); and there are nine different machine-worker combinations.

Some of the patterns represent straightforward generalizations of the static model summarized in Table 10.1. For cases in which the number of workers equals the number of machines, the discounted expected output per machine is independent of the scale of operation. The

Table 10.6. Index of Scale Effects

Scale effects
[(discounted expected rewards)/n(discounted expected rewards with one machine)]

Machines, workers	$(\lambda, \mu) = (1, 2)$			
	Asymptotic	$r = 0.01$	$r = 0.12$	$r = 1$
1, 2	1.0	1.0	1.0	1.0
2, 4	1.056	1.055	1.050	1.026
3, 6	1.080	1.080	1.076	1.053
5, 10	1.104	1.102	1.097	1.066

Machines, workers	$(\lambda, \mu) = (2, 4)$			$(\lambda, \mu) = (0.1, 0.2)$		
	$r = 0.01$	$r = 0.12$	$r = 1$	$r = 0.01$	$r = 0.12$	$r = 1$
1, 2	1.0	1.0	1.0	1.0	1.0	1.0
2, 4	1.055	1.054	1.046	1.053	1.036	1.007
3, 6	1.080	1.078	1.065	1.077	1.050	1.009
5, 10	1.102	1.099	1.081	1.098	1.061	1.010

Machines, workers	$(\lambda, \mu) = (2, 1)$			$(\lambda, \mu) = (2, 10)$		
	$r = 0.01$	$r = 0.12$	$r = 1$	$r = 0.01$	$r = 0.12$	$r = 1$
1, 2	1.0	1.0	1.0	1.0	1.0	1.0
2, 4	1.089	1.085	1.068	1.020	1.020	1.020
3, 6	1.128	1.124	1.099	1.025	1.025	1.023
5, 10	1.164	1.162	1.142	1.028	1.028	1.025

reason for this constant returns-to-scale phenomenon is that increasing returns enter only when there is a precautionary labor reserve.

The presence of increasing returns in situations in which there is a buffer labor stock can be seen more clearly using Table 10.6, in which the discounted expected output has been divided by the number of machines multiplied by the discounted expected output level in the one-machine case. This index of scale effects is presented only for the situations in Table 10.5 in which there are twice as many workers as machines.

To facilitate comparison with the asymptotic case, a similar scale effect index has been included for the asymptotic production function, where the long-run probability π_k that there will be k job vacancies in a work force of M individuals is given by

$$\pi_k = \binom{M}{k} \frac{\lambda^k \mu^{M-k}}{(\lambda + \mu)^M}. \quad [22]$$

22. For a derivation of this result, see chapter 12 of Howard (1971).

The average gain for the process is simply the summation over all $k + 1$ states of π_k multiplied by the output level associated with that state. The scale index associated with the average grain is provided in Table 10.6.

Increasing returns with respect to the rewards of the choice problem can be observed for each of the cases considered. The increasing returns phenomenon is greatest in the asymptotic situation and becomes less important in the nonasymptotic instances as the interest rate is increased. The principal benefits from a precautionary labor reserve in such stochastic contexts pertain to the long-run flexibility it provides in diminishing the drop in output associated with the probabilistic declines in work-force size.

The rate of increase of these scale effects with firm size diminishes quite rapidly, as discounted expected payoffs approach a constant rate of increase. This result is identical to that illustrated in Figure 10.1 for the static model and in the existing literature on the asymptotic production function for the repairman problem. It should be observed, however, that while the results approach the constant returns case, the scale indices in Table 10.6 remain above 1—implying that the rate at which discounted expected payoffs increase may be constant, but is nevertheless greater than in situations in which there is no precautionary labor reserve.

The impact of increasing returns also is influenced by the level of quit and layoff rates. Consider the case in which λ/μ equals 0.5, but the absolute value of each term changes, that is, the (λ, μ) pairs are given by (0.1, 0.2), (1, 2), and (2, 4). As can be seen, scale effects become more frequent. Variations in only one of these parameters produces the patterns one might expect. For example, as μ increases, worker turnover is of less consequence because of the reduced time required to replace workers. As a result, scale effects are more pronounced when the (λ, μ) pair is (2, 1) than (2, 10). The opposite result would occur if λ were increased independently.

The principal implication of these results is that when a firm has a precautionary labor reserve, there are diminishing productivity losses from labor turnover as the size of the enterprise increases. Although these scale effects taper off fairly rapidly in the homogeneous worker case, in more realistic contexts in which worker skills are quite diverse they may remain important.

These results are pertinent to the situation in which work-environment investments are designed to improve safety and health, and the turnover includes workers injured or killed on the job. Since productivity losses from injured workers decline with firm size, larger enterprises should tend to be more hazardous. Although this may be a frequent result, it need not occur since scale effects may influence firm decisions other than the safety investment.

Table 10.7.   Data for Work Environment Investment Problem

	Case 1	Case 2
Turnover Rate	$\lambda = 1 - 14c_1 - c_2$	$\lambda = 1 - c_1 - 30c_2$
Accession Rate	$\mu = 2 + c_2$	$\mu = 1 + 20c_2$
Two worker–one machine case		
Optimal c_1	0.22	0
Optimal c_2	0	0.03
Four worker–two machine case		
Optimal c_1	0.10	0
Optimal c_2	0	0.02

Consider the following two cases in which the only types of expenditure are work-environment investments c_1 and wages c_2. The interest rate is 12 percent. The other basic problem data are summarized in Table 10.7. In case 1, the turnover rate is

$$\lambda = 1 - 14c_1 - c_2,$$

while the accession rate is

$$\mu = 2 + c_2.$$

In case 2,

$$\lambda = 1 - c_1 - 30c_2,$$

while

$$\mu = 1 + 20c_2.$$

The process begins in the no-worker state. The value-determination operation described by equation (1) is used to determine the optimal values of c_1 and c_2, which must be non-negative.

For case 1, as the production process changes from the two worker–one machine case to the four worker–two machine situation, the optimal level of c_1 declines from 0.22 to 0.10, while the optimal c_2 remains at zero. The safety investment declines with the scale of operation. For case 2, c_1 is zero for both production situations, while c_2 drops from 0.03 to 0.02 with the doubling of the scale of operations. Although the diminishing of productivity losses with enterprise scale may reduce the safety investment, it need not since firms may alter other policies, such as wage levels.

Safety investments in larger enterprises are further diminished because the ratio of workers to machines may change with the scale of operations due to the indivisibility of individual workers. In the one worker—one machine situation, it may not be worthwhile to increase the size of the workplace unless λ is very high and μ is very low. For the five worker—five machine case, however, an extra worker may be warranted. For the static model in Table 10.1, for example, the value of a marginal worker increases from 0.25 to 0.47 in these two situations. An addition to the precautionary labor reserve becomes worthwhile in larger enterprises, and this also diminishes the expected productivity losses from job injuries, consequently reducing the incentive to provide a safe environment.

10.7 Conclusions

The probabilistic nature of accessions and turnover implies that the labor supply to firms is stochastic in nature. This chapter incorporated this feature of the labor market into a Markovian model of firm decisions, which was then used to analyze the optimal acquisition and retention of workers. In addition to creating an economic rationale for a precautionary labor reserve, probabilistic labor supply introduces increasing-returns aspects into a constant-returns production process, implying that larger firms should be more hazardous, other things being equal. The analysis also formalized the relation between turnover and the training investment in workers, as well as the characteristics of decisions when the supply of labor is stochastic. The insights provided by these investigations are substantively different from the results obtained with more conventional enterprise choice models.

11

THE ROLE OF UNIONS

11.1 INTRODUCTION

In a competitive market, firms with unsafe or otherwise unpleasant
working conditions will pay higher wages, while enterprises with
lower levels of risk will pay lower wages. Individuals who are less
averse to job risks, perhaps because of differences in taste or wealth,
will be hired by the more unsafe enterprises, since they will require
less compensation to incur the hazards. This process leads to socially
optimal outcomes, where workers are perfectly informed of the risk
and the social welfare criterion is the maximization of the surplus received by employers and workers.[1] This result is simply a generalization of the analysis of Hicks (1941) for competitive markets in general, where work at some quality q is the good being traded.[2]

The discussion in the previous chapters focused on otherwise competitive markets in which workers or employers may not have full information about the hazards that are present. Although this particular
market imperfection is of central importance, other deviations from
competitive conditions, especially the presence of market power, may
also influence the level of occupational hazards and their implications
for social welfare. Imperfect job risk information and labor market
power, such as monopsonistic influences, are not entirely unrelated

---

1. For simplicity, income effects are ignored. As Willig (1976) has demonstrated for
the product market context, this approximation is likely to involve very small errors.
2. See Oi (1973, 1974) and Thaler and Rosen (1976) for a fuller description of competitive outcomes.

market imperfections, since worker uncertainties may be an important contributor to monopsonistic elements in the market, as I indicated in Chapter 10.

Section 11.2 will consider the sources and implications of monopsonistic power. If the firm faces an upward-sloping supply curve for labor, will the level of job hazards be socially optimal? Section 11.3 addresses the potential role for unions in affecting the level of hazards. Market outcomes cannot be improved by union action in an otherwise competitive world. Consequently, my primary emphasis will be on the role of unions in offsetting concentration on the other side of the market. Since I have already considered potential benefits of union action in situations in which unions have better job risk information than do workers, I will not address these issues here. The subsequent discussion will utilize the simplest possible model in which workers perceive risks correctly and respond to them optimally. The ramifications of this analysis are summarized in Section 11.4.

11.2 Causes and Implications of Monopsony Power

A. Sources of Monopsony Power. The standard labor-economics literature treats monopsonies largely as a curiosity pertinent only in discussing the somewhat strained textbook example of a company town. However, as was indicated in Chapter 10, the labor supply curve to the enterprise is upward sloping, since the firm can increase the flow of new workers by raising its wage. That analysis also indicated a third source of monopsony power, which derives from the finite worker turnover rates in response to changes in the wages or perceived working conditions. Differences in the on-the-job experiences of workers in adaptive situations and differences in the transactions costs of changing jobs are likely to be two important contributors to monopsonistic elements on the quit rate margin. In effect, probabilistic aspects of labor supply with respect to hiring rates or turnover rates generate a form of monopsonistic power as the firm becomes its own internal labor market. To facilitate the exposition, the implications of monopsonistic elements will be explored within the context of a conventional production process, rather than using a more complicated stochastic production function.

B. Monopsony and Work Quality. For a monopsonistic firm, the pertinent market context to consider is the enterprise itself, since it has its own upward sloping labor supply curve and downward sloping demand curve. Consider a representative firm that has two inputs— capital K, which has a price per unit r, and labor L, which is paid a wage rate $w(q, L)$, where q is the level of workplace health and safety. The inverse supply curve $w(q, L)$ gives the wage rate required to attract L workers at safety level q. For a monopsonistic firm, $w_L > 0$ and $w_q < 0$, since workers require compensating wage differentials for higher levels of hazards.

The restriction of the analysis to a single job-risk index simplifies the presentation but is not essential. What is important is that because of the fixed costs associated with job hazard options, the enterprise does not vary the risk on an individual basis, but instead selects an overall level of hazards for the workplace. This assumption captures the non-excludability aspects of many work quality components, such as the speed of the assembly line, the existence of grievance procedures, the scheduling of work time, and levels of noise and noxious fumes.

The production process yields two joint products—job safety q and output x. For given levels of K and L, the enterprise can produce different combinations of health and safety and product output levels. The firm must choose both the optimal level of inputs and the appropriate trade-off between these Marshallian joint products.[3] The analysis could also be developed by viewing q as an input rather than as a joint product, but this modification would not affect the spirit of the results. The output x is sold in the market at price p, while the workplace health and safety output reduces labor costs through its influence on the wage rate.

The implicit form of the production function to be utilized is $G(x, q, L, K)$, which is assumed to be convex, continuous, twice differentiable, and closed in the non-negative orthant for these four variables. Following standard conventions, I assume that

$$G_x > 0, \; G_q > 0, \; G_K < 0, \text{ and } G_L < 0.[4]$$

The analysis is restricted to finite input values, which are assumed to yield finite values of the two outputs.

The monopsonistic enterprise's surplus value (or profit) E is given by

(1) $\qquad E = \pi = px - w(q, L)L - rK + \lambda G(x, q, K, L).$

Unlike the situation in a competitive market, the surplus value V reaped by workers is not independent of the actions of the enterprise due to the presence of monopsonistic elements in the market. The eco-

3. The Marshallian joint-products analysis of work quality was introduced by Oi (1973).

4. Alternatively, one could reverse the inequality signs, changing also the sign of the Lagrange multiplier.

nomic rents V reaped by workers are given by[5]

$$V = Lw(q, L) - \int_0^L w(q, v)dv.$$

Total surplus S is the sum of worker and enterprise surplus and consequently is

(2) $$S = E + V = px + \lambda G(x, q, K, L) - \int_0^L w(q, v)dv.$$

The following analysis assumes that income effects are sufficiently small so that this total surplus measure can be taken as an index of social welfare.

The firm selects x, q, K, and L to maximize π, not S. As is well known, the monopsonistic enterprise hires a suboptimal amount of workers since it will set

$$w(q, L) + Lw_L = -p(G_L/G_x),$$

where the Lw_L term is the only difference from the first-order condition for an optimizing competitive firm. The matter of concern here is whether, for given levels of the other choice variables, the level of hazards selected by the enterprise is also inappropriate.[6] The enterprise selects q so that

(3) $$\pi_q = 0 = -Lw_q + \lambda G_q.$$

However, the optimization of the total surplus S with respect to q would yield the optimality condition

(4) $$\partial s/\partial q = 0 = \lambda G_q - \int_0^L w_q dv.$$

To analyze whether workplace health and safety is too high or too low when the enterprise selects its optimal level of q, substitute the value of λG_q from equation (3) into equation (4) so that

$$\partial S/\partial q = Lw_q - \int_0^L w_q dv.$$

---

5. Alternatively, one could take the integral along the w axis, yielding a value of

$$V = \int_0^{w(q, L)} L(q, v)dv.$$

The expression in the text is somewhat simpler to manipulate since the $Lw(q, L)$ term cancels when the worker and enterprise surplus terms are added.

6. Analysis of the combined effect of the monopsonist's choice of L and q will not be presented here, since it closely parallels the analysis by Spence (1975) for the product monopoly case.

Job risks are at their optimal level if the valuation of workplace health and safety by the marginal worker is the same as the average of the marginal valuations, that is, if

$$w_q = (1/L) \int_0^L w_q dv,$$

where the left-hand term is the marginal valuation term and the right-hand term is the average marginal valuation term. This result is similar in spirit and mathematical form to that obtained in Spence's (1975) seminal analysis of the provision of product quality by a monopolistic firm.

Workplace health and safety is too low (that is, $\partial S/\partial q > 0$) if the marginal valuation term exceeds the average marginal valuation term, and conversely. It is important to note that since w_q is negative, safety is below the socially optimal amount when the marginal worker will not accept as great a decrease in wages for a marginal improvement in safety as the average worker will. On an empirical basis one would expect the marginal worker to be younger and less experienced.[7] The inframarginal workers, who are older and wealthier, will tend to place a greater valuation on work quality since they have greater wealth and family obligations. Consequently, monopsony power should result in suboptimal levels of workplace health and safety.

In all market contexts, workers have different attitudes toward job hazards, and enterprises are assumed to be able to select only a single job-risk level for the enterprise, because of the nonexcludability aspects of job hazard decisions. However, unlike a competitive enterprise, the monopsonist typically will not face flat labor-supply curves for different levels of q. Whereas all workers at a competitive enterprise can be viewed as marginal workers who would quit if w or q were lowered, at a monopsonistic enterprise employees' hazard preferences and perceptions will be varied, so that there will be many inframarginal workers who will quit only if q or w drop dramatically.

The source of the difficulties with a monopsony's selection of q is that the preferences of the marginal worker motivate profit-maximizing decisions, whereas the preferences of the inframarginal workers are critical to the social welfare calculation. It is an oversimplification to suggest that this problem is due to inadequate information, since the enterprise does know the labor supply with complete certainty. Rather, the difficulty is that market incentives are linked to the preferences of the worker on the margin rather than those of the enterprise's entire work force.

---

7. This characterization of turnover propensities is borne out in the empirical analyses of quit behavior in Chapter 13.

C. *Wage Discrimination.* One might ask why the inframarginal workers do not reveal their true preferences with respect to job risks and the wages they require to offer their labor for particular levels of q. Instead of simply knowing the labor supply curve, the firm could then match these workers to points on the labor supply curve, pay a wage to each worker dependent on his preferences, and set the health and safety level taking workers' diverse preferences into account.

The optimal wage policy for the enterprise would be to offer each worker his reservation wage, so that the monopsony now selects x, q, K, and L to maximize

(5) $$\pi = px - \int_0^L w(q, v)dv + \lambda G(x, q, K, L),$$

where the integral term represents the wage bill with wage discrimination. Enterprise profits are now identical to total surplus to society S given by equation (2), so that maximization by the monopsony will lead to a welfare-maximizing outcome, as can be readily verified.[8]

The distributional aspects of this efficient outcome are quite unattractive for workers, since the monopsonistic enterprise reaps the entire surplus. Consequently, workers do not even receive the surplus they would have obtained in the pure monopsony case. Consider the outcome prior to the workers' revelation of their preferences. The enterprise selected a health and safety level q', employed L' workers, and paid a wage level $w(q', L')$. All workers except the marginal employee earned an economic rent, with the total surplus, V', equal to

$$V' = L'w(q', L') - \int_0^{L'} w(q', v)dv$$

Suppose that workers were to permit wage discrimination, provided that they would also be paid the economic rents they would have received for that level of L and q in a regular monopsony situation. Thus, the profit function for the wage discrimination case (equation [5]) would be reduced by a transfer equal to the worker surplus V, yielding

$$\pi = px - \int_0^L w(q, v)dv + \lambda G(x, q, K, L)$$

$$- [Lw(q, L) - \int_0^L w(q, v)dv],$$

8. This result can be viewed as a monopsonistic analog of the guaranteed annual wage contract theory of Leontief (1946). In that analysis, a labor union would specify the wage and amount of labor to be hired, subject to the constraint that the employer not be made worse off. The union extracted the entire surplus, resulting in an efficient market outcome.

where the bracketed term is the worker surplus V. But this objective function simplifies to the same functional form as in the conventional monopsony case (equation [1]) since the $\int_0^L w(q, v)dv$ terms cancel. The enterprise consequently will behave no differently than would a standard monopsonist.

The fundamental problem with the wage discrimination solution to the welfare losses associated with monopsonies is that workers have no incentive to reveal their preferences unless they are compensated appropriately. If workers are compensated sufficiently, enterprises have no incentive to behave in a socially optimal fashion. Worker revelation of preferences will neither be a desirable nor an effective method of promoting worker interests.

11.3 THE POTENTIAL FOR UNION ACTION

A. *Unions as Labor Market Monopolies.* In the subsequent analysis, I will treat the labor union as the labor market equivalent of a monopoly. The objective of the union is assumed to be the maximization of total worker surplus, where wages, health and safety, and the quantity of labor are the three variables of interest. The union determines job risks and the quantity of labor, while wages are determined by the labor demand curve.

In actual practice, unions have considerable, but partial, influence over each of the three variables. The unions have a major impact on working conditions, as stressed in the institutional labor economics literature and in the empirical chapters in this volume. The union's impact on relative wages of 10–15 percent is equally well documented.[9] Union influence over the quantity of labor hired by an enterprise is perhaps most diverse. Labor supply can be controlled directly, as in the case of the American Medical Association and craft unions. However, the unions do not appear to have widespread control over entry into apprenticeship programs. Perhaps their most pervasive control over labor supply is through union influence over the employment of workers once they are hired. Seniority provisions, layoff procedures, and union involvement in firing decisions all enable unions to impinge on the amount of labor employed through control of work-force reductions.[10] Although unions do not completely control any of the three variables, it seems reasonable to regard them as exerting monopolistic control over two of the three.

9. See, in particular, the classic investigation of the relative wage effect by Lewis (1963).

10. Slichter, Healy, and Livernash (1960) provide a very detailed description of these techniques for controlling the level of employment. The influence of unions on layoff policies is documented in Medoff (1976).

Many previous attempts to formulate an objective function focused on the wage rate and level of employment as the key variables of interest. Dunlop (1944), for example, specified seven possible variants of this type. Efforts along these lines have been criticized both because of their neglect of the nonpecuniary aspects of work and because they did not yield testable implications.[11] The total worker welfare function that I am utilizing extends Dunlop's analysis by making job safety and worker preferences regarding the type and amount of work matters of central concern. In addition, the implications of the analysis are quite specific and potentially testable.

Although any effort to impute an objective function and consistent choices to a collective organization is at best a hazardous undertaking, my approach appears to be the simplest technique for gaining some insight into the role unions serve in influencing work quality. An alternative formulation of union behavior that has gained some recent popularity is the majority-rule voting model, in which median worker preferences determine union actions. That approach shares with the surplus maximization format a concern with the preferences of the inframarginal workers. However, unlike the total worker welfare approach, this formulation neglects the intensity of worker preferences. In reality, union actions appear to be quite responsive to strongly held attitudes of minorities of the membership, as most union contracts include a diverse mix of benefits that make the entire package attractive to all groups of workers. It should be noted that the surplus maximization approach also makes strong assumptions, particularly those regarding the union's knowledge of worker preferences, its responsiveness to worker's desires, and the division of the surplus in multiemployer contexts. The principal advantage of the surplus-maximizing format is its greater analytic tractability.

The analysis of monopolistic union influence in an otherwise competitive market parallels that of the monopsony case. Trade unions can never enhance social welfare in this instance. Since the optimizing union is concerned with enterprises' marginal demand for workers, not their inframarginal preferences, union actions will produce an optimal level of q for a given level of L only in exceptional instances. In particular, the marginal reduction in the firm's wage offer in response to a marginal increase in q must equal the average of the marginal reductions.

Even though a union may reduce social welfare in an otherwise competitive market, an optimizing union will enhance unionized workers' welfare. When workers have heterogeneous preferences with

11. Rees (1962) provides a critique of such formulations and opts for a more qualitative discussion of union actions.

respect to hazards, unions will be able to increase worker rents if they can select q as well as another variable, such as L or w. This result is quite general. Collective bargaining agreements typically include provisions relating to wages, fringe benefits, grievance procedures, promotion policies, and other features of the employment relationship. When workers have heterogeneous preferences with respect to the different pecuniary and nonpecuniary components of their jobs, unions can increase worker rents by influencing aspects of employment other than wage rates. If unions serve as a countervailing source of market power, they may affect not only the well-being of the affected workers but also the social implications of market outcomes.

B. Bilateral Monopoly. Unionized enterprises typically are characterized by the features that were identified as sources of monopsony power in Section 11.2. In particular, workers at unionized enterprises have more years of experience at their current place of employment than do nonunion workers.[12] This additional experience reflects not only differences in enterprise-specific skills, but also differences in seniority rights and pension benefit rights that will be lost if the worker leaves the enterprise. It is in such situations that monopsony power is most likely to be present, since the firm has, in effect, acquired its own internal labor market.

The monopsonist's inverse demand curve for labor will be represented by $u(q, L)$. This function indicates the wage that will be offered for L workers at health and safety level q.[13] Similarly, let $w(q, L)$ be the wage at which labor will supply L workers at health and safety level q.

The surplus accruing to the workers and the company consequently will be given by

$$V = Lu(q, L) - \int_0^L w(q, v)dv,$$

and

$$E = \int_0^L u(q, v)dv - Lw(q, L),$$

respectively. If the monopsonist is dominant in that he controls the choice of L and q, the result is no different than the monopsony model

12. In a more complete model, one would make monopsonistic influences such as seniority rights and fringe benefits endogenous. Workers are more willing to accept these immobilizing influences if unions are present to bargain on behalf of their interests.

13. I have assumed that the firm has solved for the optimal levels of K and x as functions of q and L. As a result, the analysis of profits can focus on the derived demand curve for labor rather than the fuller version of the problem.

in Section 11.2. Similarly, if the union's power is sufficiently great, the analysis reduces to the analogous situation of a monopoly model. In either case, the element of market concentration can never raise the surplus value above that that would be reaped if the competitive outcome prevailed, and it will usually result in a nonoptimal level of safety.

The case of greatest interest is the cooperative solution to the bilateral monopoly situation in which the parties select the levels of q and L that maximize their joint surplus S, given by

$$S = V + E = Lu(q, L) - \int_0^L w(q, v)dv + \int_0^L u(q, v)dv - Lw(q, L)$$

or

$$S = \int_0^L u(q, v)dv - \int_0^L w(q, v)dv$$

since $u(q, L)$ equals $w(q, L)$ at the market-clearing wage rate. This equation for S is identical to that for the wage discrimination case. The parties choose the levels of L and q that maximize the area between the inverse supply and demand curves, thus maximizing social welfare.

For any given value of L, the level of the optimal q satisfies the condition that

$$\partial S/\partial q = 0 = \partial/\partial q \int_0^L u(q, v) - w(q, v)dv,$$

or

$$\int_0^L u_q(q, v)dv = \int_0^L w_q(q, v)dv.$$

The optimal level of q is obtained where the partial derivative with respect to q of the area between the supply and demand curves (that is, the total surplus) equals zero. Unlike the monopsony and monopoly solutions, the optimal q is not set at a level that is unresponsive to the preferences of the inframarginal workers.

The principal result is that while the cooperative solution need not prevail, it may. If it does, unions will have served a productive function by leading a monopsonistic enterprise to choose a socially optimal level of health and safety and employment. Moreover, unlike the wage discrimination solution, the optimality of the outcome does not depend on the union's ability to ascertain the reservation wage of each worker. Since all that is required is that the general shape of the labor supply curve be known, there are no special informational requirements for productive union action. The source of a union's beneficial effects is that it may represent the preferences of inframarginal workers, which would otherwise be ignored.[14]

11.4 CONCLUSIONS

Although unions can serve no socially productive purpose in competitive contexts, they can in market situations in which there are elements of monopsony power, such as those present within internal labor markets. Union bargaining on behalf of the hazard preferences of inframarginal workers may not only promote worker interests but also those of society at large, since the cooperative solution to the bilateral monopoly problem will be socially efficient.

An analysis of this type is applicable to aspects of employment other than job risks, such as fringe benefits.[15] Fringe benefits will be undersupplied by a monopsonist if the inframarginal worker's valuation of fringes is greater than that for the marginal worker, and conversely. The marginal workers tend to be the lower income, inexperienced employees. Since there is a strong positive income elasticity of demand for fringes, union actions that boost the level of fringe benefits may lead to a socially efficient outcome, just as in the case of union influence over safety.[16] Even if the socially optimal outcome is not realized, the direction of union influence is beneficial and will enhance social welfare for given levels of L, provided that the level of fringes or work quality does not exceed the socially optimal level by too great an amount.

Union bargaining over fringe benefits, working conditions, and other aspects of employment will typically result in greater worker rents than if unions focused on wages alone. The mix of compensation, not just its level, has important implications for worker welfare when workers have heterogeneous preferences. If unions serve as a source of countervailing power in an otherwise monopsonistic context, these impacts may also promote the efficiency of the resulting mix and level of compensation.

14. Unions may, of course, have an informational advantage over the enterprise. In situations in which the labor supply curve is uncertain since the response of workers to different levels of q may be unknown, the union may have better knowledge of workers' preferences than does the company. This situation is discussed by Freeman (1976a).

15. In particular, one need only let q be the level of fringe benefits and $c(q, L)$ be the cost of providing fringe benefits at level q to L workers. The new profit function for a monopsonist will be given by $pF(K, L) - w(q, L)L - rK - c(q, L)$, where F is a conventional production function. The remainder of the analysis is qualitatively similar to that presented in the text for work quality.

16. For an empirical analysis of unions' impact on fringe benefits, see chapter 15 of Goldstein and Pauly (1976) and work in progress by Richard Freeman.

PART THREE

Empirical Evidence

12

INTRODUCTION TO THE EMPIRICAL EVIDENCE

12.1 INTRODUCTION

The previous chapters have introduced a variety of conceptual hypotheses that are potentially testable. Owing to the limited data available, however, only the most salient features of the theories will be examined. This empirical effort will, however, be sufficiently detailed so that it will be possible to ascertain whether the general conceptualizations of individual and enterprise decisions are in error.

The four principal areas of empirical concern are the determinants of worker quit rates, job hazard perceptions, earnings, and the economic response to health and safety hazards. These topics are dealt with in Chapters 13, 14, 15, and 16, respectively. Within these subject areas, I will consider hypotheses pertaining to a world with known risks and those arising in a more uncertain world in which there is both learning and adaptive behavior. It is this latter effect which is perhaps the most distinctive portion of the empirical inquiry. Section 12.2 describes the structure of the empirical model that will be employed in investigating these concerns, while Section 12.3 summarizes the principal conceptual hypotheses associated with each empirical area. All of the subsequent lines of empirical analysis will utilize large sets of survey data pertaining to individual worker behavior.

12.2 THE STRUCTURE OF THE MODEL

Perhaps the most convenient analytic structure for the quit-rate, earnings, and job-hazard-perception equations is the recursive model illustrated in Figure 12.1. The arrows indicate the predetermined vari-

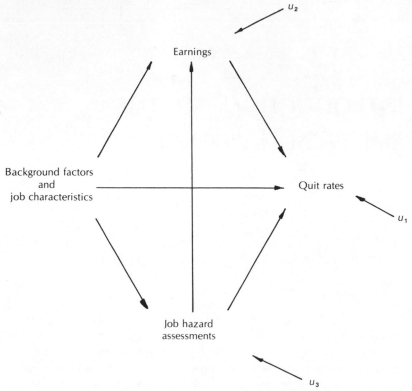

Figure 12.1 The Recursive Model Structure

ables included in subsequent equations, while the u_i's are the distur-
bance terms for the three equations of interest. These errors are assumed to be mutually independent.

The final equation in the system is the quit-rate equation, which is
the focus of Chapter 13. All preceding variables in the system—
earnings, job hazard assessments, and background factors and job
characteristics—enter the equation as explanatory variables. The principal justification for the recursive formulation of the quit equation is
that the explanatory variables are determined prior to the quit decision. The pivotal test of the adaptive model is the direct effect of job
risks on quit behavior.

The earnings equation to be estimated in Chapter 15 consists of a regression of worker earnings on background factors, job characteristics,
and variables pertaining to the risk of the worker's job, such as the
worker's job hazard assessment. This equation is intended to represent
the equilibrium market earnings schedule discussed in Chapter 2. For
workers to be willing to be employed at each level of risk, the financial

rewards for the job must increase with the magnitude of the hazard. The coefficient of the job risk variable represents both the workers' marginal supply price for risk and the enterprises' marginal demand price for risk.[1]

The first equation in the recursive system considers the determinants of workers' job hazard assessments. In particular, the regression analysis in Chapter 14 assesses the influence of background factors and job characteristics on workers' subjective perceptions of dangerous or unhealthy conditions. Due to the assumed recursive relationship between job hazard perceptions and worker earnings, this equation abstracts from the influence of worker earnings on job risks. In a simultaneous version of this model in which earnings enter the job hazard equation, workers would be viewed as being willing to accept an increase in the job risk in return for a marginal increase in earnings. The recursive model in effect assumes that the supply of workers to jobs of differing risk is inelastic with respect to monetary compensation.

This assumption does not seem too unrealistic, since the severity of the health outcomes involved implies that workers must receive extremely large wage premiums to alter their willingness to accept even modest risks. Ultimately, the choice between a recursive and simultaneous formulation must be based on empirical grounds. Since the two-stage least squares estimates of the simultaneous version of the model presented in Section F.2 of Appendix F are consistent with the recursive format, the analysis in subsequent chapters follows the recursive model sketched in Figure 12.1.

12.3 The Theoretical Hypotheses to Be Tested

The recursive relationship between job hazard assessments, worker earnings, and quit rates permits one to analyze each of these areas of empirical concern separately. The first of these topics to be considered will be the quit rate relationship—the subject of Chapter 13. The nature of the empirical tests described is dictated to a great extent by the types of data that are available.

The analysis of worker quitting will be devoted primarily to testing the predictions of the adaptive job choice models of Chapter 4. In that analysis, workers learn about job hazards through their on-the-job experience and, if their experiences are unfavorable and compensation is insufficient, they will quit. This relationship will be tested by examining the impact of workers' job hazard assessments and industry injury rates on workers' quit intentions, actual quit rates, and years of experience with their present enterprise. The quit-rate analysis also

---

1. See Thaler and Rosen (1976) for a more detailed discussion of the properties of competitive market equilibrium and the underlying econometric issues.

will consider whether quits decline with worker age, years of experience with the enterprise, and transactions costs of changing jobs (such as loss of pensions), as the adaptive models predict. The focus on the relation of the adaptive job choice model to worker quitting not only will be helpful in testing the validity of the conceptual formulations, but also may serve to provide a more appropriate theoretical rationale for an important labor market phenomenon.

Chapter 13 will also delve briefly into the relationship of job hazards to worker training. The enterprise decision model of Chapter 10 indicated that a company's training investments in its workers should be lower where workers face a higher risk of injury or death. This theoretical relationship will be tested by examining the impact of industry injury rates on workers' participation in training programs and on their years of experience with the enterprise—a variable that should be positively correlated with an enterprise's investment in its work force.

Workers base their adaptive behavior on job risks they learn about through on-the-job experience. Chapter 14 addresses the fundamental issue of the determinants of job hazard perceptions of workers. In particular, it examines whether experiencing on-the-job injuries and observing job characteristics that are likely signals of job hazards influence workers' perceptions of employment dangers. The existence of worker learning of this type serves as the motivation for workers' subsequent adaptive responses through quitting.

The empirical analysis of the role of personal and enterprise characteristics in influencing job risks also is pertinent to other theoretical hypotheses. The analysis in Chapter 3 indicated that the relationship between worker age and the optimal hazard was not theoretically clearcut, an ambiguity that can be resolved on an empirical basis. Chapter 2's prediction of a negative relation of the optimal hazard to worker wealth and Chapter 10's prediction of a positive effect of enterprise size on job riskiness also will be investigated.

The empirical chapter most closely related to economic concerns traditionally raised by job hazards is Chapter 15, which investigates the existence and magnitude of compensating wage differentials for job hazards and other job characteristics. This responsiveness of workers' job choices to monetary incentives was a central feature of the models of individual choice in this volume and has been a pivotal concept in labor economics since Adam Smith's classic contribution. Although the basic compensating wage differential theory has been in existence for almost two centuries, its validity has long been questioned by those who have observed that the most attractive jobs in society also tend to be the most well-paid.

Chapter 16 considers the differing aspects of health hazards and safety hazards. As a rough rule, one would expect workers' prior information about safety hazards to be more accurate than for health hazards due to the larger probabilities involved, the greater visibility of the hazards, and the greater observability of the job lottery outcomes. Although such a view is not inconsistent with the data, the findings are more tentative than in the preceding chapters. Chapter 17 summarizes the implications of these findings for the assessment of labor market performance.

13

JOB HAZARDS AND WORKER QUIT RATES: AN EMPIRICAL ANALYSIS OF ADAPTIVE WORKER BEHAVIOR

13.1 INTRODUCTION

Individuals starting work on a job are seldom informed about the job hazards they will encounter. This imperfection in workers' information combines with the possibility of learning from one's on-the-job experiences to provide the motivation for the adaptive job choice models in Chapter 4, which formed the basis for much of the analysis in subsequent chapters. The principal prediction for worker behavior is that individuals with unfavorable job experiences will quit unless compensated sufficiently.

Although the quit-rate literature is very extensive, there has been no investigation of the impact of job hazards or other job characteristics on worker quit rates. The four principal studies of quit rates by Stoikov and Raimon (1968), Burton and Parker (1969), Pencavel (1970), and Parsons (1972) all examined aggregative data for 49–52 industries at the three-digit (SIC code) level, producing two principal conclusions. First, higher wages reduce worker quitting, since workers respond to the financial rewards of their job in the expected fashion. Second, worker quitting is negatively related to proxy variables for worker experience, such as the rate of new hires. The absence of a consensus regarding the relative importance of other quit-rate determinants, such as workers' personal characteristics, may be due largely to the limitations of the data being analyzed.

More recently, the concurrent research by Freeman (1976a, b) has examined the impact of unions on quit behavior. Freeman's analysis is an application of Hirschman's (1970) exit-voice theory to labor unions. His empirical work explores the negative impact of unions on quits using a variety of data sets. I will not dwell on the union impacts in my results, since Freeman's analysis is quite thorough.

The next section presents the quit-rate results for aggregative data, exploring the impact of industry injury rates on quit behavior. Section 13.3 presents the quit-intention results, examining the relation of workers' assessments of job hazards to workers' quit intentions. Section 13.4 considers individual quit behavior of young men, mature men, and groups of all workers.

13.2 THE DETERMINANTS OF AGGREGATIVE QUIT RATES

The most aggregative of the industry-wide quit rate analyses deals with 1970 data for 21 two-digit manufacturing industries.[1] The dependent variable in the regressions is the industry quit rate (QUIT).[2] In each of the regressions the quit-rate variable assumes the log-odds form, where the dependent variable is the natural logarithm of QUIT/(100 − QUIT). If the quit rate is interpreted as the probability of quitting multiplied by one hundred, then the dependent variable in the log-odds form reduces to simply the logit of quitting. This transformation of the dependent variable eliminates the constraint on the permissible values for the dependent variable, which formerly ranged from zero to a hundred. Moreover, the logistic form provided a somewhat better fit than did the linear form of the equation.

The central explanatory variable of interest is the 1970 BLS injury frequency rate, that is, the number of disabling injuries per million hours worked (INJRATE). The financial rewards of the job are reflected in the average hourly earnings variable (WAGE). Other enterprise characteristics include the percentage of union members (UNION), the percentage change in the level of employment from 1969 to 1970 (EMPLOY%), and the rate of new hires in 1969 (HIRES69). The variable EMPLOY% is intended to reflect the relative growth of the industry. Expansion of an industry should increase worker quitting to the extent that it reflects the availability of alternative jobs in the industry, and it should diminish worker quitting in so far as internal promotion prospects and job security are increased. The net effect is unclear. The final variable is HIRES69, which reflects the experience mix of the industry and should exert a positive effect on worker quitting. The personal characteristics variables included in the equations are the percentage of white workers (WHITE), the percentage of female workers

1. An example of an industry group with a two-digit SIC code is the fabricated metal products industry.

2. Part F.4 of the Appendix F provides the data sources for the quit-rate regressions in this section.

Table 13.1. Variable Definitions for Two-Digit Industries

Symbol	Definition
AGE16–24	Workers in the age range 16–24 (%)
AGE45+	Workers in the industry 45 years old or older (%)
EDUC	Mean years of schooling
EMPLOY%	Change in employment from 1969 to 1970 (%)
FEMALE	Female workers in industry (%)
HIRES69	Rate of new hires in 1969
INJRATE	1970 BLS injury frequency rate
QUIT	Industry quit rate
UNION	Union members in industry (%)
WAGE	Average hourly wage (dollars)
WHITE	White workers in industry (%)

(FEMALE), mean years of schooling (EDUC), the percentage of workers who are in the age range 16–24 (AGE16–24) or who are 45 years old and above (AGE45+). Personal characteristic variables such as EDUC and FEMALE may reflect in part the differing job mix in the industries. Similarly, the age variable may not reflect the impact of age alone, but also age-related differences in experience and health. The definitions of these variables are summarized in Table 13.1.

The regression results in Table 13.2 provide strong support for the adaptive choice models. The job risk variable INJRATE is an important determinant of the industry quit rates. Equation (1) includes the two dominant determinants of worker quitting—the familiar wage effect and the job hazard variable. The INJRATE coefficient is remarkably robust as it differs by only 0.001 once the seven enterprise and personal characteristic variables are added in the second equation. Of these other variables, only AGE16–24, which has the expected positive influence on worker quitting, is statistically significant.[3]

The inclusion of HIRES69 in equation (3) represents a very demanding test of the relationship between job hazards and quits, owing to the strong relationship between quits and new hires. Although INJRATE is the only variable whose coefficient remains larger than its standard error, it is no longer statistically significant. This set of data does not appear to be rich enough to distinguish the determinants of quit rates once the new hires variable is included in the analysis. As a result, one cannot rule out the possibility that the positive relationship between the injury rate and the quit rate may be due to the fact that in-

---

3. Throughout this chapter, references to statistical significance refer to one-tailed *t*-tests at the 5 percent level.

Table 13.2. Quit-Rate Regression Results for Two-Digit
Industries, 1970

Independent variable	Coefficients and standard errors		
	(1)	(2)	(3)
WAGE	−.586	−.339	−.180
	(.069)	(.184)	(.217)
INJRATE	+.022	+.023	+.013
	(.005)	(.008)	(.011)
UNION		+.251	+.095
	—	(.210)	(.238)
WHITE		+.400	+.333
	—	(1.462)	(1.421)
FEMALE		+.0031	+.0049
	—	(.0054)	(.0054)
EDUC		−.097	−.072
	—	(.090)	(.090)
AGE16−24		+4.406	+2.333
	—	(2.086)	(2.589)
AGE45+		−.845	−.565
	—	(1.789)	(1.752)
EMPLOY%		+.0026	+.96E − 4
	—	(.0089)	(.0089)
HIRES69			+.140
	—	—	(.109)
R^2	.858	.940	.949
SEE	.483	.203	.174

dustries with higher quit rates will have a more inexperienced and accident-prone work force. The observed correlation might then occur irrespective of whether workers act in accordance with the adaptive model.

More robust results can be found in an examination of the quit-rate determinants for 95 three-digit industries.[4] This sample is roughly twice as large as in all previously published analyses of quit-rate behavior. The dependent variable in the equations is the 1974 industry quit rate (QUIT).[5] As in the earlier analysis, this variable takes on the log-odds form. The variable definitions are summaried in Table 13.3.

The job risk variable is the 1974 industry injury rate (INJRATE), which is the number of recordable injuries per hundred full-time

4. An example of a three-digit industry is the metal can industry.
5. Data sources are provided in Section F.4 of Appendix F.

Table 13.3. Variable Definitions for Three-Digit Industry Results

Symbol	Definition
AGE16–24	Workers in the age range 16–24 (%)
AGE45+	Workers in the industry 45 years old and older (%)
EMPLOY%	Change in employment from 1973–74 (%)
FEMALE	Female workers in industry (%)
HIRES71	Rate of new hires in 1971
HIRES72	Rate of new hires in 1972
HIRES73	Rate of new hires in 1973
HOURS	Mean hours worked per week, multiplied by 10
INJRATE	1974 BLS injury and illness frequency rate
INJRATE1	1969 BLS injury frequency rate
INJRATE2	1972–73 average of BLS injury and illness rate
OVERT	Mean number of overtime hours worked per week, multiplied by 10
PRODN	Fraction of production workers in industry
QUIT	Industry quit rate
UNION	Union members in industry (%)
WAGE	Average hourly wage (cents)

employees. This variable differs from that used in the analysis of two-digit data, because of the change in the BLS reporting procedures required by the 1970 Occupational Safety and Health Act. Apart from minor changes in the definition of a job injury, the principal difference is that injuries were reported on a voluntary basis in 1970 and on a mandatory basis in 1974.

The variable reflecting the financial rewards of the job is the industry wage rate in cents (WAGE). Other enterprise characteristic variables include the percentage of union members (UNION), weekly work hours multiplied by 10 (HOURS), overtime work hours multiplied by 10 (OVERT), the fraction of production workers (PRODN), the percentage change in employment from 1973–74 (EMPLOY%), and the rate of new hires for 1973, 1972, and 1971 (HIRES73, HIRES72, HIRES71). Finally, the personal characteristic variables are the proportion of female workers (FEMALE), the proportion of black workers (BLACK), the proportion of workers in the age range 16–24 (AGE16–24), and the proportion of workers 45 years old and above (AGE45+).

The columns in Table 13.4 yield the estimated coefficients for different equation specifications. Equation (1) regresses the logistic form of the quit variable on all of these explanatory variables except for the new hires variable. The addition of HIRES73 in equation (2) is intended to reflect the experience mix of the industry and represents a strong test

Table 13.4. Quit-Rate Regression Results for Three-Digit Industries, 1974

Independent variables	Coefficients and standard errors		
	(1)	(2)	(3)
WAGE	−.011	−.0084	−.0074
	(.001)	(.0009)	(.0011)
INJRATE	+.026	+.0180	+.0162
	(.007)	(.0063)	(.0064)
UNION	+.26E − 3	+.37E − 3	.30E − 3
	(.60E − 3)	(.51E − 3)	(.52E − 3)
HOURS	−.017	−.010	−.011
	(.004)	(.004)	(.004)
OVERT	+.018	+.012	+.014
	(.006)	(.005)	(.005)
PRODN	+.430	+.447	+.309
	(.342)	(.290)	(.312)
FEMALE	−1.023	−.574	.324
	(.320)	(.281)	(.318)
BLACK	−.423	−1.149	−1.122
	(.923)	(.791)	(.787)
AGE16−24	−.507	−.488	−.348
	(1.190)	(1.007)	(1.009)
AGE45+	−.429	−.187	−.123
	(.406)	(.346)	(.347)
EMPLOY%	+.0061	+.0048	+.0043
	(.0030)	(.0025)	(.0026)
HIRES73		+.018	+.0087
	—	(.003)	(.0072)
HIRES72			+.021
	—	—	(.013)
HIRES71			−.011
	—	—	(.009)
R^2	.866	.905	.908
SEE	.260	.220	.219

of the job hazard−quit relation due to the close relationship of quits and new hires. Finally, equation (3) includes three lagged hires variables whose coefficients were estimated using a free-form lag distribution.

The performance of the INJRATE variable in all three equations is quite impressive, as it exerts a consistently powerful positive effect on quitting. The inclusion of the new hires variables diminishes the magnitude of the injury rate effect by less than 40 percent. Unlike the results for two-digit industries, inclusion of variables reflecting the experience mix of three-digit industries does not make the INJRATE effect statistically insignificant.

Job risks also have a powerful effect on quit behavior. The relatively conservative measure of their influence in equation (3) corresponds to a mean increase in worker quit percentages of 12 points above what one would observe if there were no health and safety risks. This impact represents a relative increase in worker quit probabilities of one-half, which indicates that job risks are a major contributor to worker turnover.

As expected, workers respond to financial incentives and are less likely to quit if their wages are high. The hours of employment also appear to be important quit determinants. Higher weekly work hours reduce worker quitting, presumably because workers prefer a full-time work week, while additional overtime hours increase quit behavior.

Expanding industries with high EMPLOY% experience higher quit rates as the increased availability of alternative jobs diminishes the costs of searching for a new position. Industries with high rates of new hires also experience greater quit rates, although the effect appears to be concentrated in the first two years of work experience.

The other findings are more mixed, since the economic influences associated with these supplementary variables may not pertain to the particular variable label, but rather to pertinent forces correlated with it. In the case of FEMALE, for example, the consistent negative impact suggests that the variable may be capturing aspects of the job mix rather than impacts directly attributable to sex-related differences. Since I have included these variables primarily in an effort to control for interindustry differences rather than for the purpose of testing specific hypotheses, this difficulty poses no great problems.

Similar impacts of job hazards on worker quitting can be obtained for worker quit behavior for different time periods. In particular, consider the determinants of worker quitting for 1970, a 5-year average, and a 15-year average. The QUIT variable for each of these years will be indicated by QUIT-70, QUIT-5, and QUIT-15, respectively. All variables in the quit equations are on the same temporal basis except for UNION and the two injury rate variables.

Since the definition of the job risk variable changed after 1970, I will consider the sensitivity of the job hazard–quit rate relation to the particular type of job risk variable employed. The two job risk variables will be indicated by INJRATE1 and INJRATE2. The first of these variables is the 1969 injury frequency rate for the industry, that is, the number of disabling work injuries per million hours worked. To be disabling, an injury must have caused permanent impairment or the loss of the ability to work at a regularly established job for a complete day following the injury. This index was computed by the Bureau of Labor Statistics using survey reports supplied by establishments on a voluntary basis.[6] The INJRATE2 variable is the 1972–73 average of the incidence rate of occupational injuries and illnesses, that is, the number of recordable injuries per hundred full-time employees. Recordable injuries include: fatalities, lost workday cases, and nonfatal cases without lost workdays; for example, the worker quits after the injury or loses consciousness. The injury reports are provided to the Bureau of Labor Statistics on a mandatory basis. The change in the reporting system and injury definitions resulted from the 1970 Occupational Safety and Health Act, which sought to improve the quality of job hazard statistics. The variable INJRATE employed in the regressions reported in Table 13.4 was defined on the same basis as INJRATE2.

In each of the regressions the quit rate variable takes on the log-odds form, as before. The results reported in Table 13.5 are similar to the earlier findings. Both INJRATE1 and INJRATE2 are consistently powerful determinants of worker quit rates, although INJRATE2's performance is somewhat better. The existence of a positive influence of job risks on worker quitting is not particularly sensitive to either the particular job risk variable one utilizes or the particular time frame for the empirical analysis.

The final empirical matter of interest is the interactive effect of unionization and job risks. Regression results are reported for the three quit-rate variables used in Table 13.5 as well as for the 1974 quit rate, which is indicated by QUIT-74. The results in Table 13.6 indicate a consistently negative UNION × INJRATE2 impact.[7] This influence may derive largely from unions' impact on the job hazards themselves. The evidence presented in Chapter 16 indicates that in unionized contexts health risks tend to be somewhat lower and safety risks tend to be greater. Since, as will be verified in Chapter 16, health hazards are a more important determinant of worker quit rates than are safety hazards, the altered hazard mix may contribute to the negative interaction effect.

A closely related, but simpler explanation is that the INJRATE2 variable primarily reflects safety impacts, since health impacts are more difficult to monitor. As a result, the actual job risk variable in unionized industries relative to the risk in nonunionized industries is less than its measured value, because of the differences in measurement error and in hazard mix in the union and nonunion sectors. If worker

6. In 1970, for example, enterprises employing about 49 percent of all manufacturing workers responded to the survey.

7. Corresponding results for the INJRATE1 variable have not been included, since the patterns of empirical interest are quite similar for the two injury-rate variables.

Table 13.5. QUIT-15, QUIT-5, and QUIT-70 Regressions for Three-Digit Industries

Independent variables	Coefficients and standard errors					
	QUIT-15	QUIT-15	QUIT-5	QUIT-5	QUIT-70	QUIT-70
WAGE	−2.139	−2.523	−2.723	−3.089	−2.889	−3.308
	(.273)	(.246)	(.267)	(.238)	(.285)	(.253)
INJRATE1	+.012	—	+.012	—	+.014	—
	(.004)		(.004)		(.004)	
INJRATE2	—	+.029	—	+.030	—	+.032
		(.007)		(.006)		(.007)
UNION	−.84E − 3	−.42E − 3	−.58E − 3	−.14E − 3	+.28E − 3	+.72E − 3
	(.53E − 3)	(.52E − 3)	(.50E − 3)	(.49E − 3)	(.52E − 3)	(.50E − 3)
HOURS	−9.904	−9.385	−9.633	−8.872	−5.456	−4.989
	(1.762)	(1.634)	(1.773)	(1.612)	(1.635)	(1.521)
OVERT	+.905	+.887	+.981	+.956	+6.49	+.661
	(.180)	(.166)	(.192)	(1.76)	(.170)	(.156)
FEMALE	−.475	−.203	−.814	−.485	−.514	−.198
	(.310)	(.303)	(.285)	(.280)	(.290)	(.291)
PRODN	−.359	−.931	+.130	−.449	+.023	−.592
	(.327)	(.337)	(.286)	(.296)	(.306)	(.316)
R^2	.811	.830	.863	.880	.837	.854
SEE	.239	.227	.224	.209	.234	.221

Note: The dependent variable in these equations is LOG(QUIT/(100 − QUIT)). The logarithm of the following independent variables was employed instead of the usual form: WAGE, HOURS, and OVERT.

Table 13.6. Supplementary Quit-Rate Regressions for Three-Digit Industries

Independent variables	Coefficients and standard errors			
	QUIT-15	QUIT-5	QUIT-70	QUIT-74
UNION	+.0031	+.0026	+.0017	+.0026
	(.0012)	(.0011)	(.0012)	(.0012)
INJRATE2	+.058	+.053	+.041	+.061
	(.011)	(.010)	(.011)	(.011)
UNIONx	−.41E − 3	−.32E − 3	−.12E − 3	−.26E − 3
INJRATE2	(.12E − 3)	(.11E − 3)	(.12E − 3)	(.13E − 3)
R^2	.850	.890	.856	.883
SEE	.214	.201	.221	.235

Note: The dependent variable in these equations takes the general form: $LOG(QUIT/(100 − QUIT))$. The logarithms of the following dependent variables are included in the equations: WAGE, HOURS, and OVERT. In addition, the variables FEMALE and PRODN are included in the equations.

quits are determined by the overall job risk, the nature of the INJRATE2 variable itself will lead to a negative value of UNION × DANGER.[8]

13.3 QUIT INTENTION RESULTS

In this section I will explore the impact of individuals' job hazard perceptions on their quit intentions. The data source for this inquiry is the 1969–1970 University of Michigan Survey of Working Conditions (SWC), which provides the most detailed data available concerning the nature of individual workers' jobs.[9] The SWC, which is the principal data set used in all subsequent chapters, was a national survey of 1,533 workers undertaken from December 1969 to January 1970.[10] Farmers and self-employed workers were omitted from the subsample that I considered, since they did not respond to the job characteristic questions. In addition, white-collar workers were also excluded from

8. A final possibility is that UNION × INJRATE2's effect may be due to the union's impact on worker compensation. However, exploratory work in which separate compensation measures for unionized and nonunionized contexts were included did not eliminate the negative impact of this interaction term.

9. The Michigan Survey of Working Conditions was undertaken by Robert Quinn, Stanley Seashore, and Thomas Mangione of the University of Michigan Survey Research Center. A description of the variables is available as ISR Social Science Archive Study no. 3507.

10. Since this survey was undertaken before the passage of the Occupational Safety and Health Act in 1970, the complicating influence of this policy need not be considered.

Table 13.7. Geographical, Industrial, and Occupational
Characteristics of the SWC Sample

Variable	Percentage of sample[a]
Location	
Northeast (NORTH)	32
Southeast and South Central (SOUTH)	21
URBAN	15
Industry	
Mining	3
Construction	11
Manufacturing durables	31
Manufacturing nondurables	14
Transportation, communication, and other utilities	8
Wholesale and retail trade	13
Miscellaneous services	15
Public administration	5
Occupation	
Craftsmen, foremen, and kindred workers	34
Service workers	17
Private household workers	1
Laborers	5
Operatives and kindred	43

[a] The standard deviations of these variables are given by $100(m - m^2)^{.5}$, where m is the fraction in the sample.

the analysis, since the job characteristic questions were inappropriate for this group.[11] There were 496 full-time blue-collar workers in the subsample that was analyzed.

As the data in Table 13.7 indicate, the subsample being considered reflects substantial geographical and occupational diversity. The regional distribution appears representative of the working population, as is the proportion in major SMSA's. In terms of industrial distribution, there are large numbers of manufacturing and service workers. Especially hazardous industries, such as mining, were not oversampled. Over three-fourths of the workers were either operatives or craftsmen, foremen, and kindred workers. In short, the sample is representative of the blue-collar population.[12]

11. Results for the pooled sample are presented in Section F.3 of Appendix F.
12. It should be emphasized that the sampling procedure was based on a random sampling approach. Since the observations were not generated from a choice-based sampling technique, the logit analysis in this and the following chapter will not be biased by the nature of the sampling procedure.

Table 13.8. Glossary of SWC Variable Definitions and Variable Lists

Symbol	Definition
AGE	Age in years
BLACK	Black race d.v.[a]
CREAT	Job creativity d.v.
DANGER	Job hazard perceptions d.v.
EARNG	Annual earnings from main job
EDUC	Years of schooling
FAST	Fast work-speed d.v.
FEMALE	Female sex d.v.
FRINGE	Fringe benefit d.v.
HEALTH	Health limitations d.v.
ID	Set of 25 industry d.v.'s
LIST1	SINGLE, SIZE, NORTH, SOUTH, URBAN, ID, OD
LIST2	LIST1, AGE, FEMALE, BLACK, EDUC, HEALTH, UNION, EARNG, FAST, NODEC, SECURITY, PSYCH, PHCOND, TRAIN, CREAT, FRINGE
NODEC	No worker decisions on job d.v.
NORTH	Northern region d.v.
OD	Set of three occupational d.v.'s
PHCOND	Pleasant physical conditions d.v.
PHYSC	Physical effort d.v.
QUIT1	Strong quit intentions d.v.
QUIT2	Strong and moderate quit intentions d.v.
SECURITY	Job security d.v.
SINGLE	Single marital status d.v.
SIZE	Enterprise size (number of employees)
SOUTH	Southeastern region d.v.
TENURE	Years of experience with present employer
TRAIN	Training program d.v.
UNION	Unionization d.v.
URBAN	Urban area d.v.

Note: Complete definitions are provided in Section F.5 of Appendix F.
[a] d.v. equals dummy variable.

Table 13.8 provides a glossary of variable definitions, which are presented in greater detail in Section F.5 of Appendix F. The means and standard deviations of several key variables used in this and subsequent chapters are presented in Table 13.9. The extensive information on personal characteristics is comparable to that contained in other surveys. The SWC provides information pertaining to the worker's age (AGE), sex (FEMALE), race (BLACK), education (EDUC), health impairments (HEALTH), years of experience with his present employer (TENURE), and union membership (UNION). Close to half of the

Table 13.9. Means and Standard Deviations of Selected Variables in the SWC Blue-Collar Subsample

Variable	Mean or fraction in sample	Standard deviation[a]
Personal background		
AGE	39.71	13.71
FEMALE	0.234	—
BLACK	0.123	—
EDUC	10.30	3.03
HEALTH	0.266	0.918
TENURE	9.09	10.03
SINGLE	0.101	—
Enterprise characteristics		
SIZE	562.2	915.3
UNION	0.492	—
Job characteristics		
EARNG	6,809.9	2,870.7
DANGER	0.522	—
FAST	0.363	0.481
SECURITY	0.544	0.499
PHYSC	0.627	0.484
FRINGE	0.883	—
INJRATE	15.93	9.26
DEATH	5.91	8.29
NONFATAL	1,586.55	921.18
Quit intentions		
QUIT1	0.147	—
QUIT2	0.302	—

[a] The standard deviations of the zero-one dummy variations are omitted, since they can be computed from their fraction m in the sample, where the standard deviation is $(m - m^2)^{0.5}$.

workers are union members. Although this fraction is double the nationwide average for the workforce as a whole, it does not appear disproportionately large for the blue-collar, nonfarm population. The two variables reflecting the financial rewards of the job are annual earnings (EARNG) and a dummy variable for whether the worker is covered by a pension plan or other fringe benefits (FRINGE). The distinctive aspect of the data source is the extensive job characteristic data, including information regarding the speed of work (FAST), whether the worker is not allowed to make decisions (NODEC), job security (SECURITY), physical effort required (PHYSC), pleasantness of the physical conditions (PHCOND), training program availability (TRAIN), and the creativity required by the job (CREAT).

The inclusion of a diverse mix of explanatory variables should increase one's confidence that any relation of job risks to quit behavior is not due to specification bias. The health status variable (HEALTH) is particularly important in this regard, since workers with hazardous jobs would be more prone to quit—even apart from any learning effect—because an injury or illness may make them physically unable to perform their job tasks. Regression results for all data sets to be analyzed in the remainder of this chapter include measures of health status and a variety of other important variables pertaining to the worker and his job.

The variables of greatest interest are DANGER, QUIT1, and QUIT2. The variable DANGER is the worker's subjective assessment of whether his job exposes him to dangerous or unhealthy conditions.[13] Detailed comparisons of the particular hazard cited and the worker's job suggested that the responses were plausible and did not simply reflect underlying job dissatisfaction. The job hazard responses will be analyzed in detail in the following chapter. Inclusion of DANGER in an analysis of compensating wage differentials in Chapter 15 yields annual earnings premiums comparable to those implied by the industry injury rate.[14] Unlike that objective index, DANGER pertains to the worker's particular job and consequently should be subject to less measurement error than an industry-wide job hazard index.

Although 52.2 percent of the workers in the sample viewed their jobs as hazardous in some respect, the workers in the sample do not appear to be concentrated in especially hazardous pursuits. The mean value of the BLS industry injury rate (INJRATE) for the worker's three-digit (SIC Code) industries is only 15.93 per million hours worked, which is slightly greater than the manufacturing average of 14.8 but is less than several nonmanufacturing levels, such as the 18.4 average for transportation and public utilities.

My central hypothesis is that workers are more likely to quit jobs that they consider hazardous. The two quit intention variables represent alternative formulations of workers' qualitative quit intention responses.[15] QUIT1 takes on a value of 1 if the worker is very likely to make a genuine effort to find a new job with another employer in the next year and is zero otherwise. QUIT2 assumes a value of 1 if the

13. This variable is a zero-one dummy variable. Ideally, one would like information regarding the worker's probability assessments for different health state outcomes, but such detailed data are not available. Experimentation with other job hazard variables, such as those based on the number of hazards cited, did not alter the results.

14. In addition, the hypothesis that on-the-job injury experiences influence one's job hazard perceptions was also borne out, as is reported in Chapter 14.

15. The sample size was not sufficiently large to permit reliable estimation for the polytomous formulations of the quit intention variable. The similarity of the results for the two binomial cases considered suggests that the impact of DANGER on quit intentions is quite robust.

worker is very likely or somewhat likely to undertake such a job search. The variables differ in that QUIT2 includes weaker quit intentions.

The analysis below assumes that the quit intention probabilities p can be described by the logistic probability function

$$p = 1/(1 + e^{-\theta'x}),$$

where θ is the n-dimensional parameter vector to be estimated and x is a vector of n attributes of the worker and his job. The maximum likelihood estimate of θ for QUIT1 and QUIT2 are presented in Table 13.10.[16] The empirical findings are similar for both variables, providing very strong support for the adaptive models of job choice, since every statistically significant variable has the effect predicted by the theory.[17]

Job hazards and other characteristics are pivotal determinants of workers' quit intentions, a result consistent with the analysis in Chapter 4. Although job hazards were selected as the primary focus of the analysis because of the great imprecision of workers' prior information regarding hazards, the analysis is equally applicable to other job attributes and job matching problems. The DANGER variable exerts a powerful influence both on strong intentions to quit (QUIT1) and intentions to quit that also include less of a commitment to switch jobs (QUIT2).

If all variables except for DANGER assume their mean values, the mean quit intention probability is 0.10 for QUIT1 and 0.25 for QUIT2. If the worker regards his job as hazardous (if DANGER equals one instead of zero), each of these quit probabilities increases by 0.11. Subjective perception of job hazards consequently doubles the likelihood of strong quit intentions and increases the likelihood of strong and moderate quit intentions by 50 percent.

Even this substantial impact is likely to understate the role of job hazards in the quit process. The cross-sectional nature of the survey data leads to an underestimation of the impact of job hazards and other unfavorable job characteristics on worker quitting, since workers

16. The logistic curve estimates were obtained using the conditional/polytomous logit program developed by C. F. Manski. This program is based on the work of McFadden (1973), who also analyzed the formal properties of the estimates.

17. Throughout this chapter, references to statistical significance refer to one-tailed t-tests at the 5 percent level, where $t_{.95}$ for an infinite sample size is 1.645. For simplicity, the asymptotic t values are treated as being comparable to conventional t statistics. Performance of likelihood ratio tests, which are both more expensive and theoretically preferable, for a few representative variables yielded similar results. Inspection of the likelihood ratio tests in Chapter 14 indicates findings similar to t tests for the hypothesis tests for the significance of a single variable.

Table 13.10.   Logistic Parameter Estimates for
Quit Intention Determinants

| Independent variables | Coefficients and standard errors | |
	QUIT1	QUIT2
AGE	−.016	−.015
	(.014)	(.011)
FEMALE	−.530	+.300
	(.557)	(.428)
BLACK	+.581	+1.106
	(.485)	(.382)
EDUC	−.020	+.052
	(.057)	(.043)
HEALTH	+.231	+.439
	(.150)	(.135)
UNION	+.322	+.139
	(.429)	(.304)
TENURE	−.062	−.068
	(.026)	(.019)
EARNG	$-.12E-3$	$-.24E-4$
	$(.87E-4)$	$(.65E-4)$
DANGER	+.886	+.522
	(.354)	(.264)
FAST	+1.187	+1.837
	(.361)	(.278)
NODEC	−.110	−.116
	(.162)	(.125)
SECURITY	−.599	−.671
	(.358)	(.268)
PHYSC	−.832	+.205
	(.345)	(.274)
PHCOND	−.559	−.497
	(.374)	(.277)
TRAIN	−.235	−.514
	(.382)	(.292)
CREAT	−.298	−.058
	(.160)	(.121)
FRINGE	−.891	−.708
	(.429)	(.369)
Log likelihood	−146.79	−225.98

Note: Each equation also includes the variables in
LIST1.

who quit immediately after work injuries or other extremely unfavorable experiences are never captured in the sample.

The impact of the other job characteristics on quit intentions also follows the expected patterns. Workers are especially likely to quit jobs that require them to work FAST—a variable that reflects not only the rapidity of the job, but also the appropriateness of the worker's skills for the job tasks. Workers at enterprises with pleasant physical conditions or with training programs quit less frequently. The impact of the other nonpecuniary variables is more mixed.

Workers also respond to the financial rewards of their job. The two most powerful financial variables are SECURITY and FRINGE. Application of the conceptual analysis to uncertainties regarding one's financial prospects would imply that workers who are less likely to keep their jobs will be more likely to switch to alternative employment. This prediction is borne out by the strong negative impact of SECURITY on quit intentions.

Fringe benefits differ from wage compensation, since they also impose transactions costs on job changes when the workers' benefit rights are tied to his place of employment. This is particularly true of pension plans, which typically have imperfect portability and vesting provisions. The impediments that these transaction costs pose for adaptive behavior are suggested by the impressive magnitude of the FRINGE coefficients, which imply that fringe benefit coverage reduces the quit intention probabilities by 0.14 and 0.27 for QUIT1 and QUIT2, respectively. For each of these variables, fringe benefit coverage reduces the quit intention probability by over half of the value obtained when all variables except for FRINGE assume their mean levels. It should be noted that the mobility-reducing influence of pension plans may not be undesirable. By tying the worker to the firm, pension plans promote the company's investment in specific training—a phenomenon first noted by Becker (1964).

The inclusion of FRINGE and SECURITY in the regression also reduced the magnitude of the EARNG effect so that it became statistically insignificant. The traditional importance assigned to the negative effect of wages on quitting may be attributable to omitted-variables bias, since the conventional wage variables may reflect the role of omitted financial characteristics, such as fringe benefits and job security, which are positively correlated with wages. The results for the Parnes' older men's sample, which are reported in Section 13.4, are consistent with this view.

Workers' personal characteristics also are important determinants of quit behavior. Increased job experience reflected in the TENURE variable has the expected negative impact on worker quitting. The TENURE effect reflects three types of influences. First, as Becker (1964) has noted, worker mobility will be reduced by the acquisition of enterprise-specific skills. Specific training and seniority rights were incorporated into the model in Chapter 4 through the analysis of transactions costs of job changing. To the extent that TENURE serves as a proxy for specific training, this hypothesis receives additional support. The negative effect of the company training program variable TRAIN, particularly in the QUIT2 equation, also is consistent with the specific training hypothesis. The second type of TENURE effect is that workers with long tenure have revealed themselves to be nonquitters. As a result, the TENURE variable may reflect not simply the impact of experience per se, but rather the fact that experienced workers have personal attributes that make them stable employees. Finally, TENURE should have a negative effect on quitting, since more experienced workers have acquired more information about the job than new employees. To the extent that these workers have sharper probability assessments of different job outcomes, they will be less likely to acquire new information that will substantially alter these judgements.[18] As a result, they will be less likely to quit after an unfavorable work experience.

The other personal characteristics that appear to be important determinants of quit behavior are whether one is black or has a health impairment, each of which influences quit intentions positively. The HEALTH variable is of special interest, since it suggests that blue-collar workers with health impairments may have a more difficult time in finding a job appropriate to their capabilities than those who do not.

13.4 Job Hazards and Individual Quit Behavior

While the results in the previous section indicated that workers in hazardous contexts are more likely to plan to quit, the SWC survey that produced the data did not ascertain whether the workers' quit intentions were fulfilled. The analysis in this section will analyze actual quit behavior using several large sets of data on employment patterns. In particular I will focus on the University of Michigan's Panel Study of Income Dynamics (PSID) and the U.S. Department of Labor's National Longitudinal Survey (NLS) of young men and mature men. Since these data sources do not provide detailed job characteristic information, I will utilize the BLS injury rate for each worker's industry as the job risk variable.

18. Suppose that a worker has the Beta prior $B(\gamma p, \gamma)$, where p is the mean initial probability of success and γ is a measure of the sharpness. After m successes and n failures, one obtains

$$p(m, n) = (\gamma p + m)/(\gamma + m + n).$$

As the values of m and n increase, the effect of an additional observation on the assessed probability of success is diminished.

A. Quit Behavior of All Workers. The PSID data set offered the largest and most representative sample of workers. The particular portion of this panel study that I analyzed was the group of workers who were employed in 1975. If the worker quit his job between 1975 and 1976, the dependent variable QUIT assumed a value of 1; otherwise it equalled 0.

There were almost 6,000 workers in the subsamples analyzed, consisting of a representative selection of both sexes, all ages, and diverse occupations. The only new variable definitions pertain to whether the worker was married (MARRIED), his hourly wage rate in dollars (WAGE), a zero-one dummy variable for whether the worker had been employed by the firm for less than a year (TENURE1), and the 1975 BLS injury and illness frequency rate per hundred full-time workers in the industry. Since this injury variable was matched to the worker using information regarding his industry at the relatively broad two-digit level, the measurement error involved will bias the injury variable's coefficient downward, leading to an underestimate of the job risk–quit rate relationship.

Two samples of workers with jobs in 1975 were considered. The quit-rate equations were estimated both for all workers and for full-time workers (at least 30 hours per week) below age 65. The reason for distinguishing part-time and elderly workers is that they may have looser job attachments that do not reflect typical quit behavior. The full sample consisted of 5,787 individuals, while the full-time nonelderly subsample included 5,308 workers.

Table 13.11 summarizes the characteristics of these samples by worker sex. In each instance, the mean annual quit for the sample was 0.12. The workers appear to be concentrated in industries with representative levels of health and safety risks as the average INJRATE value is almost identical to the 1975 incidence rate for the private sector of 9.1 injuries per 100 full-time workers.

In obtaining the logistic parameter estimates for these very large samples, which greatly exceeded available computer limits, I employed a variant of the Theil-Goldberger Mixed Estimation Technique.[19] In particular, I divided each sample into k random subsamples and estimated separate logit equations for each. These maximum likelihood estimates for the k subsamples were then weighted by the covariance matrices to obtain the estimates for the entire sample. More specifically, let $\hat{\beta}_i$ be the estimated parameter vector for the i'th subsample and let $\hat{V}_i$ be its associated estimated covariance matrix. The

19. The consistency and efficiency of this procedure in the logit case is analyzed by Gregory M. Duncan in "Data Sets that Exceed Computer Limits: Efficient Estimation and a Test of the Reliability of the Normal Approximation," Washington State University (1978).

Table 13.11.   Summary of Sample Characteristics

| | Means and standard deviations[a] | | | |
| | All workers | | Full-time, nonelderly workers | |
Variable	Males	Females	Males	Females
QUIT	.084	.167	.079	.172
AGE	36.47	35.49	36.01	34.32
	(12.83)	(13.23)	(12.26)	(12.56)
BLACK	.285	.340	.287	.349
EDUC	11.83	11.93	11.84	12.00
	(3.79)	(2.94)	(3.75)	(2.92)
KIDS	1.46	1.31	1.49	1.28
	(1.60)	(1.50)	(1.61)	(1.47)
MARRIED	.872	.705	.875	.700
HEALTH	.081	.086	.077	.077
TENURE	7.42	3.93	7.30	3.71
	(8.19)	(5.90)	(7.99)	(5.63)
TENURE1	.276	.488	.277	.501
WAGE	4.48	2.86	4.55	2.92
	(3.03)	(2.06)	(3.00)	(2.04)
UNION	.343	.141	.347	.147
INJRATE	10.46	7.04	10.52	7.20
	(5.39)	(4.03)	(5.40)	(4.08)
Sample Size	3,178	2,609	3,075	2,233

[a] The standard deviations of the zero-one dummy variables are omitted since they can be computed from their fraction m in the sample, where the standard deviation is $(m - m^2)^{.5}$.

full sample estimates indicated by $\boldsymbol{\beta}^*$ and V^* were obtained using the covariance matrices as weights, or

$$\boldsymbol{\beta}^* = \left(\sum_{i=1}^{k} \hat{V}_i^{-1} \right)^{-1} \left(\sum_{i=1}^{k} \hat{V}_i^{-1} \hat{\boldsymbol{\beta}}_i \right),$$

and

$$V^* = \left(\sum_{i=1}^{k} \hat{V}_i^{-1} \right)^{-1}.$$

The logistic parameter estimates reported in Table 13.12 are remarkably similar to the quit-intention results. The INJRATE coefficients for both samples are statistically significant and of almost identical magnitude. In each case, the mean effect of the INJRATE variable is to raise workers' quit probabilities by 0.03 above what would be observed if there were no health and safety risks. This effect represents a 35 percent increase in workers' quit propensities—an estimate that is likely to be quite conservative in view of the aforementioned measurement error problems.

The other variables included in the analysis also are consistent with

Table 13.12. Logistic Parameter Estimates for PSID Quit-Rate Equations[a]

Independent variables	Coefficients and standard errors	
	All workers	Full-time nonelderly workers
AGE	−.024	−.029
	(.004)	(.005)
BLACK	−.521	−.556
	(.125)	(.126)
EDUC	+.039	+.029
	(.019)	(.020)
KIDS	−.066	−.056
	(.035)	(.036)
MARRIED	−.411	−.349
	(.119)	(.123)
HEALTH	+.466	+.524
	(.157)	(.163)
TENURE	+.007	+.002
	(.010)	(.011)
TENURE1	+.907	+.929
	(.129)	(.133)
WAGE	−.286	−.278
	(.022)	(.023)
UNION	+.024	+.106
	(.137)	(.136)
INJRATE	+.035	+.035
	(.013)	(.013)
Sample size	5,787	5,308

[a] Each equation also includes an intercept and sex-specific constant term, three occupational dummy variables, two regional dummy variables, the area unemployment rate, and the percentage of women in the industry.

the adaptive model of quit behavior. Workers are less likely to quit as they grow older (AGE) and are more likely to quit during the initial period of experience at the firm (TENURE1). One's experimentation with different jobs is likely to be greatest during the early periods of work experience since the gains from changing jobs diminish over time and the additional information acquired after substantial experience is also less. Individuals with health impairments (HEALTH) are more likely to quit since it may be more difficult for them to find jobs appropriate to their particular needs.

Black workers are less likely to quit, perhaps because their prospects for finding an attractive alternative position are not bright. The stabilizing influences of marriage, children, and higher wages are also borne out.

B. *Quit Behavior of Young Men.* The first NLS data set to be analyzed is the NLS of Young Men, whose ages ranged from 14–24 in 1966. I will examine the quit behavior from 1969–1970 for 2,017 workers in the subsample to be considered. Table 13.13 summarizes the variables that will be used, which for the most part are similar to those employed earlier. Complete definitions are provided in Section F.5 of Appendix F. The three quit variables pertain to total worker quits (QUIT1), quits motivated by dissatisfaction with working conditions

Table 13.13. Glossary of Variable Definitions for NLS Survey of Young Men

Symbol	Definition
AGE	Age in years
EARNG	Hourly wage rate
EDUC	Years of schooling
HEALTH	Health limitations d.v.[a]
INJRATE	1969 BLS injury frequency rate
MISC	Set of three regional d.v.'s, SMSA d.v., area unemployment rate, marital status d.v.
NONWHITE	Nonwhite race d.v.
OD	Set of six occupational d.v.'s
QUIT1	Quit 1969–1970 d.v.
QUIT2	Working conditions quit 1969–1970 d.v.
QUIT3	Working conditions quit intention d.v.
UNION	Wages set by collective bargaining d.v.

Note: Unless otherwise indicated, all variables pertain to 1969. Complete definitions are provided in Section F.5 of Appenddix F.

[a] d.v. = dummy variable.

(QUIT2), and quits motivated by worker dislike of the kind of work or working conditions (QUIT3). Since all of these dependent variables are zero-one dummy variables, the logistic parameters will be estimated using maximum likelihood techniques. An important limitation of the quit-rate data for this sample is that individuals were not asked explicitly whether they had quit their 1969 positions. I determined whether workers had quit their 1969 jobs using a complicated computer algorithm and information concerning the individual's work history.

The independent variables are similar to those present on the SWC data set except that the job attribute information is less extensive. All variables pertain to the worker's 1969 job and his personal characteristics in that year.[20] Each regression includes variables pertaining to the worker's age (AGE), race (NONWHITE), years of schooling (EDUC), health impairments (HEALTH), union membership (UNION), hourly wage rate (EARNG), the 1969 BLS injury rate for the worker's industry (INJRATE), the number of years the individual had worked for his present employer (TENURE), and a group of 12 zero-one dummy variables pertaining to the worker's occupation, regional economic conditions, and marital status.

Table 13.14 reports the maximum likelihood estimates of the logistic forms of the regression equations. Each of the quit-rate regressions is performed with and without the TENURE variable, since TENURE reflects past quit behavior, and inclusion of this variable serves as a very rigid test of the strength of the INJRATE effect. Although the effect of INJRATE on quits is consistently positive, the magnitude of the impacts is not as great as in the quit intention results. The mean effect of the INJRATE variable in the QUIT1 and QUIT2 equations omitting the TENURE variable is to raise the quit probability by only 0.01, an amount that represents 6 percent and 12 percent of the mean quit probabilities for QUIT1 and QUIT2, respectively. The effect is somewhat larger for QUIT3, which reflects worker dislike of working conditions. The mean effect of INJRATE is to raise the QUIT3 probabilities from a level of 0.20 to 0.26.

The comparatively small magnitudes of impacts are coupled with a lack of statistical significance at the usual confidence levels. The weakest results are for overall quitting (QUIT1), for which the INJRATE coefficient is much smaller than its standard error. The results for the other quit variables are somewhat better. The impact of INJRATE on quits stemming from working conditions (QUIT2) is quite sizable, although the coefficient is about the same size as its standard error. No such difficulty affects the very strong QUIT3 results, which pertain to dissatisfaction of workers with their working conditions.

20. Experimentation with other variables, such as measures of a change in the worker's health status from 1969 to 1970, did not alter the results.

Table 13.14. Logistic Parameter Estimates of Quit-Rate Determinants for Young Men

Independent variables	Coefficients and standard errors						
	QUIT1	QUIT1	QUIT2	QUIT2	QUIT3	QUIT3
AGE	−.013	−.073	−.049	−.020	−.0023	−.0049
	(.027)	(.027)	(.030)	(.030)	(.020)	(.021)
NONWHITE	−.077	−.131	−.092	−.153	−.276	−.271
	(.162)	(.162)	(.193)	(.193)	(.136)	(.137)
EDUC	+.057	+.044	+.027	+.015	+.043	+.044
	(.035)	(.034)	(.039)	(.038)	(.027)	(.027)
HEALTH	+.031	−.0059	−.555	−.599	+.206	+.209
	(.244)	(.245)	(.357)	(.358)	(.196)	(.196)
UNION	−.274	−.258	−.107	−.078	−.183	−.185
	(.165)	(.165)	(.192)	(.192)	(.126)	(.126)
EARNG	−.158	−.144	−.119	−.108	−.124	−.125
	(.077)	(.076)	(.089)	(.088)	(.055)	(.055)
INJRATE	+.0050	+.0028	+.0090	+.0067	+.018	+.018
	(.0080)	(.0080)	(.0091)	(.0091)	(.006)	(.006)
TENURE	—	−.227	—	−.208	—	+.014
		(.537)		(.587)		(.028)
Log likelihood	−791.27	−780.37	−607.26	−599.70	−1126.3	−1126.2

Note: Other variables included are given by MISC and OD.

The weak nature of these results may be attributable to three factors. First, the aforementioned problems in constructing the quit-rate variable may have affected the results. Second, there may be insufficient information in the sample to estimate the quit-rate effect reliably—a factor that may have contributed to the superiority of the QUIT3 results to the QUIT1 and QUIT2 regressions. While 517 workers were dissatisfied with their working conditions, only 291 quit overall, with 187 of these quits being related to working conditions. Even more dramatically, only eight workers in the sample identified ill health or disability as the reason for their quitting.

Third, the INJRATE variable is not an accurate measure of the true job risk for a particular job. The BLS index tends to neglect hazards that are difficult to monitor, such as health risks. This shortcoming is particularly important because, as the analysis in Chapter 16 suggests, health risks affect worker quitting more than do safety hazards. The INJRATE variable also is an industry-wide average based on the SIC Code, and it is matched imperfectly to individual workers, who are classified according to a different industry index (Census Code). The undoubtedly substantial measurement error involved may create large downward biases in the INJRATE coefficient.[21] Following the error-in-variables analysis of Griliches and Ringstad (1972), suppose that the true value of the job risk variable is z' and its measured value is z, where

$$z = z' + v,$$

and z is uncorrelated with z', the other independent variables in the quit-rate equation, and the error term for the quit rate equation.[22] Then the true job risk coefficient α is related to its estimated value $\hat{\alpha}$ by

$$\alpha = \frac{\text{plim } \hat{\alpha}}{1 - \dfrac{[\sigma_v^2/(\sigma_v^2 + \sigma_z^2)]}{1 - r_{zx}^2}},$$

where the σ^2 terms represent the error variance ratio and r_{zx}^2 pertains to the regression of z on all other independent variables in the quit rate equation.

21. Indeed, if INJRATE is used instead of DANGER in the quit intention regressions in the previous section, the job risk coefficient will always be smaller than its standard error.

22. The errors-in-variables analysis of Griliches and Ringstad (1971) that I follow is strictly applicable to ordinary least-squares regression equations, not logit analysis. However, the procedure suggested by Haggstrom (1974) transforms OLS coefficients into logit parameters by multiplying the coefficients and standard errors by a common factor, leaving the t values unaffected. The transformed OLS estimates were almost identical to the logit estimates of the coefficients and standard errors in this instance, so the procedure to be described below should be suggestive of the likely influence of errors in variables on the maximum likelihood estimates.

Table 13.15.   Glossary of Variable Definitions for NLS Survey of Mature Men

Symbol	Definition
AGE	Age in Years
COTRAIN	Company training program d.v.[a]
EARNG	Hourly wage rate
EDUC	Years of schooling
HEALTH	Health limitations d.v.
INJRATE	1969 BLS injury frequency rate
MISC	Set of three regional d.v.'s, SMSA d.v., area unemployment rate, marital status d.v.
NONWHITE	Nonwhite race d.v.
OD	Set of seven occupational d.v.'s
OTHTRAIN	Other training d.v., that is, TRAIN-COTRAIN
OVERT	Overtime work d.v.
PENSION	Pension benefits d.v.
QUIT1	Quit 1969–1971 d.v.
QUIT2	QUIT1 or job search 1966–1971 d.v.
TENURE	Years of experience with present employer
TRAIN	Training program d.v.
UNION	Wages set by collective bargaining d.v.

Note: Unless otherwise indicated, all variables pertain to 1969.
Complete definitions are provided in Section F.5 of Appendix F.
   [a] d.v. = dummy variable.

Assuming as a rough approximation that $\hat{\alpha}$ equals plim $\hat{\alpha}$, one can now determine the extent of the measurement error that is required to substantially lower the value of α. An instructive standard is the error required for the true values of α associated with the first QUIT2 equation in Table 13.14 to pass the usual tests for statistical significance at the 5 percent level.[23] The job risk effect would pass this test if σ_v^2 is at least 52 percent of the size of σ_z^2. Measurement errors of this magnitude are not implausible.

B. Quit Behavior of Older Men.   The impact of job risks on quit rates of older men can be examined using the NLS Mature Men's data set. The variable definitions are provided in Table 13.15 and are quite similar to those already employed. Complete definitions are provided in Appendix F. The 1,932 individuals in the subsample were 45–59 years old in 1966. The focus of this analysis is on the relationship of workers' personal and job characteristics in 1969 to their quit behavior

23. Here I treat asymptotic *t* values as being comparable to regular *t* statistics.

from 1969 to 1971. The first quit rate variable pertains to actual job quitting (QUIT1), while the second (QUIT2) includes quitting and job search efforts to find a new job. In addition to the explanatory variables included in the analysis of younger workers, the regressions for older men include variables for 1969 pertaining to participation in a training program (TRAIN), coverage by a retirement plan (PENSION), and overtime work (OVERT).

The adaptive models predict that job changing should be greatly diminished for older workers. Individuals near the end of their work lives should exhibit much greater employment stability, since less revision of one's probabilistic judgments occurs at that time, and the gains from job switching are relatively less. This stability is reflected in the fact that only 77 of the 1,932 workers in the sample quit their jobs in the two-year period under scrutiny.

The logit regressions in Table 13.16 present evidence consistent with this view of adaptive behavior. As in the regressions for young men, AGE and TENURE bear a strong negative relationship to quitting. These are the variables that are largely responsible for the aforementioned stability of individuals near the end of their work lives. Pension benefits, which rarely are fully portable or vested, in effect impose transactions costs on job changes and should reduce adaptive behavior. This impact is borne out by the very strong PENSION impact on QUIT1 and QUIT2.

A conservative estimate of the pension effect is obtained by considering the equations in which a TENURE variable has been included. If PENSION assumes a value of zero and all other variables take on their mean values, the quit probabilities are 0.069 for QUIT1 and 0.409 for QUIT2. Coverage by a pension plan reduces these probabilities by 0.038 and 0.252, respectively, thus diminishing the likelihood of quitting or searching for a new job by over half.

Inclusion of the PENSION variable also affects the coefficient of the wage variable in much the same manner as FRINGE affected the EARNG coefficient in the SWC results. In particular, the pension variable eliminates the dominant role traditionally assigned to wage compensation. While workers respond to financial incentives, companies may prefer to use pension plans rather than wages as a mobility-reducing device, because of the substantial tax breaks accorded to pensions and because they are more closely linked to job changes when they are not fully vested or portable.[24]

The effect of INJRATE on worker quitting is comparable to that observed for younger men. The INJRATE coefficient in the QUIT1 equa-

24. As Becker (1964) has observed, pensions also serve as a form of insurance reimbursement for companies, since they are not liable for the pension benefits of a worker who quits and who has not yet attained full rights to his accrued benefits.

Table 13.16.   Logistic Parameter Estimates of Quit-Rate Determinants
for Older Men

Independent variables	Coefficients and standard errors			
	QUIT1	QUIT1	QUIT2	QUIT2
AGE	−.086	−.077	−.023	−.012
	(.031)	(.031)	(.010)	(.010)
NONWHITE	−.507	−.467	−.255	−.303
	(.325)	(.327)	(.138)	(.144)
EDUC	−.035	−.043	+.014	+.0021
	(.045)	(.045)	(.019)	(.020)
HEALTH	+.277	+.144	+.274	+.230
	(.293)	(.299)	(.137)	(.146)
UNION	−1.709	−1.622	−.552	−.438
	(.425)	(.426)	(.127)	(.133)
TRAIN	+.058	+.068	+.239	+.265
	(.396)	(.395)	(.166)	(.175)
EARNG	−.083	−.011	−.102	−.049
	(.083)	(.069)	(.036)	(.034)
INJRATE	+.013	+.0073	+.017	+.012
	(.015)	(.015)	(.006)	(.007)
PENSION	−1.081	−.832	−.958	−.769
	(.281)	(.285)	(.121)	(.129)
OVERT	−.832	−.828	−.101	−.012
	(.278)	(.281)	(.127)	(.134)
TENURE	—	−.093	—	−.079
		(.019)		(.006)
Log likelihood	−267.85	−251.51	−1064.3	−966.37

Note: Other variables included in the regression are given by OD and MISC.

tions is smaller than its standard error. The inclusion of an additional 480 workers in the QUIT2 variable may contribute to the fact that in the equations pertaining to workers' attempts to find an alternative job over a five-year period, the INJRATE coefficient is statistically significant. For each of the equations in Table 13.14 there is also the aforementioned measurement error problem, which biases the injury-rate coefficient.

D. An Analysis of Paths of Employment.   The problem of the small samples encountered in the analyses of worker quitting can be alleviated by analyzing longer periods of worker behavior. The numerical examples in Chapter 4 have illustrated that the relation of job hazards to adaptive behavior is essentially dynamic. Workers acquire information and once their experiences have become sufficiently unfavorable they quit. On an empirical basis, one would expect to find not only a job hazard–quit rate relationship, but also an influence of job risks on workers' paths of employment. More specifically, the period of time a worker remains with an employer should be shorter in hazardous contexts.

The dependent variable for this analysis is the worker's TENURE. For the young men's sample, TENURE has a mean value of 1.39 years and a standard deviation of 1.98. This variable in effect provides a longer time frame for analyzing turnover during the early portion of the careers of these individuals. For the older men's sample, TENURE takes on a mean value of 13.2 years and a standard deviation of 11.3. TENURE for older men represents a retrospective look at the duration of the paths of employments near the end of an individual's work life.

Tables 13.17 and 13.18 report the TENURE regressions for the two groups. Both during the early and later stages of the employment process, job hazards exert an important influence on the stability of the

Table 13.17. Tenure Regression Results for Young Men

Independent variables	Coefficients and standard errors
AGE	+.221
	(.015)
NONWHITE	−.459
	(.101)
EDUC	−.054
	(.019)
HEALTH	−.175
	(.157)
UNION	+.127
	(.091)
INJRATE	−.012
	(.005)
OTHER VARIABLES	MISC, OD
R^2	.170
SEE	1.81

Note: Other variables included are given by OD and MISC.

Table 13.18.   Tenure Regressions
for Older Men

Independent variables	Coefficients and standard errors
AGE	+.403
	(.063)
NONWHITE	−.549
	(.630)
EDUC	+.119
	(.090)
HEALTH	−.962
	(.656)
UNION	+3.66
	(.56)
INJRATE	−.101
	(.028)
R^2	.082
F	9.01

Note: Other variables included are given by OD and MISC.

worker's attachment to the enterprise. As might be expected, the size of the INJRATE effect is about an order of magnitude larger for older workers. The mean effect of INJRATE is to reduce worker experience by 2 months for young workers and 1.5 years for older workers, each of which represent relatively important effects. Job hazards consequently shorten the duration of worker experience with a firm at both ends of an individual's work life.

E. Job Hazards and Worker Training.   The TENURE regression also is pertinent to Chapter 10's prediction that an enterprise's training investment in its workers will be lower in high-risk situations. Empirical analyses of human-capital formation have traditionally employed the TENURE variable as a proxy for the worker's enterprise-specific training. To the extent that TENURE serves as a reasonable measure of the specific skills in which the company has invested, the negative relation between tenure and job risks is consistent with the theoretical predictions.

Three other training measures are available for the NLS Mature Men's Survey. These variables provide information on whether a worker has participated in any training program from 1969–1971 (TRAIN), whether he has participated in a training program at a com-

Table 13.19.   Training Regressions for Mature Men,
Logistic Curve Approximations

Independent variables	Coefficients and standard errors		
	TRAIN	COTRAIN	OTHTRAIN
AGE	−.080	−.026	−.098
	(.019)	(.288)	(.023)
NONWHITE	−.279	+.079	−.440
	(.179)	(.029)	(.213)
EDUC	+.120	+.156	+.074
	(.030)	(.041)	(.031)
HEALTH	+.919	+.456	+.185
	(.189)	(.288)	(.227)
UNION	−.189	−.360	−.060
	(.169)	(.264)	(.197)
INJRATE	−.033	−.036	−.027
	(.008)	(.012)	(.010)
F	11.02	13.94	7.75

Note: Logistic curve estimates were obtained from the OLS results using the method of Haggstrom (1974). Other variables included in the regression are given by MISC, OD, and TENURE.

pany training school (COTRAIN), or whether he has participated in a training program other than at a company school (OTHTRAIN). The approximations to the logistic parameter estimates are presented in Table 13.19 for each of these variables. These approximations reflect patterns of influence similar to those displayed in the maximum likelihood estimates provided in Table 13.20 for TRAIN. The negative INJRATE effect on these worker training variables provides very strong support for the probabilistic labor supply model of enterprise decisions. The relation between job risks and training is a more refined and a much more meaningful test of the specific predictions in Chapter 10 than are the TENURE results, since it does not compound the impact of job risks on worker training with the quit-rate effect.

13.5 Conclusions

The principal intent of this chapter has been to ascertain whether workers quit after learning about the job hazards they face, as predicted by the adaptive models. The evidence supporting this hypothesis is both diverse and quite strong. On an industrywide basis, in two-digit and three-digit industries, the injury rate is an important determinant of the aggregative quit rate. Examination of the behavior of

Table 13.20. Logistic Parameter
Estimates for the Probability of
Participating in a Training Program,
Mature Men's Sample

Independent variables	Coefficients and standard errors
AGE	−.071
	(.014)
NONWHITE	−.384
	(.199)
EDUC	+.142
	(.267)
HEALTH	+.272
	(.189)
UNION	−.132
	(.171)
INJRATE	−.042
	(.010)
Log likelihood	−635.05

Note: Other variables included in the equation are given by MISC, OD, and TENURE.

individual workers yields similar results. The analysis of workers' quit intentions in Section 13.3 has indicated that the likelihood that a worker will attempt to switch jobs is dramatically altered by his subjective job hazard perceptions. Strong quit intention probabilities are more than doubled if the worker views his job as hazardous.

The analysis of quit behavior of a very large sample of workers from the Panel Study of Income Dynamics reveals a very powerful relationship between job risks and individual quit behavior. Because of data limitations, the analysis of actual individual quit behavior for the NLS surveys of young and mature men produce somewhat weaker results. Nevertheless, there is a strong positive influence of the industry injury rate on worker dissatisfaction and job search activity. Moreover, the duration of worker tenure at any enterprise is significantly shortened by job risks at both ends of the life cycle of work activity. In short, these results are consistent with the adaptive models' principal prediction for worker behavior.

14

THE DETERMINANTS OF JOB HAZARD ASSESSMENTS

14.1 INTRODUCTION

Workers who consider their jobs to be dangerous are more likely to quit than those who do not, as shown in Chapter 13. These results are consistent with the central behavioral hypothesis of the adaptive models of job choice. Underlying this adaptive behavior is the process of learning about the risks posed by a job through on-the-job experience. The analysis in this chapter will attempt to ascertain whether workers' perceptions of job hazards are consistent with the hypothesis that workers learn about job hazards through observation of job characteristics and injury experiences.

To analyze the learning process, ideally one would like information on the revision over time of the probabilities for different health state outcomes, as well as information regarding the types of experiences that contributed to this updating. The best data available—the 1969–1970 Michigan Survey of Working Conditions (SWC)—is from a cross sectional survey, so that the actual updating process cannot be monitored. One can, however, ascertain the relative contribution of job characteristics and injury experiences in influencing the hazard assessment variable. The impact of personal and enterprise characteristics on the riskiness of a worker's job also will be explored, providing additional tests of the validity of the conceptual formulations.

14.2 DESCRIPTION OF THE VARIABLES

The primary data source for the analysis in this chapter is the SWC, which was employed in the earlier investigation of quit intentions.[1]

Table 14.1. Glossary of SWC Variable Definitions and Variable Lists

Symbol	Definition
AGE	Age in years
BLACK	Black race d.v.[a]
DANGER	Job hazard perceptions d.v.
EDUC	Years of schooling
EXPINJURY1	Injury experience d.v.
EXPINJURY2	Weighted injury experience d.v.
FEMALE	Femal sex d.v.
HEALTH	Health limitations d.v.
INJRATE	1969 BLS injury frequency rate
IRREG	Irregular work hours d.v.
LIST1	SINGLE, OD, NORTH, SOUTH, URBAN
LIST2	LIST1, AGE, FEMALE, BLACK, EDUC, HEALTH, UNION, INJRATE, TENURE, PHYSC, IRREG, PHCOND, MISTK, NODEC, OVERT, EXPINJURY2
LIST3	LIST1, AGE, FEMALE, BLACK, EDUC, HEALTH, TENURE, IRREG, MISTK, NODEC, OVERT, SIZE
MISTK	Job requires no worker mistakes d.v.
NODEC	No worker decisions on job d.v.
NORTH	Northern region d.v.
OD	Set of three occupational d.v.'s
OVERT	Overtime work d.v.
PHCOND	Pleasant physical conditions d.v.
PHYSC	Physical effort d.v.
SINGLE	Single marital status d.v.
SIZE	Enterprise size, that is, number of employees
SOUTH	Southeastern region d.v.
TENURE	Years of experience with present employer
UNION	Unionization d.v.
URBAN	Urban area d.v.

Note: Complete definitions are provided in Section F.5 of Appendix F.
[a] d.v. = dummy variable.

Tables 13.7 and 13.9 summarize the sample characteristics. The variables and variable lists to be used in this chapter are summarized in Table 14.1. More complete definitions are given in Section F.5 of Appendix F. The key variables of interest are DANGER, EXPINJURY1, and EXPINJURY2. The latter two variables are the injury experience and

---

1. The empirical analysis will continue to focus on the 496 full-time blue collar workers in the sample since the job characteristic questions were most appropriate for this subsample. The results for the pooled sample, which are quite similar to the blue collar findings, are reported in Section F.3 of the Appendix F.

Table 14.2. Job Hazard Frequencies

Hazard	D_1	E_1	D_2	E_2	D_3	E_3	ΣD	ΣE
Inadequate protective equipment or clothing	.0040	.0020	.0020	—	—	—	.0060	.0020
Inadequate shoring	.0081	—	.0040	—	.0020	—	.0141	—
Inadequately guarded electrical apparatus	—	—	.0020	—	—	—	.0020	—
Inadequate safety procedures	.0121	.0020	.0060	—	.0020	—	.0201	.0020
Inadequate guards on machinery	.0040	—	.0020	.0040	.0020	—	.0080	.0060
Defective machines or equipment	.0081	.0020	.0141	—	—	—	.0222	.0060
Inadequate hazard warnings	.0020	—	—	—	—	—	.0020	—
Danger from exposure to animals	—	—	—	—	.0020	—	.0020	—
Violence from customers	.0141	.0060	.0101	.0020	—	—	.0242	.0080
Other exposures to violence	.0121	.0020	.0020	—	.0020	—	.0161	.0020
Inherently dangerous materials	.1008	.0121	.0585	.0161	.0141	—	.1734	.0282
Inherently hazardous equipment	.0786	.0202	.0181	.0040	.0101	.0040	.1068	.0282
Inherently hazardous procedures	.0625	.0121	.0181	.0020	.0121	.0020	.0927	.0161
Dangerous exposures to dust, etc.	.0383	.0060	.0161	.0081	.0040	—	.0584	.0141
Inappropriate job for physical capabilities	.0020	—	.0020	—	—	—	.0040	—
Inadequate help	.0141	.0040	.0101	.0020	—	—	.0242	.0060
Poor sanitation	.0060	—	.0060	.0020	—	—	.0120	.0020
Slippery floors or footing	.0060	.0040	.0121	.0040	.0040	.0020	.0221	.0100
Excessive noise	.0060	.0020	—	—	—	—	.0060	.0020
Temperature or humidity extremes	.0202	.0040	.0181	.0020	.0081	.0060	.0464	.0120
Placement hazards	.0242	—	.0343	.0060	.0141	.0020	.0726	.0080
Exposure to the elements	.0181	.0081	.0060	.0040	.0060	.0040	.0301	.0161
Transportation hazards	.0282	.0020	.0081	—	—	—	.0363	.0020
Exposure to communicable diseases	.0202	.0020	.0020	.0020	.0040	.0020	.0262	.0060
Other illness or injury	.0081	.0040	—	—	.0060	.0040	.0141	.0080

Note: The D columns present the frequencies of the job hazards cited, where the subscripts refer to the first, second, and third hazards cited. The E columns list the frequencies in the sample of job hazards that have also been accompanied by on-the-job injury experiences.

the severity-weighted injury experience dummy variables. Since on-the-job learning serves as the motivation for adaptive behavior, a fundamental prediction of the adaptive models of job choice is that these variables will be important determinants of job hazard assessments.

The DANGER variable is the dummy variable for whether or not the worker's job exposes him to physical dangers or unhealthy conditions. The frequencies of the particular hazards facing workers are presented in Table 14.2, where columns D_1, D_2, and D_3 list the frequencies for the first, second, and third hazards mentioned by workers, and ΣD is a simple summation of these values. The E columns are defined similarly and represent the frequencies for which these hazards are cited and are also accompanied by an on-the-job injury within the past three years. I will defer the interpretation of the injury experience data until Section 14.6.

The workers in the sample mentioned most frequently the risks posed by inherently dangerous materials (such as chemicals, gases, smoke, and fumes), inherently hazardous equipment, inherently hazardous procedures, placement hazards, and dangerous exposures to dust and other materials. Detailed examination of the hazards reveals that the risks are consistent with the individual's particular job. For example, temperature and humidity extremes are cited by a truck driver for a canning company, inadequate shoring is listed by a construction worker, and slippery floors or footing is cited by a manufacturing worker in the plastic products industry. It should be emphasized that the danger variable pertains only to those hazards that are perceived by the worker. Risky conditions that are associated with a job but which are not identified by a worker are not reflected in the data.

14.3 REGRESSION RESULTS AND THE ROLE OF PERSONAL CHARACTERISTICS

The worker's assessment of the risks posed by his job depends on the contribution of his personal characteristics to that risk, the nature of the job itself, and his on-the-job experiences. In this section I will introduce the regression results and focus on the first of these determinants of worker perceptions—the personal characteristics of the worker. Table 14.3 reports the maximum likelihood estimates of the logistic parameters pertaining to the probability of danger perception.

Different groups of variables have been added to each of the five equations in an effort to measure the relative contribution of variables observable at different points in the employment process. Equation (1) includes only the worker's personal characteristics and will be used to ascertain the total effect (that is, direct effects plus indirect effects via subsequent variables in the system) of these variables on assessed job hazards. Equation (2) introduces enterprise characteristics, including

Table 14.3. The Determinants of Danger Perception, Logistic Curve Estimates

Independent variables	Coefficients and standard errors				
	(1)	(2)	(3)	(4)	(5)
AGE	-.0066 (.0048)	-.015 (.006)	-.017 (.008)	-.018 (.008)	-.019 (.009)
FEMALE	-.633 (.219)	-.485 (.259)	-.450 (.283)	-.436 (.285)	-.427 (.286)
BLACK	-.516 (.284)	-.556 (.298)	-.592 (.318)	-.599 (.319)	-.601 (.320)
EDUC	+.051 (.019)	+.0015 (.024)	-.024 (.029)	-.024 (.030)	-.026 (.030)
HEALTH	+.090 (.103)	+.105 (.105)	+.094 (.111)	+.079 (.112)	+.060 (.113)
SIZE		+.16E-3 (.11E-3)	+.27E-3 (.13E-3)	+.26E-3 (.13E-3)	+.26E-3 (.13E-3)
UNION		+.105 (.215)	-.027 (.230)	-.014 (.232)	-.0039 (.233)
INJRATE		+.048 (.011)	+.039 (.012)	+.039 (.012)	+.039 (.012)
			+.0094	+.0062	+.0071

TENURE			(.013)	(.013)	(.013)
PHYSC			+.718 (.212)	+.658 (.214)	+.661 (.215)
IRREG			+1.501 (.660)	+1.465 (.659)	+1.474 (.660)
PHCOND			−.825 (.205)	−.799 (.207)	−.789 (.208)
MISTK			+.135 (.095)	+.136 (.096)	+.130 (.096)
NODEC			−.174 (.092)	−.158 (.093)	−.150 (.093)
OVERT			+.151 (.072)	+.126 (.073)	+.124 (.073)
EXPINJURY1				+.853 (.314)	
EXPINJURY2					+.349 (.107)
Other variables	SINGLE	LIST1	LIST1	LIST1	LIST1
Log likelihood	−334.08	−321.78	−298.09	−294.18	−292.21

the BLS injury rate for the worker's industry. The variables in this equation can be observed by the worker prior to employment.[2] The variables introduced in equation (3) are on-the-job experience variables that primarily consist of job characteristics observed by the worker. These variables might be used by the worker in updating his prior probability assessments after work on the job. Finally, equations (4) and (5) introduce the unweighted and severity-weighted injury experience variables.

Whether the addition of each of these sets of variables significantly affects the explanatory power of the regression can be determined using likelihood ratio tests. In particular, let $\hat{\theta}^*$ be the estimated parameter vector with q coefficients constrained to be zero and $\hat{\theta}^{**}$ be the unconstrained estimates. If L represents the likelihood of the observed sample, then

$$-2 \log [L(\hat{\theta}^*)/L(\hat{\theta}^{**})] = -2[\log L(\hat{\theta}^*) - \log L(\hat{\theta}^{**})],$$

which is approximately chi-square with q degrees of freedom. The log likelihoods from Table 14.3 can be used to calculate the test values for this equation, which are given in Table 14.4. These magnitudes are considerably larger than the critical $\chi^2(q)$ for 95 percent confidence levels, which are given in the last column of Table 14.4. One must consequently reject the hypothesis that the coefficients in each of the sets of variables added to equations (2–5) equal zero.

In each equation the first group of variables pertains to the personal characteristics of the worker. The individual attribute of greatest conceptual interest is the worker's AGE. This variable captures the influence of the shorter time horizon of older workers, physical deterioration, and job sorting with age.[3] The time horizon effect was examined in Chapter 3. That analysis suggested that no unambiguous theoretical relationship exists between the optimal job risk and the length of the time horizon. The effect of physical deterioration with age also was not clearcut. Although a deterioration of one's physical capabilities should increase the risk of any particular job, the job selected by a worker also may vary with his age, leading to a net impact whose direction cannot be predicted. Older workers may have learned how to reduce the risks posed by a job, further complicating the productivity effect. The final age-related influence is that older workers are in the latter stages of their lifetime adaptive process. To the extent that these individuals have quit jobs that they considered too risky and have

2. The extent of an individual's knowledge about a job prior to working on it no doubt lies somewhere between equations (2) and (3). Interpreting the results in this manner would not affect the conclusions.

3. There also may be age-related changes in worker preferences, such as an increase or decrease in risk aversion.

Table 14.4. Summary of Likelihood Ratio Tests

Equation	Variables added	$-2(\log L(\hat{\theta}^*)$ $- \log (\hat{\theta}^{**}))$	$\chi^2(q)$
(2)	SIZE, UNION, INJRATE	24.6	7.81
(3)	TENURE, PHYSC, IRREG, PHCOND, MISTK, NODEC, OVERT	47.38	14.1
(4)	EXPINJURY1	7.82	3.84
(5)	EXPINJURY2	11.76	3.84

sorted themselves into more desirable occupational pursuits, one would expect age to have a negative effect on the riskiness of a worker's job.

On an empirical basis the net effect of these influences is clearcut. The AGE variable has a consistently significant and negative effect on the riskiness of a worker's job except in equation (1), which does not include any job characteristic variables.[4] The total AGE effect reflected in its coefficient in equation (1) is only a third of the size of the AGE effect once the attributes of the worker's job are taken into account. Most of the increase in the AGE coefficient occurs when the three enterprise characteristic variables are introduced in equation (2). This result suggests that the diminishing of job risks with worker age is accomplished largely by working at a safer job than one would predict in view of the general characteristics of one's place of employment and one's personal attributes. The underlying economic effect responsible for this pattern cannot be distinguished.

The influence of the FEMALE variable is somewhat different. Its coefficient in equation (5) is two-thirds the size of its original value in equation (1). The lower riskiness of female employment reflects the fact that women have different kinds of jobs, work at different kinds of establishments, and have different work histories than do men.

A personal characteristic of particular interest is the worker's race. In particular, is there evidence that black workers are discriminated against in terms of the riskiness of their jobs? Such a job discrimination hypothesis is not supported by the results. Indeed, the BLACK coefficient is negative and quite large. This result is consistent with workers' own assessments, since only 1 of the sixty-one blacks in the sample

4. Throughout this chapter, references to statistical significance refer to tests at the 5 percent level. The value of $t_{.95}$ for a one-tailed t-test with an infinite sample size is 1.645. Treatment of the asymptotic t values as being comparable to regular t statistics is considerably cheaper than performing repeated likelihood ratio tests. The likelihood ratio test results for EXPINJURY1 and EXPINJURY2 in Table 14.4 are quite similar to what one would obtain using conventional t-tests.

Table 14.5. Regression of INJRATE
on Worker's Personal Characteristics

Independent variables	Coefficient and standard errors
AGE	−.068
	(.033)
FEMALE	−6.67
	(.934)
BLACK	−2.80
	(1.23)
EDUC	−.313
	(.141)
HEALTH	−.171
	(.434)
SINGLE	−2.38
	(1.40)
R^2	.120
SEE	8.74
F	11.13

complained that he got a worse, dirtier, or harder job because of racial discrimination.

Race-linked differences in perceptions of job attractiveness do not appear to be an important cause of this result, since the pattern is consistent with patterns reflected in objective measures of risk. Black workers tend to be employed in industries with low BLS injury rates. The regression of INJRATE on workers' personal characteristics reported in Table 14.5 yields a negative BLACK coefficient, as in the subjective job hazard assessment results. A similar result is reported for the larger National Longitudinal Survey data set in Table 14.11.[5] Indeed, the supplementary regressions presented in Section F.2 of Appendix F indicate that apart from the lower safety risks faced by blacks, the only statistically significant impact of race on job characteristics is that blue-collar blacks are more likely to be supervisors.[6] There is no available evidence suggesting that there is any racial discrimination against blacks in terms of the riskiness of their jobs.

The two other personal characteristics—EDUC and HEALTH—are relatively unimportant empirically, perhaps because these variables

5. These results are for blue-collar workers and white-collar workers combined.
6. None of these regressions include any ability or family background measures other than the level of education; as a result the pure race effect cannot be identified as precisely as one might like.

capture a variety of influences of differing direction. For example, EDUC may exert a negative influence to the extent that better-educated workers have access to more attractive jobs, but a positive influence if workers with more schooling are better able to identify the hazards they face. Such an interpretation is consistent with the empirical results, since the EDUC coefficient is statistically insignificant with varying signs in the DANGER regressions, but negative in the INJRATE regression reported in Table 14.5.

The health limitation variable likewise is conceptually ambiguous, since the decreased ability to avoid accidents on a particular job would lead to a negative coefficient for HEALTH, while the desire of impaired workers to seek safe employment appropriate for their capabilities would represent an opposite influence. The positive coefficient for HEALTH in the DANGER regressions and the negative coefficient in the INJRATE regressions indicates that each of these opposing impacts may be present, although the effects are not statistically significant.

14.4 ENTERPRISE CHARACTERISTICS

The inclusion of enterprise characteristics in the second equation in Table 14.3 completes the group of variables observable by an individual before employment. This regression equation will serve as the benchmark for assessing the impact of on-the-job learning on workers' danger perceptions. The enterprise characteristic variables are also of substantial interest in their own right.

The SIZE variable reflects the influence of enterprise size on the risks faced by the worker. In Chapter 10, the productivity losses from job risks were shown to diminish with increases in the scale of the enterprise, suggesting that SIZE should have a positive sign. Five other possible effects that were not matters of theoretical inquiry also may be pertinent. First, job risks may decrease with enterprise size to the extent that there are economies of scale in safety provision. Second, an opposite influence would be exerted if the adverse externalities among workers, such as those associated with safety mishaps, increased disproportionately with enterprise size. This effect could result if worker actions became more difficult to coordinate as the scale of the enterprise increased. Third, a positive learning effect might be observed if, because of the larger number of workers in a large establishment, the job risk information available to workers increased, thus boosting the workers' assessments of the dangers involved. Alternatively, there might be a negative learning effect if workers in small establishments knew much more about their coworkers' experiences, offsetting the fact that there are fewer individuals to observe. Finally, the extent of merit rating for workmen's compensation benefits increases with firm

Table 14.6. Logistic Estimates of the Relationship of
Enterprise Size to Danger Perceptions

Independent variables	Mean and standard deviation	Coefficients and standard errors
SIZE	562.2	+.67E − 3
	(915.3)	(.46E − 3)
SIZE × SIZE	+.12E + 7	−.14E − 6)
	(.27E + 7)	(.15E − 6)
Other variables	— —	LIST2
Log likelihood	—	−291.78

size. Larger enterprises consequently will have a financial incentive to reduce the types of risks that are covered by this program. Since workmen's compensation primarily affects safety risks, there should be a differential policy impact for different kinds of risks. This differential effect is explored in Chapter 16.

The net empirical impact of these influences is negative and statistically significant once the characteristics of the worker's job are included in the regression (that is, equations [3–5] in Table 14.3). The nature of the influence of enterprise scale is illuminated further by adding the SIZE×SIZE term to equation (5), as is reported in Table 14.6. The positive SIZE coefficient is more than double its previous value. Coupled with the negative sign of the SIZE×SIZE coefficient, this result suggests that there may be a concave functional relationship between job hazards and enterprise scale.[7] This pattern is consistent with the predictions of Chapter 10's model of enterprise decisions, since the economies of scale associated with the probabilistic labor supply model diminish with enterprise size.

A potentially important determinant of job risks is the presence of a union to bargain for worker interests. The role of unions derives from

7. This relationship is not as strong as one requires to be able to reject the hypothesis that the SIZE×SIZE coefficient equals zero. In particular, the likelihood ratio test statistic has a value of 0.86, which is far below the 3.84 critical χ^2 value at the 95 percent confidence level. Although the starker inverted U-shaped relationship of injury rates to enterprise size found by Oi (1974) for several particular industries may be attributable in part to his failure to adjust for inter-firm differences in occupational mix or for differences in worker characteristics, the most likely contributor to the differences in our results is that the BLS injury rate data pertain primarily to safety risks for which the merit rating of workmen's compensation may offset the stochastic economies of scale at large enterprises. This hypothesis is consistent with the results in Chapter 16 for health and safety risks.

the advantages of collective action in this market context. First, unions can serve a coordinating function in promoting patterns of work effort and safety precautions that further the employees' group interests.[8] A second possible role is that of influencing workplace characteristics with nonexcludability aspects, such as noise, chemical vapors, and radiation. With bargains on an individual basis, the provision of favorable job conditions of this type will be suboptimal. Union bargaining on behalf of all workers may serve as a more effective mechanism for expressing worker preferences and promoting their collective interests. A closely related union function is the provision of job hazard information to workers. Apart from the public-goods aspect involved, perhaps the most important advantage of unions is their permanency. Workers switch jobs and enterprises fairly frequently, whereas unions exhibit much greater stability and are able to acquire job hazard information over a longer time span and for a greater number of jobs than is any individual worker.

The superiority of unions' information about job hazards and their ability to promote workers' interests on a collective basis would lead one to predict a negative union impact on job hazards. Yet the UNION coefficients in Table 14.3 display insignificant varying signs, with no apparent net influence.

The absence of any evidence of a significant union reduction of hazards runs counter to the conclusion one might draw on the basis of one's observation of actual union actions. For example, building trade unions have traditionally opposed piece rates since accident rates would be higher with such incentive systems.[9] More recently, the United Steelworkers alleviated the safety hazards posed by the incentive system for coke ovens.[10] The data presented in Table 14.7 indicate that impacts such as these are widespread. Millions of workers are affected by collective bargaining provisions for safety committees, safety inspections, safety equipment, workplace sanitation, physical examinations, first aid facilities, protection against a variety of specific job hazards, and other matters likely to affect workplace health and safety. In view of the insignificant union impact in the regression analysis, one might conclude that such improvements would have occurred in the absence of union influence.

8. Although the strategic possibilities are many, a common situation resembles the widely discussed Prisoner's Dilemma, where in this particular context the workers' dominant strategies may involve careless work habits that lead to injuries to coworkers. A Pareto-superior improvement from the careless worker equilibrium might result if all workers were more cautious and did not inflict adverse externalities on their coworkers.

9. See Dunlop (1958), p. 259.

10. See U.S. Dept. of Labor, Occupational Safety and Health Administration, *Job Safety and Health*, vol. 3, no. 5 (May 1975), p. 15.

Table 14.7. Collective Bargaining Provisions Affecting Job Hazards, 1974–1975

Provisions	Agreements with such provisions	Workers covered (in thousands)
General safety and health provisions	1,607	7,197.4
Union-management cooperation on safety	757	3,946.3
Safety committees	567	3,222.1
Employer compliance with health laws and regulations	585	2,665.6
Employee compliance with safety and health rules	805	3,282.6
Employee discipline for noncompliance	349	1,521.8
Safety inspections	335	2,356.9
Safety equipment	847	4,294.9
Safe tools, equipment, and materials	164	783.2
Crew-size safety regulations	222	870.1
Sanitation, housekeeping, and personal hygiene	673	2,994.3
Physical examinations	554	2,963.0
Accident procedures	459	2,745.9
First aid and hospital facilities	492	3,019.9
Specific hazard protection		
Adequate lighting	104	564.1
Eye and face protection	338	1,427.0
Protection from noxious gases and dust	285	2,218.0
Protective clothing	367	2,373.4
Gloves	297	1,568.6
Safety shoes	168	462.2
Hearing protection	67	1,286.0
Falls	146	777.3
Falling objects	174	705.0
Machinery guards and safety devices	115	439.5
Protection from electrical hazards	80	305.3
Radiation	72	520.1
Fire protection	188	1,006.9
Hazard to fellow employee	128	355.9
Total sample size	1,724	7,868

Source: U.S. Dept. of Labor, Bureau of Labor Statistics, *Major Collective Bargaining Agreements: Safety and Health Provisions,* Bulletin 1425–16 (Washington: U.S. Government Printing Office, 1976).

An alternative and more likely possibility is that unions boost worker wages and the wage premiums for job hazards, as I will show in the following chapter. A normal enterprise response would be to reduce workplace safety in much the same way as landlords often respond to rent control laws. The failure to observe such a quality decline might be attributed to the offsetting union influence. Furthermore, the empirical findings would understate the union impact if the types of enterprises that were unionized tended to be more hazardous than those that were not. The mean injury rate is 17.19 for the unionized workers in the sample and 14.70 for the nonunionized workers. The regression analysis takes this influence into account. However, if within industry groups the enterprises that become unionized are the more hazardous firms, the extent to which unions reduce job risks would be understated by the regression results. A final explanation of the union results is based on the differential union impact on health and safety risks (see Chapter 16).

The third enterprise characteristic included in the regressions is INJRATE—the 1969 BLS injury frequency rate (the number of disabling work injuries for each million hours worked). This variable is the principal index of job hazards available on a public basis. The strong positive relationship between INJRATE and DANGER exhibited in Table 14.3 suggests that workers' danger assessments are well-founded.

The variation of danger perceptions with INJRATE is displayed in more detail in Table 14.8. The second column lists the fraction of workers in the sample in each of the nine INJRATE groups. The fraction of workers who consider their jobs dangerous is presented in the third

Table 14.8. Danger Assessments and the Injury Rate for the Worker's Industry

INJRATE (IR)	Proportion of workers in category	Proportion of workers who consider job hazardous	Proportion of workers in IR category who consider job hazardous
0 ≤ IR < 5	0.504	0.120	0.237
5 ≤ IR < 10	0.178	0.076	0.426
10 ≤ IR < 15	0.076	0.036	0.472
15 ≤ IR < 20	0.077	0.041	0.534
20 ≤ IR < 25	0.062	0.042	0.678
25 ≤ IR < 30	0.070	0.046	0.657
30 ≤ IR < 35	0.012	0.007	0.636
35 ≤ IR < 40	0.015	0.009	0.600
40 ≤ IR	0.005	0.005	1.00

column. The final column shows the fraction of workers in each injury rate interval who consider their jobs dangerous. This fraction steadily increases with the industry's injury rate.[11] Indeed, all workers in industries for which INJRATE is greater than or equal to 40 consider their jobs hazardous. In short, the strong relationship between INJRATE and DANGER in this tabulation provides additional evidence of the plausibility of workers' prior probability assessments to the extent that the INJRATE variable reflects the state of worker knowledge before obtaining any on-the-job experience.

14.5 JOB CHARACTERISTICS

The job characteristic variables are added in equation (3) of Table 14.3 in order to capture the influence of the incremental learning about job risks that arises through observation of job characteristics affecting the worker's conditional assessments of likely hazards. These variables include years of experience with the enterprise (TENURE), physical effort required by the job (PHYSC), irregular work hours (IRREG), pleasantness of the physical conditions (PHCOND), whether the job requires that the worker not make mistakes (MISTK), whether the worker is not permitted to make decisions (NODEC), and the extent of overtime work (OVERT). As a group, these variables dramatically increase the explanatory power of the equation, easily passing the test for statistical significance in Table 14.4. This finding is consistent with a fundamental tenet of the models of adaptive job choice—that on-the-job experiences are critical to workers' judgments regarding job hazards.

The job characteristics with statistically significant coefficients are PHYSC, IRREG, PHCOND, NODEC, and OVERT.[12] As one would expect, jobs requiring substantial physical effort (PHYSC), irregular work (IRREG), and overtime work (OVERT) tend to be more dangerous, while those associated with a pleasant physical environment (PHCOND) are less hazardous. The negative coefficients of the no-decisions variable (NODEC) and the statistically insignificant positive effect of the no-mistakes variable (MISTK) are difficult to interpret. A possible explanation of the negative NODEC effect is that this variable may capture the job attributes associated with lighter and less-

11. The failure of the DANGER-INJRATE relationship to be steadily increasing for all intervals is due to several factors. First, INJRATE is the injury rate for the worker's three-digit industry. Unlike DANGER, this variable does not pertain to the worker's particular job or occupation within that industry. Second, INJRATE is reported on a voluntary basis and may involve substantial measurement error. Third, the sample size is rather small, particularly for the higher injury-rate groups.

12. Reference to the significance of individual coefficients refers to t-tests using the asymptotic t values.

demanding blue-collar work, which typically permits fewer worker decisions. The positive MISTK influence may derive from the greater risks posed by tedious assembly-line jobs and other repetitive tasks for which the avoidance of mistakes is of particular importance.

The TENURE variable has little direct effect on workers' danger perceptions. The insignificance of this variable may be attributable to the presence of two possible opposing influences—the different information possessed by more experienced workers and the different kinds of job tasks that they perform. What is most important is that the worker's observation of job characteristics influences his assessment of job hazards. The most important form of on-the-job experience is incurring an on-the-job injury—the subject of the next section.

14.6 INJURY EXPERIENCE

The adaptive models of worker behavior assumed that workers learn from their experiences of job injuries and update their probability assessments using this information. On an empirical basis, one would predict that a worker's injury experiences on his present job should be a very important determinant of his danger perceptions. Both the injury experience dummy variable EXPINJURY 1 and the severity-weighted version of that variable EXPINJURY2 contribute substantially to danger perceptions, as is evidenced by the results in equations (4) and (5) of Table 14.3 and the likelihood ratio test results in Table 14.4.

The influence of EXPINJURY1 in the fourth regression equation is suggestive of the magnitude of this effect. If all variables except for EXPINJURY1 assume their mean values, the probability that the worker will view his job as hazardous is 0.42. After experiencing an on-the-job injury (that is, if EXPINJURY1 equals one instead of zero), the probability that the job will be regarded as hazardous increases by 0.21. This amount represents a 50 percent increase in the likelihood of a subjective job hazard assessment.

The strength of this effect is especially impressive since these empirical results are likely to understate the impact of injury experiences on hazard assessments, owing to the cross-sectional nature of the data. Many workers who experience injuries may update their probabilities of injury and switch jobs very quickly, never being captured in the survey. The data reflect the injury experiences of only those workers who do not intend to change jobs or have not yet had the opportunity to do so.

The cross tabulation of danger perceptions and injury experience frequencies in Table 14.9 indicates that 71 percent of the workers who have experienced an injury consider their jobs dangerous, while 19 percent of the workers on dangerous jobs have experienced an injury at that position. Whether or not a worker experiences an injury on a

Table 14.9. Danger Perceptions and Injury Experience
Breakdown for Blue-Collar Workers

	Proportion of workers who consider job hazardous	Proportion of workers who do not consider job hazardous
Experienced injury	0.10	0.04
No injury	0.42	0.44

job he considers hazardous depends on the nature of the danger and on the other information available to the worker. Returning to Table 14.2 one finds that six of the perceived dangers were accompanied by no injury experiences at all: inadequate shoring, inadequately guarded electrical apparatus, inadequate safety procedures, inadequate hazard warnings, dangerous exposures to animals, and inappropriate work for one's physical capabilities. The visible nature of these hazards seems largely responsible for workers' ability to identify these risks without actually incurring an injury.

An analytic result of substantially greater interest is that 29 percent of the workers who have experienced injuries do not consider their jobs dangerous. This seemingly aberrant behavior can be explained in a variety of ways: (a) the worker's job may have changed after the injury; (b) the worker may view the source of the hazard to be personal error rather than an intrinsic aspect of his job; (c) workers may have different perceptions regarding the level of risk that is dangerous; (d) workers may have sharp prior assessments that are updated very slowly; and (e) workers may not learn at all.[13]

Further insight into the nature of the learning process can be obtained by analyzing the danger perceptions associated with different injury experiences, as is presented in Table 14.10. The E_1, E_2, and E_3 columns list the frequencies of different injury experiences in the sample, where the subscripts refer to the first, second, and third most-recent injuries. The D values are the corresponding frequencies of danger perception in the sample. The injuries least likely to be associated with danger perceptions are: muscle or joint inflammation; other injuries from movement; poisoning; dermatitis; and a job-aggravated ailment. These injuries consist almost exclusively of health outcomes dependent on the worker's own physical condition before the injury (a job-aggravated ailment, for example) or a likely act of carelessness (such as poisoning) that he does not consider to be an

13. Explanation (e) is simply the limiting case of reason (d).

Table 14.10. Danger Perceptions (D) for Different Injury Experiences (E)

Injury experience	E₁	D₁	E₂	D₂	E₃	D₃	ΣE	ΣD
Heat burns, or scalds	—	—	—	—	.0020	.0020	.0020	.0020
Other burns	.0020	.0020	—	—	—	—	.0020	.0020
Contusion, bruise	.0040	.0040	.0020	—	—	—	.0060	.0040
Fracture, broken bones	.0222	.0181	.0020	.0020	.0020	.0020	.0262	.0221
Other injuries from hit or fall	.0121	.0121	—	.0040	.0020	.0020	.0141	.0141
Cuts, lacerations, etc.	.0181	.0141	.0040	—	—	—	.0221	.0181
Dislocation	.0020	.0020	—	—	—	—	.0020	.0020
Sprains, strains	.0222	.0121	.0060	.0040	.0020	.0020	.0302	.0181
Muscle or joint inflammation	.0060	.0020	—	—	.0020	.0020	.0080	.0040
Hernia, rupture	.0081	.0060	—	—	—	—	.0081	.0060
Other injuries from movement	.0040	.0020	—	—	—	—	.0040	.0020
Poisoning	.0020	—	—	—	—	—	.0020	—
Asphyxia, strangulation	—	—	.0020	.0020	—	—	.0020	.0020
Dermatitis	.0020	—	—	—	—	—	.0020	—
Contagious disease, cold	.0081	.0060	.0040	.0040	—	—	.0121	.0100
Heart attack, hypertension	.0060	.0060	.0040	.0020	.0020	.0020	.0120	.0100
Job-aggravated ailment	—	—	—	—	.0020	—	.0020	—
Other disease or injury	.0242	.0181	.0101	.0101	.0020	.0020	.0363	.0302

Note: Subscripts 1, 2, and 3 refer to the first, second, and third most recent injuries. All numbers are frequencies for the entire blue collar sample.

inherent part of the job. The hypothesis that workers don't learn at all about job hazards is certainly not borne out by these data, since only two workers with multiple injuries did not view their jobs as hazardous. The probable explanation for these exceptional instances is that the injuries involved (a heart attack and a job-aggravated ailment) were very dependent on the worker's own physical condition, rather than on the job alone.

14.7 THE ROLE OF WORKER ASSETS

The final matter of empirical interest is the influence of worker assets on optimal job risks. The conceptual analysis in Chapter 2 indicated that the optimal job risk would necessarily decrease with the worker's wealth, provided that certain mild restrictions on the worker's preferences and employment opportunities were imposed. The validity of this result cannot be tested using the SWC data, owing to the absence of any worker asset variables. One can, however, use the 1969 data from the National Longitudinal Survey of Mature Men, in conjunction with the 1969 BLS industry injury rates, to ascertain whether there is

Table 14.11. Regression of INJRATE on Assets and Other Pertinent Variables

Independent variables	Coefficients and standard errors
AGE	−.018
	(.052)
NONWHITE	−1.38
	(.499)
EDUC	−.629
	(.063)
ASSETS	−.81E − 5
	(.38E − 5)
Other variables[a]	—
R^2	.090
SEE	8.91
F	15.83

[a] Other variables included were: an area unemployment variable, three regional dummies, one SMSA dummy, union membership, and health status. The sample size was 1,932.

any systematic relationship between the injury rate of the worker's industry and his wealth.

These results are reported in Table 14.11. The variables used either have the same definitions as do the Michigan survey variables (AGE, EDUC) or else are self-explanatory (NONWHITE). Complete definitions were provided in Chapter 13. The variable ASSETS is the worker's net assets and has a mean value of $21,717. ASSETS has a statistically significant coefficient with the expected sign. The magnitude of the coefficient is rather small, however, implying an elasticity of the worker's industry injury rate with respect to his net assets of only −0.011.

Much of the wealth effect undoubtedly is reflected in the individual's choice of a particular job or occupation within an industry, so that these empirical results should significantly understate the magnitude of the wealth effect. If more appropriate data were available, one could obtain a more accurate estimate of the extent of this influence. However, even the underestimate of the wealth effect is statistically significant. This result consequently provides empirical support of the overall conceptualization of individual job choice presented in Chapter 2.

14.9 CONCLUSIONS AND CAVEATS

Overall, 52 percent of the workers in the sample of blue-collar workers viewed their jobs as hazardous in some respect. Detailed analysis of individuals' responses to the survey questions indicated that the types of hazards cited were consistent with the worker's job. Moreover, there was a strong positive correlation between the worker's danger perceptions and both the pertinent BLS industry injury rate and his direct injury experiences. These findings were also supported by the regression results, which suggested that job characteristics correlated with likely hazards and direct injury experiences were important determinants of workers' danger perceptions.

Together the findings in this chapter suggest that one should not accept without supporting evidence the common assertion that workers systematically underestimate the job risks they incur and are generally ignorant of the hazards they face. Indeed, all available evidence indicates that, while workers may not have perfect information, their hazard perceptions appear to have been formed in a systematic manner that is quite consistent with the conceptual analysis of individual behavior. The existence and magnitude of wage premiums for these perceived hazards will be investigated in the following chapter.

It should be noted that the cross-sectional data base that was used was not ideally suited to the analysis of the actual learning process. The principal limitation is that the inclusion of variables that reflect the state of the worker's knowledge before work on the job, such as the industry injury rate, is an imperfect technique for controlling for the worker's prior knowledge of job risks. As a result, part of the influence of the worker experience variables may reflect the different work histories of individuals who have risky jobs, wholly apart from any learning effect. A worker who views his prospective job as being hazardous is more likely to experience an injury—a result that would appear in the regression results as a learning effect even though there may have been no alteration of the worker's prior probability assessments. It is the time when workers' assessments are formed, not the assessments themselves, which remains questionable.

Although the empirical tests are not as refined as one would like, difficulties of this type necessarily accompany any empirical investigation. One can only determine whether a particular hypothesis is consistent with the data, not whether it is the only hypothesis that is consistent. The most convincing evidence that workers learn on the job is that they behave as if they are learning. Workers quit their jobs if they are too hazardous.

15

COMPENSATING EARNINGS
DIFFERENTIALS FOR
JOB HAZARDS

15.1 INTRODUCTION

The conceptual analysis in Chapter 2 formalized Adam Smith's claim that workers will require additional compensation for jobs that pose health and safety risks. Even in the adaptive contexts considered in Chapter 4, one obtains a similar finding, although the analysis must be modified to take into account the precision of the worker's prior assessment. The theory of compensating wage differentials has played a central role in the labor economics literature for the past two centuries.

It has only been recently, however, that this theory has been subjected to successful empirical tests. The first of these studies was Thaler and Rosen's (1976) analysis of death risks, which will be discussed in Section 15.3. The primary difficulty encountered in earlier investigations, which typically utilized aggregative data, was that unless one had detailed information pertaining to the worker's personal characteristics and his job, one could not disentangle the compensation for job risks from compensation for other attributes of the worker and his job. The resulting empirical estimates consequently were seriously biased.

The empirical results in this chapter extend our knowledge in several ways. First, the results in Section 15.2 represent the first attempt to analyze job hazard premiums using an equation that also includes other job attributes. One can consequently be more confident that the resulting wage premium estimates do not reflect compensation for attributes correlated with riskiness, such as the speed of work. These earnings premiums are estimated both for objective and subjective measures of job risks, providing additional evidence regarding the influence of individuals' job hazard perceptions on their behavior.

241

The magnitude of the job risk compensation will depend not only on the worker's willingness to incur the risk, but also on the magnitude of the risk. A useful measure of the extent of wage compensation for risks is the value of life and limb implied by these results, which I consider in Section 15.3. The role of unions in altering the extent of wage compensation for job risks is the principal interactive effect analyzed in Section 15.4. An alternative to wage compensation is ex post compensation for injuries in forms such as medical insurance. The role of these fringe benefits is the subject of Section 15.5. The principal implications of this analysis are summarized in Section 15.6.

15.2 ANALYSIS OF COMPENSATING EARNINGS DIFFERENTIALS

The data source that I will use to investigate compensating earnings differentials is the 1969–1970 Michigan Survey of Working Conditions (SWC), which was also employed in the quit intention and danger perception analysis in Chapters 13 and 14. This data base pro-

Table 15.1. Glossary of SWC Variable Definitions and Variable Lists

Symbol	Definition
AGE	Age in years
BLACK	Black race d.v.[a]
DANGER	Job hazard perceptions d.v.
DEATH	1969 BLS fatal injury frequency rate
DEATH1	DEATH × DANGER
EARNG	Annual earnings from main job
EDUC	Years of schooling
FAST	Fast work speed d.v.
FEMALE	Femal sex d.v.
FRINGE	Fringe benefit d.v.
HEALTH	Health limitations d.v.
ID	Set of 25 Industry d.v.'s
INJRATE	1969 BLS injury frequency rate
INJRATE1	INJRATE × DANGER
IRREG	Irregular work hours d.v.
LIFEINS	Life insurance d.v.
LIST1	ID, LIST2
LIST2	OD, NORTH, SOUTH, URBAN
LIST3	AGE × AGE, UNION, LIST2, LIST4
LIST4	AGE, FEMALE, BLACK, EDUC, HEALTH, SINGLE, SIZE, TENURE, SUPER, FAST, NODEC, MISTK, SECURITY, OVERT, TRAIN, LIST1

Note: Complete definitions are provided in Section F.5 of the Appendix F.
[a] d.v. = dummy variable.

Table 15.1. (Continued)

Symbol	Definition
LOGEARNG	Natural logarithm of EARNG
MEDINS	Medical insurance d.v.
MISTK	Job requires no mistakes d.v.
NODEC	No worker decisions on job d.v.
NONFATAL	1969 BLS nonfatal injury frequency rate
NONFATAL1	NONFATAL × DANGER
NORTH	Northern region d.v.
OD	Set of three occupational d.v.'s
OVERT	Overtime work d.v.
PENSION	Pension plan d.v.
PHCOND	Pleasant physical conditions d.v.
PHYSC	Physical effort d.v.
PROFIT	Profit-sharing plan d.v.
SECURITY	Job security d.v.
SICKLV	Sick leave d.v.
SINGLE	Single marital status d.v.
SIZE	Enterprise size, that is, number of employees
SOUTH	Southeastern region d.v.
STOCK	Stock option plan d.v.
SUPER	Supervisor d.v.
TENURE	Years of experience with present employer
TRAIN	Training program d.v.
UNION	Unionization d.v.
URBAN	Urban area d.v.

vides the most extensive information available about the nature of particular jobs, including information on hazardous conditions. My analysis will focus on 496 full-time blue-collar workers in the sample, since the survey questions are not particularly appropriate for white-collar workers.[1] The variables and variable lists that will be employed are summarized in Table 15.1 and are very similar to those encountered in the previous chapters. Tables 13.7 and 13.9 summarize the sample characteristics.

Since the survey did not ascertain the worker's hourly wage rate, I will use the worker's annual earnings from his principal job (EARNG) and the natural logarithm of this variable (LOGEARNG) as the two dependent variables of interest.[2] The two forms of equations to be esti-

1. Findings for the entire sample are provided in Section F.3 of Appendix F.
2. Differences in worker hours are not of great importance since I focus on full-time workers and include an overtime work variable. The absence of a weeks-worked variable prevents the construction of a wage variable.

mated are

$$\text{EARNG} = \alpha + \sum_{k=1}^{m} \beta_k X_k + u,$$

and

$$\text{LOGEARNG} = \alpha' + \sum_{k=1}^{m} \beta_k' X_k + u',$$

where α and α' are constant terms, β_k and β_k' are coefficients, the X_k's are worker characteristics and job characteristics, and the u and u' are error terms. The linear form of the earnings equation implies a constant supply price per job characteristic unit, while the semilogarithmic form implies a rising supply price per characteristic unit. The procedure of viewing worker earnings as being dependent on the attributes of the job in effect involves the estimation of a hedonic earnings function, which is econometrically similar to the hedonic price index analysis.[3]

The major regression results are reported in Table 15.2 for both the EARNG and LOGEARNG equations. A variety of job characteristics and worker attributes were included in each equation. Equations (1) and (3) include the DANGER variable, which is the worker's perception of dangerous or unhealthy conditions. An alternative objective hazard index is the BLS injury rate for the worker's industry — INJRATE — which has been included in equations (2) and (4).[4]

The coefficients for the first ten variables in the equations, which represent personal and enterprise characteristics, reflect familiar patterns of influence. Better-educated workers earn more, as do those who belong to a union. Females and workers with health impairments earn less. The magnitudes of the effects are less than in other studies, since much of the impact of these exogenous variables is indirect, through job characteristic variables, such as whether the worker is a supervisor.[5]

The two job risk variables each reflect positive and statistically significant earnings premiums for hazardous work.[6] The results in equation (1) indicate that workers on jobs perceived as being dangerous

3. For a survey of the hedonic price index literature, see Griliches (1971). Thaler and Rosen (1976) present a more detailed motivation of the hedonic approach to analysis of compensating wage differentials.

4. These equations omit the industry dummy variables since INJRATE is the industry injury rate matched to the workers in the sample using information pertaining to their three-digit SIC industry code.

5. The reduced form estimates are more comparable to the results in the human capital literature.

6. Throughout this chapter, references to statistical significance refer to tests at the 5 percent level. The value of $t_{.95}$ for a one-tailed t-test with an infinite sample size is 1.645.

Table 15.2. EARNG and LOGEARNG Regression Results

Independent variables	EARNG		LOGEARNG	
	(1)	(2)	(3)	(4)
AGE	+138.22	+163.74	+.025	+.030
	(45.50)	(44.40)	(.0072)	(.0070)
AGE × AGE	−1.63	−1.96	−.28E − 3	−.34E − 3
	(.53)	(.51)	(.083E − 3)	(.082E − 3)
FEMALE	−2,585.9	−2,809.3	−.507	−.534
	(278.9)	(244.8)	(.044)	(.039)
BLACK	−382.38	−429.00	−.063	−.067
	(276.19)	(269.54)	(.044)	(.043)
EDUC	+128.84	+136.14	+.024	+.025
	(33.34)	(32.76)	(.0053)	(.0052)
HEALTH	−194.91	−168.92	−.019	−.017
	(93.88)	(93.14)	(.015)	(.015)
SINGLE	−1,088.6	−981.16	−.231	−.210
	(343.9)	(328.75)	(.054)	(.052)
SIZE	+.233	+.305	+.25E − 4	+.38E − 4
	(.119)	(.104)	(.19E − 4)	(.16E − 4)
UNION	+543.07	+645.05	+.109	+.113
	(206.88)	(196.53)	(.033)	(.031)
TENURE	+.12.40	+6.25	−.13E − 3	−.0015
	(11.28)	(10.87)	(1.78E − 3)	(.0017)
DANGER	+374.82	—	+.055	—
	(177.67)	—	(.028)	—
INJRATE	—	+26.37	—	+.0040
	—	(10.14)	—	(.0016)
SUPER	+372.24	+414.69	+.032	+.043
	(193.89)	(191.43)	(.031)	(.030)
FAST	+519.54	+460.82	+.072	+.063
	(189.64)	(184.22)	(.030)	(.029)
NODEC	−121.78	−146.67	−.016	−.021
	(83.85)	(82.38)	(.013)	(.013)
MISTK	−127.91	−140.29	−.023	−.027
	(85.31)	(82.79)	(.013)	(.013)
SECURITY	+521.27	+496.28	+.093	+.097
	(177.90)	(172.06)	(.028)	(.027)
OVERT	+170.12	+191.76	+.032	+.037
	(67.41)	(64.66)	(.011)	(.010)
TRAIN	+362.08	+519.59	+.059	+.099
	(201.14)	(193.27)	(.032)	(.031)
Other variables	LIST1	LIST2	LIST1	LIST2
R^2	.641	.611	.698	.669
SEE	1,813.5	1,836.6	.286	.291

earn an annual earnings premium of $375. Although this amount represents only 5.5 percent of the workers' mean earnings of $6,810, the low level of compensation is not implausible in view of the large percentage of workers (52.2 percent) who claim that their jobs expose them to dangerous or unhealthy conditions. Moreover, the low level of the risk faced by these workers will yield low earnings premiums, as I will discuss in the following section.

An instructive check on the plausibility of the job risk premium is to compare the value generated by the worker's own perception of the risk with the average premium implied by the objective job risk variable INJRATE. Equation (2) indicates that workers receive an additional $26 for a one point increase in the frequency of disabling work injuries per million hours worked. Since the average value of INJRATE is 15.93 per million hours worked, the mean level of annual earnings compensation for injuries is $420. This amount is only $45 more than was implied by the DANGER variable—a discrepancy that is well within the bounds of error. Both job hazard variables indicate an average level of compensation for risky jobs of about $400 annually in 1969. The similarity of these findings provides additional support for the view that workers' job hazard perceptions influence their behavior.

The other job characteristic variables included in the regressions serve two functions. First, they control for a variety of job attributes, thus reducing the bias in the job hazard variable's coefficients. Second, they provide additional tests of the validity of the theory of compensating differentials.

The coefficients associated with these variables reflect the expected patterns of influence. Supervisors (SUPER) are paid more, as are employees whose jobs require them to work fast (FAST), those who work overtime (OVERT), and those who work for enterprises with training programs (TRAIN). Workers who do not make decisions (NODEC) and whose jobs require them not to make mistakes (MISTK) tend to be paid somewhat less, which is consistent with the lighter tasks and lower-level assembly-line work associated with these characteristics. The only variable with a sign opposite of what one might expect on the basis of the compensating differentials analysis is SECURITY. However, the higher earnings of individuals with job security is quite consistent with the greater security associated with upper-level blue-collar positions. This variable thus may be capturing primarily the relative ranking of the worker's job rather than any particular job attribute which is not appropriately compensated.

15.3 IMPLICIT VALUATIONS OF LIFE AND LIMB

A. Empirical Results. A more useful measure of the extent of wage compensation for job risks than the annual wage premium is the implicit value of life and limb that these premiums reflect.[7] Particularly when one is dealing with very small risks, one may conclude that the market is not working effectively because the absolute levels of compensation are not very large. However, if the risks incurred also are quite small, then modest overall levels of compensation do not necessarily imply market failure.

To analyze the implicit values of life and limb, I will use the earnings equations for the previous section, with the addition of more disaggregative job risk variables. The BLS industry data divide disabling worker injuries into three categories: deaths, permanent partial disability, and temporary total disability. On average, for the industries represented by the workers in the sample, 0.4 percent of all injuries were fatal. Permanent partial disability accounted for 2.9 percent of all injuries, and temporary total disability for the remaining 96.7 percent. For the purposes of this analysis, the two nonfatal injury rate classifications were pooled, for the data were not rich enough to distinguish the compensating differentials for all three types of hazards. The first of the disaggregative injury variables is DEATH, which is INJRATE multiplied by the percentage of injuries that were fatal in the industry. Similarly, the variable NONFATAL was obtained by multiplying INJRATE by the percentage of nonfatal injuries.

Assuming an average work week of 40 hours and an average of 50 weeks worked per year, these hazard variables can be directly converted into annual probabilities of adverse outcomes.[8] On average, the workers in the sample faced an annual probability of 0.0319 of a fatal or nonfatal job injury, a 1.18×10^{-4} probability of death, and a 0.0317 probability of a nonfatal injury. This death risk is roughly one hundred times the chance that the worker will be struck by lightning in a year. These risks are a bit higher than the average for all manufacturing industries, but lower than the hazard levels in many nonmanufacturing industries, such as mining and transportation. They are, of course, incremental death and injury risks, over and above the risks the workers face in the normal course of their daily lives.

Three job risk variables were also constructed, using the information as to whether the worker considered his job hazardous, thereby reducing some of the measurement error associated with using an industry-wide risk index. The variables INJRATE1, DEATH1, and

7. This section draws on material presented in Viscusi (1978). That essay provides a more detailed discussion of the relation of these results to earlier research and the manner in which the empirical estimates should be used for policy evaluation.

8. Since INJRATE is the number of fatalities and injuries per million hours, the number per 2,000 hours is INJRATE divided by 500. DEATH and NONFATAL are the percentages of INJRATE that are fatal and nonfatal, respectively (that is, DEATH + NONFATAL = 100 INJRATE). Hence, dividing each by 50,000 converts it to an annual probability.

NONFATAL1 were obtained by multiplying their former values by the zero-one dummy variable DANGER. Thus, these variables are identical in value to INJRATE, DEATH, and NONFATAL, except that each is zero if the worker doesn't view his job as hazardous.

After replacing the INJRATE variables in equations (2) and (4) of Table 15.2 with different combinations of job risk variables, one obtains the death risk results reported in Table 15.3. Six different specifications were estimated for both the EARNING and LOGEARNING variables. The principal differences among them are the other job risk variables that were included—the nonfatal injury rate or self-assessed dangers—and whether the hazard variables took on nonzero values only in instances in which the worker perceived his job as being hazardous. The most meaningful results are probably those given on lines 2 and 5 of Table 15.3, in which both the fatal and nonfatal components of the BLS injury rate are included in the equation. Throughout this first set of equations, the death risk coefficients tend to be somewhat lower for the job risk variables that are conditional upon self-perceived hazards.

The implied value of life estimates contained in that table pertain to implicit values when there are low probabilities of risk. These magnitudes were computed in straightforward fashion. Since each unit of the death risk variable corresponds to 50,000 deaths per year, multiplication of the death risk coefficient for the EARNING equation by that number yields the value that individuals place on their lives for small changes in the probability of death. The valuation estimates for the LOGEARNING equation were obtained similarly, taking into consideration the different functional form being used.[9]

The results from one equation to the next display striking similarity; most of the death risk equations in which other job risk variables are included indicate a value of life in the range $1 million to $1.5 million in 1969 dollars. These estimates clearly exceed the amount that a representative worker in the sample could pay to avoid certain death.

It is important, however, to note that such a magnitude is not what the valuation-of-life figures represent. Rather, individuals act as if their lives are worth the indicated amounts when they are faced with very small incremental risks of death. An individual facing an annual additional death risk of 1.18×10^{-4} (the mean for the sample) would receive additional wage compensation of $173 based on the EARNING equation coefficient on line 2. The amount that a worker would pay to eliminate the certainty of death is necessarily below the $1–$1.5 million amount, since the worker's wealth would be reduced

---

9. These estimates were obtained with respect to a one-unit change in the death risk evaluated at the mean income level for the sample.

Table 15.3. Summary of Death Risk Regression Results

Equation	Death risk variable	Other job risk variables included in equation	LOGEARNING results		EARNING results	
			Death risk coefficient and standard error	Implied value of life	Death risk coefficient and standard error	Implied value of life
(1)	Industry death risk (DEATH)	—	.00205 (.00075)	1,595,000	35.39 (10.73)	1,769,500
(2)	"	Nonfatal injury rate (NONFATAL)	.00153 (.00088)	1,185,000	29.20 (12.69)	1,460,000
(3)	"	Self-assessed dangers (DANGER)	.00183 (.00075)	1,420,000	32.13 (10.81)	1,606,500
(4)	Industry death risk conditional upon self-perceived hazard (DEATH1)	—	.00189 (.00072)	1,490,000	34.08 (10.38)	1,704,000
(5)	"	Nonfatal injury rate conditional upon self-perceived hazard (NONFATAL1)	.00076 (.00093)	600,000	18.27 (13.33)	913,500
(6)	"	Self-assessed dangers (DANGER)	.00141 (.00079)	1,080,000	27.93 (11.40)	1,396,500

Note: Regression equations are the same as equations (2) and (4) of Table 15.2, except that different job risk variables are utilized.

as he purchased reductions in the risk of death. Each purchase of an incremental reduction in the death risk would diminish the monetary value the individual attached to his life, since his willingness to incur such risks would increase as his wealth declined, as I demonstrated conceptually in Chapter 2 and empirically in Chapter 14. In short, there are likely to be important income effects so that the implicit value of life for small changes in the probability of death will greatly exceed the value workers would pay to avoid certain death.

In similar fashion, one can interpret the implied values of all injuries, including deaths. These values, which are the first implicit values of injuries ever obtained, are reported in Table 15.4. Workers act as if they view the average industrial injury as equivalent to a $13,000–14,000 drop in income. This result refers to the distribution of all industrial injuries, of which 0.4 percent overall were fatalities, 2.9 percent permanent partial disability, and 96.7 percent temporary total disability. If the death risk premium is distinguished from that for nonfatal injuries, one obtains a value for nonfatal injuries in the $6,000–$10,000 range. These results are instructive in that they indicate that in dollar terms, a probability of death is regarded as being a hundred times worse than an equal probability of a nonfatal injury.

The most immediate significance of the empirical results is their implication for labor market performance. If workers were not compensated adequately for the risks they incurred, one would conclude that the market did not function effectively, perhaps because of systematic individual misallocations. The theme of inadequate compensation runs throughout the more sociologically oriented literature on occupational safety.

As the empirical results indicate, the annual compensation per worker for all job risks totals only about $400. Unlike stuntmen and other workers who received clearly significant hazard premiums, blue-collar workers in the more hazardous occupations do not receive additional remuneration that is sufficiently great to be visible to the casual observer. It is also important to note, however, that the risks the workers incur are not very large; the probability of a fatal injury is only about 10^{-4}. To ascertain whether workers are accepting risks for amounts small enough to suggest some form of market failure, one should examine not the absolute level of compensation but the implicit values that workers associate with death or injury. The empirical results indicate that these magnitudes are quite impressive—on the order of $1–$1.5 million for fatalities and $10,000 for injuries. Although there is no way to ascertain whether these levels of compensation are above or below those that would prevail if workers were perfectly informed, the magnitudes are at least suggestive in that they indicate substantial wage compensation for job hazards. These findings do not imply that the government should not intervene. They do indicate, however, that it is doubtful that one can base the case for intervention on the absence of compensation for risks of death and injury.

B. Likely Biases and Comparison with Other Work. Although the empirical estimates of workers' valuations of their lives and limbs are quite substantial, they should be regarded as underestimates of the true implicit values. First, I have neglected the role of *ex post* compensation through medical insurance, life insurance, and workmen's compensation. Inclusion of these benefits would yield larger implied values of health status. Second, the constructed job risk variables are imperfectly related to workers' subjective assessments. If the job risk measures are randomly distributed about their true value, one will encounter a conventional errors-in-variable situation in which the empirical estimates are biased downward. Finally, suppose that the workers' prior probability assessments are not biased, but that these assessments are imprecise. The analysis in Chapter 4 demonstrated that in normal employment situations in which workers face a sequence of lotteries on life and death and in which workers learn about the risks of the job through their on-the-job experiences, workers will require less wage compensation for any mean level of risk as their initial judgments become less precise. The empirical results consequently will underestimate workers' actual value of life and health.

Yet, even the resulting conservative estimates are quite sizable and considerably larger than those found in Thaler and Rosen's (1976) analysis of implicit valuations of life in the labor market, which yielded estimates of $220,000 ± $66,000 in 1969 dollars.[10] Their seminal study focused on nine hundred adult males in very hazardous occupations. The death risk variables used were the Society of Actuaries' incremental death risks for each of 37 narrowly defined occupations. These variables reflect the death risks of the occupations per se as well as the death risks that are unrelated to work but are correlated with the characteristics and lifestyles and income levels of people in different occupations. As a result, the patterns of risk are surprising. Cooks face three times the death risk of firemen, elevator operators face twice the death risk of truck drivers or electricians, waiters face sixty-seven times the death risk of linemen or servicemen, and actors face a higher death

10. The discussion of other work presented here considers only the Thaler and Rosen (1976) analysis, which is the first and most widely discussed investigation of job risk premiums. Discussion of research by Robert Smith (1976) and others is presented in Viscusi (1978).

risk than fishermen, foresters, power-plant operatives, and individuals in many other more physically demanding occupations. These narrowly defined occupational risk indexes include death risks unrelated to work, so it is unclear whether they involve, as Thaler and Rosen argue, less measurement error than BLS industry risk data do.

The stark disparity between Thaler and Rosen's value-of-life estimates and those I have obtained does not appear to be attributable to different biases in the analyses. The first potential source of bias would be the job risk variables. If, as Thaler and Rosen suggest (p. 287), the BLS injury rate involves more measurement error, and if this error is random, my value-of-life estimates should underestimate the actual value by more than theirs. My figures, however, are already roughly five times theirs. Consequently, one cannot use measurement error to explain the difference in results, because correction for this problem would make the estimates more disparate than they already are.

A second possible bias is that my results are the only value-of-life estimates obtained from equations in which other nonpecuniary job characteristics, such as nonfatal injuries and the speed of work, were included. To the extent that job risks are positively correlated with other unattractive job attributes, the omission of these attributes will lead to overestimates of the value of life. A suggestive estimate of the extent of the bias can be obtained by examining the results in Table 15.4. Omission of the nonfatal injury rate from the equations boosts the implied value of life significantly. The increase ranges from 21 percent to 150 percent, depending on the equation in question. Omission of seven other job-attribute variables alters the value of life estimates by much less—usually by about one-third. Consequently, Thaler and Rosen's estimates would appear to be too high, and if additional job-attribute variables had been included in their analysis, their value of life would actually have been less than one-fifth of the magnitude I found.

The most salient difference between the two studies is the level of the mean death risk for the sample, 10^{-4} in my analysis versus 10^{-3} in theirs. The Thaler and Rosen analysis focuses on a group who have shown themselves to be less averse to severe death risks than the rest of the population. Unlike standard consumer items, death risks do not command a single price. The risk is inextricably linked to the job; it cannot be divided to yield a constant price per unit of risk. Those individuals who are least averse to such risks will be willing to accept a lower compensation per unit of risk than the rest of the working population. As a result, they will be inclined to accept larger risks with lower wage premiums per unit of risk. Hence, the Thaler and Rosen analysis yields a lower implied value of life.

What these differing value-of-life results suggest is that the curve that

Table 15.4. Summary of Injury Risk Regression Results

Equation	Injury risk variable	Death risk variable included in equation	LOGEARNING results		EARNING results	
			Injury risk coefficient and standard error	Implied value of injury	Injury risk coefficient and standard error	Implied value of injury
(1)	Unspecified job injury (INJRATE)	—	.0040 (.0016)	13,550	26.37 (10.14)	13,185
(2)	Unspecified job injury conditional upon self-perceived hazard (INJRATE1)	—	.0043 (.0013)	13,550	27.72 (7.83)	13,860
(3)	Industry nonfatal injury rate (NONFATAL)	Industry death rate (DEATH)	$.932E - 5$ $(.837E - 5)$	5,500	.110 (.121)	5,500
(4)	Industry nonfatal injury rate conditional upon self-perceived hazard (NONFATAL1)	Industry death rate conditional upon self-perceived hazard (DEATH1)	$.136E - 4$ $(.704E - 5)$	9,500	.191 (.101)	9,500

Note: Line 1 of this table presents the results based on equations (2) and (4) of Table 15.2. Other equations were obtained by substituting for the job risk variable other measures of the job hazard.

relates wage rates to death risks is not linear.[11] The market trade-off of dollars for risk becomes less steep as the level of the risk is increased. These findings are consistent with Chapter 2's assumptions concerning the shape of the offered wage schedule. Comparison of mine and Thaler and Rosen's analyses of the value of life also suggests that there is substantial heterogeneity in the values individuals attach to their lives. Economists should direct their efforts at estimating entire value-of-life schedules for the population rather than attempting to determine a single elusive value-of-life number.[12]

15.4 INTERACTIVE EFFECTS

Although the average level of compensation for job risks is the matter of greatest interest, the variation in job risk compensation with worker characteristics is also important to understanding the functioning of the wage differential mechanism. This section will primarily address the role of trade unions in determining the level of job risk premiums.

Unions generally are better situated to have job hazard information than are the workers themselves. Although an individual can profit from his own experiences and those of his immediate coworkers, a trade union can monitor the hazardousness of different jobs in different enterprises for a longer time than most workers can. Moreover, since job risks are an important source of worker dissatisfaction and quitting, one would expect unions to raise job risk premiums both to promote worker welfare and to insure a stable union membership.

Inspection of contract provisions, as summarized in Table 15.5, indicates that there is substantial activity of this type, ranging from hazardous duty differentials to various forms of injury compensation. The most prevalent collective-bargaining provisions continue the wages or supplemental pay of injured workers. The subsequent analysis focuses on hazard premiums for uninjured workers rather than supplemental pay for those unable to work.

The importance of union bargaining for hazard pay is reflected in

11. The SWC sample was not sufficiently rich to identify any nonlinearities. In particular, estimates of quadratic forms of death risk variables were not significant.

12. The implications of the heterogeneity of the value of life are explored more fully in Viscusi (1978). The results of the study by Robert Smith (1976) also are consistent with these findings. Converting his BLS death risk variable to an annual death risk by assuming that individuals work 40 hours per week and 50 weeks per year, one obtains the result that workers facing an average risk of 7×10^{-5} act as if their lives are worth roughly $1.5 million in 1973 dollars. His results for the 1967 CPS data, which imply an implicit value of life of $2.6 million, also may be quite reasonable if workers in the sample are concentrated in low-risk occupations. Unfortunately, mean death risk figures are not available for that earlier year. This discussion is based on Robert S. Smith, personal communication, March 6, 1978.

Table 15.5. Collective Bargaining Provisions Affecting Job Risk Premiums, 1974–75

Provision	Agreements with such provisions	Workers covered (in thousands)
Hazardous duty differentials	260	1,005.3
Falling risks	161	575.3
Excessive heat or fire	21	76.7
Radiation hazards	12	30.6
Electrical work	13	25.0
Acid, fumes, or chemicals	109	372.9
Explosives	42	249.7
Compressed air	80	293.9
Unable to determine	4	31.3
Compensation for job-related injuries	1,038	4,655.2
Temporary continuation of wages	634	2,904.9
Supplemental pay for time not worked	710	3,338.8
Red circle rate in transfer	83	250.5
Total sample size	1,724	7,878

Source: U.S. Dept. of Labor, Bureau of Labor Statistics, *Major Collective Bargaining Agreements: Safety and Health Provisions,* Bulletin 1425-16 (Washington: U.S. Government Printing Office, 1976), pp. 63–64.

the presence of strong interaction effects in the EARNG and LOGEARNG results summarized in Tables 15.6 and 15.7. Consider the EARNG equation findings, which are somewhat stronger. The presence of the union–job-risk interaction term eliminates the statistical significance (at the 5 percent level) of the job risk variables and reduces their magnitude, irrespective of the job hazard measure employed. Moreover, the interactive terms are consistently both statistically significant and larger than the hazard variables' coefficients, suggesting that most hazard compensation occurs in unionized contexts. For example, the results in equation (3) indicate that unions substantially raise the job risk compensation for both death risks (DEATH) and nonfatal injury risks (NONFATAL).

Although the findings for the LOGEARNG equations are somewhat weaker, they are consistent with the hypothesis that unions boost hazard premiums. On an individual basis, the only statistically significant coefficients are those for the UNION×DEATH coefficient in equation (1) and the UNION×NONFATAL coefficients in equations (2), (3), and (5). However, except for the results in equation (7), the group of death

Table 15.6. Estimates of Union Hazard Premiums, EARNG Equation

Equation[a]	Hazard Variables' coefficients and standard errors				Interaction variables' coefficients and standard errors			R^2, SSR
	INJRATE	DEATH	NONFATAL	DANGER	UNION × DEATH	UNION × NONFATAL	UNION × DANGER	
(1)	+10.66 (11.04)	—	—	—	+44.99 (13.31)	—	—	.616, 1565E + 6
(2)	−27.71 (14.82)	—	—	—	—	+.916 (.188)	—	.626, 1526E + 6
(3)	−27.99 (14.79)	—	—	—	+23.55 (14.25)	+.785 (.203)	—	.628, 1517E + 6
(4)	—	−10.32 (21.11)	—	—	+60.38 (24.05)	—	—	.617, 1567E + 6
(5)	—	+22.21 (23.06)	+.154 (.121)	—	+64.63 (24.26)	—	—	.617, 1562E + 6
(6)	—	—	+.282 (.149)	—	—	+.918 (.187)	—	.626, 1526E + 6
(7)	—	—	—	+60.00 (246.29)	—	—	+650.06 (353.20)	.644, 1452E + 6

[a] Each equation also includes the variables given in LIST3. Equation (7) also includes ID.

Table 15.7. Estimates of Union Hazard Premiums, LOGEARNG Equation

Equation[a]	Hazard variables' coefficients and standard errors				Interaction variables' coefficients and standard errors			R², SSR
	INJRATE	DEATH	NONFATAL	DANGER	UNION × DEATH	UNION × NONFATAL	UNION × DANGER	
(1)	+.24E − 2 (.18E − 2)	—	—	—	+.45E − 2 (.21E − 2)	—	—	.664, 40.4
(2)	−.16E − 2 (.24E − 2)	—	—	—	—	+.94E − 4 (.30E − 4)	—	.668, 40.0
(3)	−.16E − 2 (.24E − 2)	—	—	—	+.22E − 2 (.23E − 2)	+.82E − 4 (.33E − 4)	—	.669, 39.9
(4)	—	+.17E − 2 (.34E − 2)	—	—	+.40E − 2 (.39E − 2)	—	—	.661, 40.8
(5)	—	+.19E − 2 (.37E − 2)	+.25E − 4 (.19E − 4)	—	+.47E − 2 (.39E − 2)	—	—	.646, 40.2
(6)	—	—	−.16E − 4 (.24E − 4)	—	—	+.95E-4 (.30E − 4)	—	.668, 40.0
(7)	—	—	—	+.035 (.039)	—	—	+.041 (.056)	.698, 36.3

[a] Each equation also includes the variables given in LIST3. Equation (7) also includes ID.

risk variables are always jointly significant, with the largest magnitudes of impact being the union interaction terms.[13]

The only LOGEARNG equation not consistent with this view is equation (7), since the UNION×DANGER interaction effect is not consequential. However, this underlying job risk variable is a zero-one dummy variable, so that the interaction term would not reflect changes in the level of compensation per unit of risk as accurately as would a variable based on a continuous index of riskiness. In short, the available evidence suggests that unions have an instrumental effect in altering the dollars-risk trade-off for both fatal and nonfatal occupational hazards.

Although an effort was made to identify other interactive effects, the data were not sufficiently rich to make many strong inferences. The most important personal characteristic that affected the level of wage premiums was the worker's age. The AGE×DANGER interaction variable reflects three types of influences. First, the willingness of workers to accept job risks may be age-dependent. Although the analysis of Chapter 3 indicated that the direction of this time horizon effect was theoretically ambiguous, the negative relation between worker age and the job risk a worker will incur, which was documented in Chapter 14, suggests that AGE×DANGER should be positive. The second possibility is that this interaction term would reflect the greater riskiness of older workers in any particular job.[14] If older workers are less efficient in producing safety in the workplace than are younger employees, they will be paid less, as was demonstrated in Chapter 6. A third explanation is that this interaction term reflects the outcome of a self-selection process. Workers who are not averse to job risks, who are adept at reducing the risk posed by a job, or who are unproductive and consequently have few alternative job prospects will tend to remain at the risky jobs as they grow older, producing a negative AGE×DANGER effect.

The net empirical impact is negative and very sizable. The findings in Table 15.8 suggest that the influence of age on the job risk premium is independent of any affect of unions in altering the premium, as the AGE×DANGER coefficient is remarkably robust even after a union-risk interaction term is added. The direction of the age-related influence suggests that the impact of productivity and selectivity factors dominates any positive time horizon effect that may exist. Indeed, this effect

13. For example, the pertinent F statistic associated with the three risk variables in LOGEARNG equation (4) is 3.41, which exceeds the critical $F_{.05}(3,470)$ of roughly 2.62.

14. See Iskrant (1968) for extensive information on the relation of different kinds of accidents to age. Death rates for falls, fires, and explosions are steadily increasing functions of age. Motor vehicle deaths reflect a U-shaped pattern with respect to age, in large part because of different driving frequencies and differences in alcohol consumption.

Table 15.8.   AGE × DANGER Interaction Effects

Independent variables[a]	Coefficients and standard errors			
	EARNG equations		LOGEARNG equations	
DANGER	+1,291.2	+982.20	+.310	+.290
	(528.9)	(552.86)	(.083)	(.087)
UNION × DANGER	—	+656.36	—	+.043
	—	(352.24)	—	(.055)
AGE × DANGER	−23.21	−23.43	−.0065	−.0065
	(12.62)	(12.58)	(.0020)	(.0020)
R^2, SEE	.644	.647	.705	.706
	1,808.6	1,803.6	.283	.283

[a] Each equation also includes ID and LIST3.

is so strong that a worker who is 56 years old or over will be paid less for a hazardous job than for a safe position.

The addition of AGE×DANGER boosts the size of the DANGER coefficient by a factor of 3 for the EARNG equation and by a factor of almost 6 for the LOGEARNG regression. Adjusted for age-related differences in productivity and hazard propensities, the compensation for job risks may be quite large. This effect should, however, be regarded as more tentative than the earlier findings, since the available data do not permit one to disentangle age-related differences in risk and compensation for a given job, as opposed to differences that may derive from different types of jobs held by older workers.

15.5 FRINGE BENEFITS

In addition to receiving ex ante compensation for job hazards in the form of higher earnings, workers also receive ex post compensation that is dependent on their health status. These forms of remuneration include: medical insurance, pension plans, life insurance, and sick leave. In this section, I will analyze the determinants of fringe benefit coverage and, in particular, investigate the role of worker earnings, union membership, and job hazards in influencing the probability of coverage.

Table 15.9 presents the logistic curve estimates for the regression of the aggregative FRINGE benefit variable and its component parts on worker and job characteristics. These approximate results reflect patterns of influence that are roughly comparable to the coefficients and

Table 15.9. Fringe Benefit Regressions, Logistic Curve Estimates

Independent variables	FRINGE		MEDINS		LIFEINS		PENSION		SICKLV		PROFIT		STOCK	
	(1)	(2)	(3)	(4)	(5)	(6)	(7)	(8)	(9)	(10)	(11)	(12)	(13)	(14)
EARNG × E-3	+.18	+.18	+.292	+.309	+.203	+.204	+.198	+.202	+.053	+.070	+.116	+.116	+.064	+.067
	(.097)	(.098)	(.077)	(.077)	(.070)	(.070)	(.074)	(.074)	(.071)	(.073)	(.084)	(.084)	(.084)	(.084)
UNION	+1.20	+1.39	+.680	+1.31	+.874	+.950	+1.72	+1.90	-.494	+.244	-.793	-.766	+.120	+.277
	(.43)	(.58)	(.340)	(.46)	(.304)	(.411)	(.32)	(.44)	(.314)	(.427)	(.365)	(.492)	(.370)	(.499)
DANGER	-.041	+.131	-.201	+.359	-.272	-.203	-.036	+.130	-.174	+.495	-.456	-.438	-.083	+.065
	(.367)	(.508)	(.286)	(.406)	(.260)	(.361)	(.280)	(.389)	(.267)	(.373)	(.310)	(.438)	(3.22)	(.434)
UNION × DANGER	—	-.360	—	-1.18	—	-1.35	—	-.338	—	-1.40	—	-.055	—	-.305
		(.731)		(.58)		(.52)		(.554)		(.54)		(.629)		(.628)
F	2.46	2.41	3.50	3.54	4.03	3.94	6.21	6.09	5.31	5.41	2.14	2.09	2.50	2.45

Note: Logistic curve estimates were obtained from the OLS regression results using the approximation technique developed by Haggstrom (1974). Other variables included in the equations are given by LIST4.

Table 15.10. Logistic Estimates of
the Probability of Fringe Benefit
Coverage

Independent variable	Coefficients and standard errors
EARNG × E-3	+.208
	(.098)
UNION	+.906
	(.473)
DANGER	−.157
	(.370)
AGE	+.011
	(.016)
FEMALE	−.159
	(.622)
BLACK	−.070
	(.630)
EDUC	+.137
	(.067)
HEALTH	+.026
	(.163)
SIZE	+.94E − 3
	(.67E − 3)
TENURE	+.050
	(.0007)
Log likelihood	−117.26

Note: Other variables included in the equation are SINGLE, SUPER, FAST, NODEC, MISTK, OVERT, TRAIN, NORTH, SOUTH, URBAN, ID, and OD. For these maximum likelihood estimates, the number of industry (ID) and occupational (OD) dummy variables is each reduced by one.

standard errors produced by maximum likelihood techniques, as is demonstrated by the representative FRINGE regression reported in Table 15.10.[15] The EARNG coefficient is positive for all forms of fringes and statistically significant for overall fringe benefits (FRINGE), medical insurance (MEDINS), life insurance (LIFEINS), and pension plans

15. The job hazard perception and quit intention regression results were also similar for both the maximum likelihood technique and the discriminant analysis approximation method.

(PENSION). These results reflect the strong positive relationship between one's income and the demand for fringe benefits.

Unionization also has a substantial positive effect on FRINGE, MEDINS, LIFEINS, and PENSION.[16] This impact is part of the unions' general role in boosting worker compensation and may also reflect the ability of unions to avoid adverse selection problems by insuring groups of workers in many enterprises on a compulsory basis. To the extent that workers in more hazardous industries are more likely to avail themselves of this compensation, unions promote the financial interests of those in riskier jobs.

There is no similar union impact on sick leave (SICKLV), and indeed a negative effect can be observed. There are two likely explanations of this phenomenon. First, sick leave in effect may serve as random vacation time for workers who may not be in ill health. This instability may be undesirable in unionized contexts in which there is a substantial training investment in workers and a great deal of interdependence. In their classic study of collective bargaining, Slichter, Healy, and Livernash (1960) cite administrative difficulties of this type as the principal reason for union emphasis on alternative forms of health benefits, such as accident insurance. Second, sick leave may be a less expensive and inferior form of compensation that is provided in lieu of extensive insurance. The absence of any strong effect of EARNG on sick leave is consistent with this view. Finally, the absence of a substantial union impact on profit sharing (PROFIT) and stock option plans (STOCK) may be due in part to the use of these forms of remuneration to increase worker motivation and attachment to the enterprise when a union is not present. Moreover, unions have traditionally opposed fringe benefits of this type, which have been advocated primarily by enterprises seeking to increase worker commitment to the objectives of the firm.[17]

The impact of job hazards (DANGER) of fringe benefit coverage compounds two types of influences—the increased demand for compensation in hazardous jobs and the increased cost of supplying insurance in this situation. The net effect is negative and insignificant when no interaction terms are included, and sometimes positive and insignificant when they are. The DANGER variable does not exert much impact on the likelihood of worker coverage by fringe benefits.

The UNION×DANGER interaction effect is, however, consistently negative and is statistically significant for the three types of fringe benefits most directly linked to job risks—medical insurance, life insurance, and sick leave. Indeed, for life insurance benefits this interaction

16. Work in progress by Freeman and the analysis of Goldstein and Pauly (1976) indicate a similar union impact on fringe benefit provision.

17. See pp. 438–440 of Slichter, Healy, and Livernash (1960) for a discussion of union opposition to profit-sharing plans.

effect is so large that it more than offsets the UNION coefficient, implying that unionized workers in hazardous industries are covered by life insurance less frequently than are nonunionized workers.

The coupling of the negative UNION×DANGER interaction effect on fringes with the positive effect of unions on wage compensation levels per unit of risk indicates that in hazardous contexts unions may sacrifice additional *ex post* compensation in order to obtain additional *ex ante* compensation for workers. Although the actual reason for this emphasis is unclear, a likely explanation is that higher wage premiums for risky jobs may be more effective in reducing risk-induced turnover, which tends to be concentrated among young workers who have weaker preferences for fringe benefits. In addition, *ex ante* compensation may be perceived as creating a more equitable wage structure than does *ex post* compensation, which potentially benefits all workers.

15.6 CONCLUSIONS

This chapter provides strong support for the classic theory of compensating wage differentials. Both subjective and objective measures of job risks indicate that workers received an annual earnings premium for job hazards of $400 in 1969. This amount was not especially large because the annual risks incurred by workers were quite small, on the order of 10^{-4} for death risks and 10^{-2} for nonfatal injuries. Workers acted as if they placed an implicit value on their lives of $1 million and an implicit value on nonfatal injuries of $10,000. Unions appear to play a major role in this compensation process, boosting *ex ante* compensation for hazardous jobs and reducing *ex post* compensation below the levels found in other unionized contexts. Age-related differences in the production of health and safety may also be important, as older workers in hazardous industries receive lower job risk premiums.

16

An Analysis of Health and Safety Hazards

Workers' prior information about job risks, the extent of wage compensation for hazards, and their undesirability are no doubt quite different for the rather diverse types of risks facing workers. Although the data available are not sufficiently detailed to permit analysis of the economic ramifications of narrowly defined categories of job risks, the 1969–1970 Michigan Survey of Working Conditions can be utilized to investigate the differing economic implications of health hazards (HDANGER) and safety hazards (SDANGER). The other variables are defined as before.

The somewhat arbitrary division of these two types of hazards is summarized in Table 16.1. Two-fifths of the dangers cited were health hazards. As a general rule, safety hazards pose more immediate and visible threats to the worker's well-being. Safety risks involve external physical dangers, such as the chance of being maimed or bruised, whereas health risks primarily affect one's sense of well-being. The adverse consequences of health risks tend to be monitored less accurately in the BLS injury rate statistics and by prospective employees, since health hazards typically lead to deferred health effects for which the cause may be difficult to identify. In addition, health risks such as noise and radiation tend to affect workers as a group more than do safety risks, which tend to be specific to a particular job or job group.

16.2 HDANGER, SDANGER, and Quit Intentions

To the extent that it is more difficult to obtain information about health hazards prior to work on the job, one would expect that these risks

264

Table 16.1. List of Health and Safety Hazards

Health hazards (HDANGER)
1. Inadequate shielding from radiation
2. Inadequately labeled chemicals
3. Inherently dangerous materials (fumes, etc.)
4. Dangerous exposures to dust, etc.
5. Poor sanitation
6. Excessive noise
7. Temperature or humidity extremes
8. Exposure to the elements
9. Exposure to communicable diseases

Safety hazards (SDANGER)
1. Inadequate protective equipment
2. Inadequate shoring
3. Inadequately guarded electrical apparatus
4. Inadequate safety procedures
5. Inadequate guards on machinery
6. Defective machines or equipment
7. Inadequate hazard warnings
8. Danger from exposure to animals
9. Violence from customers
10. Other exposures to violence
11. Other dangers from people or animals
12. Inherently hazardous equipment
13. Inherently hazardous procedures
14. Inappropriate job for physical capabilities
15. Inadequate help
16. Slippery floors or footing
17. Inadequate space for activities
18. Placement hazards
19. Transportation hazards
20. Other illness or injury

would be more important determinants of worker quit behavior than would safety hazards. Table 16.2 presents maximum likelihood estimates of the logistic form of the quit equations. These results provide some support for the view that health hazards are more likely to produce worker quitting than are safety hazards.

The starkest difference between health and safety hazards appears in the regression involving QUIT1—a dummy variable that assumes a value of 1 only if the worker is very likely to make a genuine effort to find a new job in the coming year. The HDANGER impact on quit intentions is over two and a half times as large as the SDANGER impact. No such difference is displayed by the QUIT2 results, which include

Table 16.2. Logistic Parameter Estimates of HDANGER, SDANGER, and Other Determinants of Quit Intentions

Independent variables	Coefficients and standard errors	
	QUIT1	QUIT2
HDANGER	+1.290	+.453
	(.431)	(.328)
SDANGER	+.499	+.543
	(.399)	(.300)
AGE	−.058	−.015
	(.015)	(.011)
FEMALE	−.485	+.303
	(.562)	(.427)
BLACK	+.755	+.011
	(.490)	(.381)
EDUC	−.0052	+.050
	(.058)	(.044)
HEALTH	+.244	+.440
	(.152)	(.135)
UNION	+.364	+.121
	(.430)	(.306)
TENURE	−.058	−.068
	(.027)	(.019)
EARNG	−.11E − 3	−.22E − 4
	(.09E − 3)	(.65E − 4)
FAST	+1.202	+.182
	(.362)	(.278)
NODEC	−.131	−.112
	(.163)	(.125)
SECURITY	−.630	−.675
	(.358)	(.269)
PHYSC	−.847	+.038
	(.348)	(.273)
PHCOND	−.570	−.504
	(.377)	(.277)
TRAIN	−.216	−.522
	(.384)	(.292)
CREAT	−.288	−.054
	(.160)	(.120)
FRINGE	−1.034	−.694
	(.437)	(.371)
Other variables	LIST1	LIST1
Log Likelihood	−145.57	−226.06

workers less committed to seeking an alternative job than those in QUIT1. The variable QUIT2 assumes a value of 1 if the worker is very likely or somewhat likely to quit his job. The difference in the quit intention response to health hazards and safety hazards seems to be largely one of degree. Health hazards tend to produce stronger quit intentions than do safety hazards. The reason for this variance in worker response to the risks can be traced in part to the nature of worker information and its acquisition—matters that will be considered in the following section.

16.3 THE DETERMINANTS OF HEALTH AND SAFETY HAZARD ASSESSMENTS

The disparity in worker quit response to health and safety hazards is suggestive of an underlying dissimilarity in the nature of worker information and learning about the two types of hazards. Table 16.3 presents the logistic parameter estimates for the determinants of HDANGER and SDANGER perceptions. The empirical results are quite different for the two kinds of hazards and accord with one's expectations about the formation of worker judgments.

The BLS industry injury rate variable INJRATE has a negligible negative influence on HDANGER perceptions and the expected strong positive effect on SDANGER perceptions. To the extent that the INJRATE variable reflects workers' prior information about a job's riskiness, this result supports the hypothesis that prior information about health hazards is less accurate than that about safety hazards. The plausibility of this interpretation is enhanced by the earlier finding that health risks are especially likely to cause workers to quit their jobs. It should be noted, however, that the empirical results may overstate the actual inadequacy of prior information about health hazards since the INJRATE variable primarily reflects safety risks. As a result, the coefficient of this variable may be an inaccurate measure of prior health hazard beliefs.

Workers appear to learn about both health and safety risks from observation of job characteristics, although the role of these characteristics differs for the two classes of hazard. Physical effort (PHYSC) and physical conditions (PHCOND) serve mainly as HDANGER determinants, while the impacts of the no-mistakes (MISTK) and no-decisions (NODEC) variables are greatest in the SDANGER regression. Of particular pertinence to the models of adaptive behavior is the HDANGER equation, in which the injury experience variable (EXPINJURY2) has a statistically insignificant coefficient that is only a third of its size in the SDANGER regression. Workers appear to base their HDANGER assessments almost exclusively on observation of job characteristics, whereas the industry safety record, job characteristics, and injury experiences all contribute to SDANGER perceptions.

Table 16.3. Logistic Parameter Estimates of the Determinants of HDANGER and SDANGER Perceptions

Independent variables	Coefficients and standard errors	
	HDANGER	SDANGER
AGE	−.0083	−.028
	(.0094)	(.009)
FEMALE	−.088	−.579
	(.340)	(.334)
BLACK	−1.033	−.253
	(.467)	(.353)
EDUC	−.083	−.024
	(.034)	(.031)
HEALTH	−.0012	+.029
	(.121)	(.120)
SIZE	$+.41E-3$	$-.10E-3$
	$(.14E-3)$	$(.13E-3)$
UNION	−.730	+.486
	(.276)	(.244)
INJRATE	$-.92E-3$	+.033
	(.013)	(.012)
TENURE	−.0040	+.012
	(.015)	(.014)
PHYSC	+.524	+.116
	(.252)	(.231)
IRREG	+.826	+.731
	(.513)	(.491)
PHCOND	−.859	−.332
	(.256)	(.223)
MISTK	+.130	+.041
	(.111)	(.010)
NODEC	−.046	−.237
	(.109)	(.101)
OVERT	+.052	+.020
	(.083)	(.076)
EXPINJURY2	+.059	+.174
	(.103)	(.094)
Other variables	LIST1	LIST1
Log likelihood	−234.08	−269.18

The difference in the unions' impact on the two types of hazards also is rather stark. Health hazards are much lower in unionized contexts—a result consistent with the collective-goods aspects of many health risks, such as noise and radiation. The reduction of health risks also may reflect the general commitment of unions to a maintaining a stable work force by reducing the causes of worker quitting. No such impact can be observed for safety hazards, which are strikingly greater in unionized contexts. The interpretation of the UNION coefficient in each of the equations should be made with some caution, however, since the regression results do not distinguish between union impacts on hazards and the motivations for unionization of an enterprise.

The findings in Table 16.3 illuminate further the role of the personal characteristic variables. Older workers and females are much less likely to face safety hazards, while blacks and better-educated workers work where health hazards are lower. In view of the nonexcludability feature of health risks, these findings suggest that within enterprises women and older workers tend to have safer jobs. In contrast, better educated workers and blacks appear to work at different kinds of enterprises that typically provide healthier work environments.

A similar interpretation of the enterprise SIZE variable, which is positive and significant only in the HDANGER equation, accords with the prediction of the probabilistic labor-supply model of enterprise decisions. Diminished productivity losses of injured workers to larger firms will lead these enterprises to select higher risk levels, as reflected in the HDANGER results. The SDANGER variable, which is more indicative of the risks posed by a specific job than of the enterprise's safety policy, reflects no such influence. However, merit rating for workmen's compensation increases with firm size. Since this insurance pertains primarily to safety hazards, it may offset the impact of the stochastic economies of scale. The absence of a net scale effect is consistent with Oi's (1974) detailed analysis of the firm size effect for BLS injury rate data.

16.4 Compensation for Health and Safety Risks

Analysis of compensation for health and safety hazards does not enable one to make the sharp distinctions that the quit intention and danger perception analyses produced. Table 16.4 presents the EARNG and LOGEARNG results, which are somewhat mixed. Correspondingly higher levels of compensation for SDANGER are found in the EARNG equation, but not in the LOGEARNG equation. Overall, there is no statistical evidence that the levels of compensation for these two types of hazards are different.

The interaction of the unionization variable with these danger vari-

Table 16.4.   Selected Coefficients from Supplementary EARNG
and LOGEARNG Regressions

Independent variables	Coefficients and standard errors			
	EARNG	EARNG	LOG-EARNG	LOG-EARNG
HDANGER	+287.64 (226.17)	+71.14 (298.34)	+.050 (.036)	+.045 (.047)
SDANGER	+391.25 (208.12)	+117.42 (303.42)	+.047 (.033)	+.029 (.048)
UNION × HDANGER	— —	+485.28 (451.70)	— —	+.010 (.071)
UNION × SDANGER	— —	+524.76 (414.45)	— —	+.035 (.066)
R^2	.641	.643	.697	.698
SEE	1816.5	1816.3	.287	.287

Note: Other variables included in the regressions are given by LIST3.

ables is more clearcut, since the UNION×SDANGER coefficient is larger than the UNION×HDANGER coefficient, particularly in the LOGEARNG equation, where it is three and a half times as large. Although the limitations of the data prevent one from drawing conclusions that are supported as firmly as one would like, this preliminary investigation suggests that unions may alter the compensation levels more for safety risks than for health risks. Overall, unions appear to accept greater safety risks in return for higher levels of wage compensation. For health risks, the emphasis appears to be on reducing the hazard.

16.5 CONCLUSIONS

The economic ramifications of health and safety risks derive in large part from the nature of worker information and the potential for learning. Health risks, which tend to involve low probabilities and are not readily monitorable, appear to be associated with a considerable amount of initial worker uncertainty with regard to the nature of the risk. The formation of health hazard perceptions was found to depend almost exclusively on the observation of job characteristics, whereas the safety record of the industry, one's injury experiences, and observation of job characteristics all contribute to safety risk assessments. The more pronounced quit intention response to health hazards also reflected the rather limited information available for forming health risk assessments prior to work on the job.

17

IMPLICATIONS FOR MARKET PERFORMANCE

Economists since the time of Adam Smith have noted that individuals require higher wages to accept jobs they view as hazardous. The requirements for this result are minimal. The two principal conditions that must be met are that workers prefer being healthy to being dead or injured and that they prefer more consumption to less.

Analysis of actual employment patterns yields evidence consistent with this traditional view.[1] An average blue-collar worker receives job hazard premiums totaling about $400 annually in 1969 dollars. Although the absolute magnitude of this compensation is not especially large, one should not conclude that compensating wage differentials are unimportant. Coal miners, stuntmen, and professional athletes receive more readily visible hazard premiums since they face far greater risks. The representative group of workers that I studied incurred an annual death risk of only 1/10,000 and an annual risk of nonfatal injury of 1/100. The resulting compensating wage differentials implied that workers behaved as if they valued their lives at over $1 million and that they placed a value on nonfatal injuries on the order of $10,000. The plausibility of these results is enhanced by the fact that similar wage differential estimates were obtained using either objective measures of the risk or workers' subjective perceptions.

The apparent paradox noted by John Stuart Mill and others who have observed that the best jobs in society are the highest paid can be resolved if one takes wealth effects into account. On a conceptual

1. This chapter discusses only the main features of the findings. For a more detailed summary, see the conclusion in each chapter.

basis, the job risk a worker will select will necessarily decline with his wealth, a result that is borne out empirically. Since individual wealth and income are highly correlated, it is not at all surprising that a simple cross-sectional view should indicate that worker incomes are negatively related to the risks they incur.

The most distinctive aspect of the analysis is its treatment of the imperfections in worker information about job hazards. Critics of the efficacy of market allocations have correctly noted that individuals often do not have perfect information about the hazards they face. This informational difficulty is especially great for health hazards, such as those posed by potentially carcinogenic substances.

However, even if the worker's information is imperfect, he will require additional monetary compensation for a job that he subjectively perceives as being hazardous. The principal difference from the perfect information situation is that the mean initial risk is not a sufficient description of the attractiveness of the job. If the worker is incurring a sequence of health and safety risks, he will require less wage compensation for risks that are not known with precision. The generalizations of the two-armed bandit models used to analyze the job choice problem indicate that workers will exhibit a systematic preference for uncertain jobs, not only in adaptive situations in which they can switch jobs after unfavorable experiences, but also in nonadaptive situations, such as those involving sequential lotteries of life and death.

Previous analyses of individual choice under uncertainty have maintained that individuals may incur too great a risk if they systematically underestimate the hazards involved. Since over 52 percent of the blue-collar workers in the sample I examined viewed their jobs as hazardous in some respect, the common assumption that risks are typically underestimated should not be accepted without supporting evidence. Even if worker perceptions are unbiased, one cannot conclude that workers will choose the same job risk as in a world of perfect information. An important implication of the adaptive models is that workers will be willing to accept more hazardous jobs than they would if they were better informed. This statement about individuals' predilection for hazardous jobs is much stronger than in previous studies, since it does not hinge on any assumption of biased assessments.

In situations in which workers accept jobs with uncertain properties, there usually is the possibility of learning about the job through experience. For example, an individual can observe the speed of the assembly line, the noise level, accidents affecting others, and injuries to himself. These sources of information can be used to update his conditional judgments. If the worker's experiences are sufficiently unfavorable, he will quit. It should be emphasized that an experience need not raise the mean value of the risk in order to be unfavorable. Additional information that does not alter the assessed risk will decrease the job's attractiveness' because workers prefer jobs whose implications are dimly understood.

Enterprise actions are unlikely to eliminate learning-induced quits as an important labor market phenomenon. Because workers systematically prefer uncertain positions, it will generally not be possible or desirable to adopt a wage policy that will attract only individuals with precise initial judgments. Providing workers with job hazard information could potentially reduce turnover costs, but the added wage costs arising from the increased precision of workers' judgments combine with other deviant properties of information, such as its nonexcludability aspects, to discourage such activity.

As a consequence, learning-induced quits should be a matter of considerable empirical importance, as is borne out by the diverse evidence that job hazards induce workers to quit. Moreover, variables reflecting on-the-job acquisition of information, such as workers' injury experiences, are important determinants of the job hazard assessments that lead to these quit decisions.

Employment hazards influence economic outcomes not only by affecting wage rates, but also by influencing workers to quit if the wage level is insufficient to compensate for on-the-job experiences. Imperfections in worker information do not imply that economic mechanisms cease to function. Not only are there compensating wage differentials for perceived hazards, but since workers start with imperfect information and learn on the job, they may quit if the job proves to be too hazardous.

The adaptive models also have more general ramifications, since they provide the first formal theory of learning-induced quits. The framework is directly applicable to analysis of uncertain monetary rewards and other features of individual's lifetime patterns of employment. The early years of the worker's labor market experience and his initial period of employment at an enterprise can be profitably viewed as a period of experimentation in which worker turnover is a consequence of adaptive behavior.

Collective worker action through unions is of potential importance, particularly if unions serve as a source of countervailing market power. On an empirical basis, unions appear to sacrifice additional ex post job hazard compensation to obtain more ex ante wage compensation. Moreover, the mix of hazards is quite different in unionized industries, as health hazards are less prevalent and safety hazards more prevalent. Although I suggested possible motivations for these actions, further work needs to be done. The burgeoning interest of unions in workplace health and safety suggests that an understanding of the unions' role will be increasingly important to an analysis of the functioning of the market process.

Employment hazards also have a fundamental impact on enterprise decisions. By introducing a stochastic component into the enterprise's labor supply, a firm's production function that formerly exhibited constant returns to scale will now be characterized by increasing returns. Job hazards are positively related to the scale of the enterprise, as predicted by the conceptual analysis. Moreover, since job risks decrease the expected duration of employment through quit behavior and the disabling effects of injuries, enterprises reduce their training investments in hazardous contexts.

Although the systematic economic responses to job hazards are quite diverse, one cannot conclude that no policy intervention is warranted.[2] The imperfect nature of workers' information combines with their systematic preferences for jobs that are not fully understood to suggest that ill-informed individuals will be prone to accept more hazardous employment than they would have accepted if they had been better informed. Although subsequent learning and adaptive behavior are often important, the learning process itself may be quite costly, as in the case of disabling injuries. Moreover, if there are substantial impediments to job changing, such as enterprise-specific seniority rights and pension benefits, it may be very costly to reverse earlier decisions.

These and other shortcomings of market outcomes can potentially be alleviated by some form of governmental intervention. Nevertheless, the existence of these limitations does not imply that any form of regulation, however inefficient, is necessarily warranted. Interference with market allocations will typically undermine many of the desirable aspects of market outcomes. Moreover, policy interventions may suffer from the same limitations that hinder worker decisions. For example, recent efforts to regulate workplace conditions through health and safety standards have systematically neglected the same types of health hazards that pose special difficulties for worker behavior.[3]

Since workers appear to utilize job risk information in a systematic manner in their employment decisions, it might be desirable for the

2. Even if the market functions reasonably effectively, there may be important externalities. Society may have an altruistic concern with workers' health status. There also may be important pecuniary externalities, since job risks affect the cost of workmen's compensation benefits, social security benefits to the survivors of a worker who suffers a fatal injury, and other social insurance costs.

3. Indeed, whereas 40 percent of the hazards cited by workers are health risks, only 1 percent of the standard violations cited by the Occupational Safety and Health Administration are of this type.

government to acquire and disseminate information that would enable individuals to make more informed decisions. This governmental function has been noted in other analyses of information, such as that of Arrow (1971), and would seem to be particularly appropriate to job hazard data because of the substantial barriers to private information provision.

The economic frameworks developed in this volume also are applicable to aspects of employment decisions other than health and safety risks. With minor modifications, the analysis can be applied to worker uncertainty about wages and income. Outside the labor market, economic choice situations that raise related analytic issues are quite diverse. The formation and dissolution of marriages, sequential medical care decisions, choices involving environmental risks, and repeated consumer purchases of commodities with uncertain quality attributes are among the situations sharing the types of analytic features encountered here.

Individuals and enterprises seldom have perfect information about the risks associated with their actions. The analysis of employment hazards suggests that the existence of this imperfection does not simply diminish the effectiveness of the usual market mechanisms. Rather, these traditional modes of response are augmented by other forms of economic behavior by participants on both sides of the market.

Appendix A

Optimal Time Allocations to Risky Activities

A convenient analytic construct for determining the optimal riskiness of a worker's job is a time allocation model in which the individual divides his time between work and nonwork activities.[1] Unlike the model presented in Section 2.2, the hours one can choose to devote to each activity are assumed to be flexible, and the wage per unit of time on a job does not vary with the amount of time spent at it.

The notation is the same as in Section 2.2, except that we now let

w_i = the wage per unit of time spent in activity i, where $i = 1, \ldots, n$
T = total time available
t_i = the amount of time spent in activity i
λ_1 = the shadow price for the goods constraint
λ_2 = the shadow price for the time constraint

The wage for nonwork activities is zero. Variables t_i and x appear as subscripts to other variables to indicate partial derivatives.

The individual's objective is to pick the activity mix that maximizes his welfare. The Lagrangian L for the individual's maximization problem is given by

$$L = [1 - p(t_1, \ldots, t_n)]u^1(x, t_1, \ldots, t_n)$$
$$+ p(t_1, \ldots, t_n)u^2(x, t_1, \ldots, t_n) + \lambda_1(x - A - \sum_{i=1}^{n} w_i t_i)$$
$$+ \lambda_2(T - \sum_{i=1}^{n} t_i).$$

Optimizing with respect to x and the t_i's produces the $n + 1$ first-order conditions (in addition to the two constraint equations):

(1) $$L_x = 0 = (1 - p)u_x^1 + pu_x^2 + \lambda_1$$

---

1. The short-run time-allocation literature dealing with deterministic situations began with the contribution by Becker (1965).

and

(2) $\qquad L_{t_i} = 0 = -p_{t_i}u^1 + (1-p)u^1_{t_i} + p_{t_i}u^2 + pu^2_{t_i} - \lambda_1 w_i - \lambda_2$

for $i = 1, \ldots, n$.

Substituting the value of λ_1 from equation (1) into equation (2) and solving for w_i produces the condition

(3) $\qquad w_i = \left[\dfrac{\lambda_2 + p_{t_i}(u^1 - u^2) - (1-p)u^1_{t_i} - pu^2_{t_i}}{(1-p)u^1_x + pu^2_x} \right].$

This strict equality holds for all interior solutions in which $0 < t_i < T$. If the worker devotes no time to an activity, then the wage for that activity must be less than or equal to the right-hand side of equation (2). In the unlikely case in which all of one's time is spent in a single activity, the wage for that activity must be greater than or equal to the right-hand side of equation (3).

The interpretation of equation (3) can be facilitated by comparing it to its deterministic analogue which is given by

(4) $\qquad\qquad\qquad w_i = (\lambda - u_{t_i})/u_x,$

thus equating the wage in activity i to the difference in the shadow price of time and the marginal of time in activity i, divided by the marginal utility of consumption. In the job risk case the marginal utility of time is replaced by the expected marginal utility of time, and the marginal utility of consumption is replaced by its expected marginal utility. The distinctive feature of equation (3) is the second term in the numerator, which is the marginal increase in the probability of the undesirable state multiplied by the utility loss experienced if state 2 occurs.

Though the time allocation approach provides some insight into the role of employment hazards, the essential features of the model are not particularly realistic. In particular, the assumption that work activities are divisible at a constant wage per unit of time contrasts starkly with the quite limited control that workers exert over the hours of employment. The principal insight provided by the model is that the injury risk posed by a marginal time allocation to a job may depend on the worker's other activities. The worker allocating his time among different pursuits should take any important interactive effects into account.

APPENDIX B

OPTIMAL JOB RISKS IN A DYNAMIC CONTEXT

Section 2.3 presented numerical examples to illustrate the effect on optimal job risks of including the dynamic implications of worker actions. This appendix analyzes how the optimality conditions for the dynamic case differ from those in static models, such as that presented in Section 2.2. The variables are the same as for equations (9)–(11) in Section 2.3.

Using this notation, the myopic version of the job choice problem is to choose the value of p that will maximize

$$(1) \qquad u^1 = (1 - p)v^1(p) + pv^2.$$

The first-order condition for a maximum is that

$$(2) \qquad v_p^1 = (v^1 - v^2)/(1 - p) > 0.$$

A worker demands a positive compensating wage differential for an increased probability of an adverse outcome. The marginal increase in the value of v^1 with the value of p equals the difference in the rewards for the two states divided by the probability of a favorable outcome. The second-order condition permits v_{pp}^1 to be either negative or positive, but not too large:

$$(3) \qquad v_{pp}^1 < 2v_p^1/(1 - p).$$

The additional notation needed for the multiperiod case is that the discount factor b will equal $1/(1 + r)$, where r is the interest rate. Recall that for the infinite horizon model being considered, worker choice enters the problem only with respect to the optimal job risk when he is in state 1—a strategy that is time-invariant. To compute the discounted expected value of alternative job risk transition matrices, I will utilize Howard's (1960) value-determination operation, which implies that the value of the worker's decision problem is given by

(4) $$\mathbf{u} = [I - bP]^{-1}PV.$$

Since we are assuming that u^1 changes continuously with respect to p, the optimizing value can be determined by straightforward differentiation rather than by standard iteration techniques. In more detailed form, equation (4) can be rewritten as

(5) $$\mathbf{u} = \frac{1}{(1 - b)(1 + bp - bq)} \begin{bmatrix} 1 - bq & bp \\ b - bq & 1 - b + bp \end{bmatrix} \begin{bmatrix} (1 - p)v^1 + pv^2 \\ (1 - q)v^1 + qv^2 \end{bmatrix}.$$

Since all workers start in state 1, the only value of interest is

(6) $$u^1 = [(1 - b)(1 + bp - bq)]^{-1}[v^1(1 - p + bq - bq) + v^2 p].$$

Differentiating with respect to p produces the first-order condition for an optimum that

(7) $$0 = -[(1 - b)(1 + bp - bq)]^{-2}(b - b^2)[v^1(1 - p + bp - bq) + v^2 p]$$
$$+ [(1 - b)(1 - bp - bq)]^{-1}$$
$$[v^1(-1 + b) + v^2 + v_p^1(1 - p + bp - bq)].$$

Solving for v_p^1 produces the condition that

(8) $$v_p^1 = \frac{(v^1 - v^2)(1 - b - bq + b^2 q)}{\begin{array}{l} 1 - b + p(-1 + 3b - 2b^2) + q(-2b + 2b^2) \\ \quad + pq(b - 3b^2 + 2b^3) + p^2(-b + 2b^2 - b^3) + q^2(-b^3 + b^2) \end{array}}$$

This expression takes on a more convenient form after substituting $1/(1 + r)$ for b and simplifying, yielding

(9) $$v_p^1 = \frac{(v^1 - v^2)(1 + r - q)(1 + r)}{(1 + r)^2 - 2q(1 + r) + q^2 + p(1 - q + rq - r^2) - p^2 r}.$$

Equation (9) states the necessary condition for the selection of the optimally risky job. The worker increases the job risk he incurs until the marginal increase in the reward of state 1 just offsets the loss in lifetime welfare imposed by the increased job hazard, where all terms are appropriately adjusted both with regard to discounting and the problem's stochastic structure. For very large r, equation (9) reduces to the optimality condition for the myopic problem given by equation (2).

Casual inspection of equation (9) is not particularly helpful in allowing one to determine whether a worker necessarily will be less risky in the dynamic choice problem than he would in a myopic context involving the same function $v^1(p)$. The reason for this difficulty is that in general the consideration of the dynamic implications of the job hazard may either increase or decrease the hazard one incurs, depending on the parameters of the problem. Somewhat analogously, increasing the value of r may either increase or decrease the job hazard one chooses. Section 2.3 provided numerical illustrations of the difference in results between myopic and dynamic optimizations.

Before leaving the general version of the model, consider the role of the complicated set of adjustment factors on the right-hand side of equation (9). If we let q equal 1, state 2 becomes an absorbing state, and equation (9) reduces to

(10)
$$v_p^1 = \frac{(v^1 - v^2)(1 + r)}{r + p(1 - r) - p^2}.$$

Comparison with equation (9) reveals that the various terms involving q served to increase the desirability of job hazards, since the lower q's value was, the greater would be the likelihood that the worker would return to the healthy state after an unfavorable job transition. Alternatively, if q equaled zero, the return to state 1 would be immediate and equation (9) would take the form

$$v_p^1 = \frac{(v^1 - v^2)(1 + r)^2}{(1 + r)^2 + p(1 - r^2) - p^2 r}.$$

In relation to this result, the effect of nonzero values of q is to make transitions from state 2 probabilistic, thus leading to a series of adjustment terms capturing the uncertain duration of one's injury.

APPENDIX C

SENSITIVITY OF RESULTS TO PROBABILITY ASSESSMENTS

Prior distributions given by some Beta functions $B(d, e)$ can take on a wide variety of shapes, with different labor market consequences. Intuitively, an increase in the value of e for any particular value of d/e can be thought of as increasing the sharpness of the prior. As the value of e increases, one's probability assessments become less sensitive to additional information. The examples in this section will illustrate the sensitivity of the results of the ten-period model introduced in Section 4.2 to different prior assessments.

The following examples differ from the basic paradigm only in that $p(m, n)$ and w are varied. Suppose e equals 2. Data in the first two columns of Table C.1 indicate that the minimum wage required to get the worker to accept job I in the first period decreases as job I's probability of success increases—that is, as the value of $p(0, 0)$ or d/e increases. For any value of d/e less than q, which is 0.8, increasing the value of e sharpens the prior, thus decreasing the likelihood that job I will turn out to be more favorable than job II. As the last two

Table C.1. Minimum Value of w Required as a Function of (d, e)

$e = 2$		$d/e = 0.5$	
d	w	e	w
0.1	9.57	0.5	1.16
0.3	3.56	1.0	1.23
0.5	2.32	2.0	1.33
1.0	1.33	4.0	1.42
1.5	0.98	10.0	1.51
2.0	0.81	20.0	1.55

Table C.2.   Values of
the Beta Function for
Which Job I Is Selected
in the First Period

d/e	Maximum value of e
0.55	0.01
0.6	0.24
0.7	1.3
0.79	24
0.8	—

columns of Table C.1 indicate, the wage required to lead a worker to begin work on an uncertain job increases with the sharpness of his prior assessment of the job's lower probability of success.

It should be emphasized that even if w equals 1, the worker should not necessarily follow a myopic decision rule, that is, choose whichever job corresponds to the larger of $p(m, n)$ or q. Provided one's prior assessments are not too sharp, it will often be optimal to experiment with the uncertain job even though it offers a lower probability of success. Some ranges of values for which it is desirable in the initial period to obtain information by experience with job I are provided in Table C.2. The higher the initial probability of success on job I, the sharper the prior can be for job I to be selected. For example, if $p(0, 0)$ equals 0.79, job I is preferred for all values of e not exceeding 24.

If the probability of success on the uncertain job is greater than or equal to the certain probability q on job II, it will always be optimal to follow the myopic policy and select job I. The reason is that in such circumstances job I provides an expected immediate reward at least as great as that of job II, and it also provides increased information about job I's properties.[1] Since the stochastic properties of job II are known, experience on that job does not provide new information.[2]

1. If there is one period remaining, job I and job II are equally desirable when $p(m, n)$ equals q.

2. Within the context of the present discussion of the role of probability assessments, it is interesting to speculate on the relation of personal characteristics to the speed of the worker's adaptive response. Unfortunately, few unambiguous theoretical conclusions can be drawn. For example, increased education may facilitate adaptive behavior by enabling workers to identify pertinent work characteristics more quickly, or it may inhibit adaptation by sharpening workers' prior assessments.

APPENDIX D

GENERAL FORMULATION OF ADAPTIVE BEHAVIOR

The purpose of this appendix is twofold. First, I will analyze the principal results of Chapter 4 for the state-dependent utility function situation, thus strengthening the relationship of the adaptive models to the framework employed in earlier chapters. Second, I will let the worker's probabilistic perceptions of the hazards posed by an uncertain job be a function of the wage that is paid, since a worker may infer that a job is hazardous or otherwise unpleasant if he observes that the wage is high. It will be shown that this additional influence strengthens the nature of the results presented earlier in Chapter 4.

Consider the following two-period choice situation. In each period, the worker's job may leave him in good health (state 1) or ill health (state 2), where the ill-health state may represent death or permanent disability. The worker's state-dependent utility functions u^1 and u^2 have the properties described in Chapter 2, as the worker prefers being healthy and

$$u^1_x > 0, \; u^2_x > 0, \; u^1_{xx} \leq 0, \text{ and } u^2_{xx} \leq 0,$$

where x is the level of his consumption. For simplicity, initial worker assets and workmen's compensation benefits will be subsumed into the functional forms of the utility functions. Moreover, while I will make the wage rate paid the argument of the utility function in each state, the formulation of u^2 is sufficiently general to include payment of no compensation or positive ex post compensation levels that may be dependent on w though not necessarily equal to w. I also assume that resources and utility functions are separable across periods and that expected utility in period 2 is discounted, using a discount factor b.

Job II offers a wage rate w_0 and a probability that state 1 will occur of q, which is known with precision. The uncertain job I offers a wage rate w and an initial probability $p(0, 0)$ of a successful outcome and a probability $p(m, n)$ of a success after observing m successful outcomes and n unsuccessful outcomes

284

on that job. With no loss of generality, one can set the expected utility of working on job II for a single period at zero, that is,

$$0 = qu^1(w_0) + (1 - q)u^2(w_0).$$

The discounted expected value of job II in the initial period for the standard job injury model is given by

$$
\begin{aligned}
V = p(0, 0)u^1(w) &+ [1 - p(0, 0)]u^2(w) + bp(0, 0)[p(1, 0)u^1(w) \\
&+ (1 - p(1, 0))u^2(w)] + b(1 - p(0, 0))\max[p(0, 1)u^1(w) \\
&+ (1 - p(0, 1))u^2(w), qu^1(w_0) + (1 - q)u^2(w_0)],
\end{aligned}
$$

which was calculated using the fundamental result that the worker will not leave job I after a success.

The principal matter of concern is the determination of the value of the reservation wage level. This wage satisfies the property that the worker will accept the job initially but will necessarily quit after an unfavorable outcome, leading to an expected payoff of zero in period 2. The expression for V consequently becomes

(9) $$\quad V = p(0, 0)u^1(w) + (1 - p(0, 0))u^2(w) + bp(0, 0)[p(1, 0)u^1(w) \\ + (1 - p(1, 0))u^2(w)].$$

If one were considering lotteries on life and death, V would take on this form for all workers, not simply marginal workers. The principal modification required for the irreversible outcome case is that the value of job II would be some constant other than zero—a change that would not alter any of the subsequent results.

Consider prior probability assessments belonging to the Beta family of priors, where p is the mean value of $p(0, 0)$ and γ is a measure of its tightness where higher γ's are associated with sharper priors. After m successes and n failures, the posterior $p(m, n)$ on job I is given by

$$p(m, n) = (\gamma p + m)/(\gamma + m + n).$$

The additional influence considered here is that the mean value of the prior p may be a function of the wage offer w—that is, $p(w)$ where $dp/dw \leq 0$—so that the worker may infer that the job is more hazardous if a higher wage is paid. As a consequence, the posterior $p(m, n)$ may be reduced by a higher wage so that $\partial p(m, n)/\partial w$ is negative or zero.

The first matter of interest is the effect of more precise initial judgments on the reservation wage for the uncertain job. Upon implicit differentiation of equation (9), one obtains the result that

$$\partial w/\partial \gamma = -V\gamma/V_w,$$

where

$$V_\gamma = bp(0, 0)[u^1 - u^2][\partial p(1, 0)]/\partial \gamma < 0,$$

and

$$
\begin{aligned}
V_w = u_x^1 p(0, 0)[1 + bp(1, 0)] &+ u_x^2[1 - p(0, 0) + bp(0, 0)(1 - p(1, 0))] \\
&+ [\partial p(0, 0)/\partial w]\{u^1 - u^2 + b[p(1, 0)u^1 + (1 - p(1, 0))u^2]\} \\
&+ [\partial p(1, 0)/\partial w]\{bp(0, 0)[u^1 - u^2]\},
\end{aligned}
$$

where the first two terms are positive and the latter two terms involving $\partial p(0, 0)/\partial w$ and $\partial p(1, 0)/\partial w$ are negative, since u^1 exceeds u^2 and these probability derivatives are negative.

It can be shown using an argument parallel to that in Chapter 2 for the probability of an unfavorable outcome that

$$\partial w/\partial p = -V_p/V_w < 0$$

for the worker to choose to work at a job at any point on the available wage schedule. This compensating wage differential result requires that V_w be necessarily positive, as is $\partial w/\partial \gamma$.

The negative terms in V_w involving $\partial p(0, 0)/\partial w$ and $\partial p(1, 0)/\partial w$ consequently reduce the magnitude of V_w but do not alter its sign, thus increasing the magnitude of $\partial w/\partial \gamma$. Sharper priors lead to higher reservation wage rates, and the magnitude of this effect is enhanced if workers lower the assessed probability of a successful outcome as the wage is increased.

Other previous results are likewise reinforced by the feedback of wage rates on probabilistic perceptions. For example,

$$\frac{\partial w}{\partial b} = \frac{-V_b}{V_w} = \frac{-p(0, 0)[p(1, 0)u^1 + (1 - p(1, 0))u^2]}{V_w} < 0.$$

Since the benefits of adaptive behavior are necessarily deferred, an increase in the discount factor b raises the reservation wage rate, where the magnitude of this effect becomes more negative as V_w is reduced, that is, as the influence of w on the mean value of p is increased.

APPENDIX E

ANXIETY AND THE OPTIMAL JOB RISK

The impact of anxiety on the optimal job risk will be determined using a variant of the basic model from Section 5.2A. The Lagrangian for the worker's optimization problem is given by

$$L = (1 - p)u^1(a, x) + pu^2(a, x) + \lambda_1[x - A - w(p)] + \lambda_2[a - kf(p)].$$

This equation differs from the model in Section 5.2A only in that $f(p)$ has been replaced by $kf(p)$, where k is a constant. The parameter k will be varied to analyze the impact of different levels of anxiety on the optimal value of p.

The first-order conditions for a maximum are given by

(1) $$\partial L/\partial x = 0 = (1 - p)u_x^1 + pu_x^2 + \lambda_1,$$

(2) $$\partial L/\partial p = 0 = -u^1 + u^2 - \lambda_1 w_p - \lambda_2 kf_p,$$

(3) $$\partial L/\partial a = 0 = (1 - p)u_a^1 + pu_a^2 + \lambda_2,$$

(4) $$\partial L/\partial \lambda_1 = 0 = x - A - w(p),$$

and

(5) $$\partial L/\partial \lambda_2 = 0 = a - kf(p).$$

After appropriate substitutions, these conditions reduce to

(6) $$0 = -u^1 + (1 - p)u_a^1 kf_p + (1 - p)u_x^1 w_p + u^2 + pu_a^2 kf_p + pu_x^2 w_p.$$

Solving equation (6) for w_p yields equation (1) in Section 5.2A for the special case in which k equals 1.

One can obtain the second-order condition for a relative maximum by differentiating equation (6) with respect to p, taking into account the functional dependencies of a and x on $w(p)$ and $f(p)$, respectively. After some simplifica-

287

tion, this procedure leads to the requirement that

(7) $(w_p)^2[(1 - p)u^1_{xx} + pu^2_{xx}] + 2w_p[-u^1_x + u^2_x] + w_{pp}[(1 - p)u^1_x + pu^2_x]$
$\quad + 2kf_p\{(-u^1_a + u^2_a) + w_p[(1 - p)u^1_{ax} + pu^2_{ax}]\} + (kf_p)^2[(1 - p)u^1_{aa}$
$\quad\quad\quad\quad\quad + pu^2_{aa}] + kf_{pp}[(1 - p)u^1_a + pu^2_a] \equiv D < 0.$

The principal matter of concern is how the optimal job risk p is affected by an increase in the value of k, the factor that multiplies the anxiety function. To investigate this relationship, one can totally differentiate equation (6), if one also notes the fact that x equals $A + w(p)$ and a equals $kf(p)$. Since the primary matter of interest is the sign of $\partial p/\partial k$, the dA terms will be set at zero throughout. Total differentiation of equation (6) yields

(8) $0 = -u^1_a kf_p dp - u^1_a f_p dp - u^1_x w_p dp - u^1_a kf_p dp + (1 - p)u^1_{aa}(kf_p)^2 dp$
$\quad + (1 - p)u^1_{aa} k(f_p)^2 dk + (1 - p)u^1_{ax}w_p kf_p dp + (1 - p)u^1_a f_p dk$
$\quad + (1 - p)u^1_a kf_{pp} dp - u^1_x w_p dp + (1 - p)u^1_{ax} kf_p w_p dp$
$\quad + (1 - p)u^1_{ax} f_p w_p dk + (1 - p)u^1_{xx}(w_p)^2 dp + (1 - p)u^1_x w_{pp} dp$
$\quad + u^2_a kf_p dp + u^2_a f_p dk + u^2_x w_p dp + u^2_a kf_p dp + pu^2_{aa}(kf_p)^2 dp$
$\quad + pu^2_{aa} k(f_p)^2 dk + pu^2_{ax}w_p kf_p dp + pu^2_a f_p dk + pu^2_a kf_{pp} dp + u^2_x w_p dp$
$\quad + pu^2_{ax} kf_p w_p dp + pu^2_{ax} f_p w_p dk + pu^2_{xx}(w_p)^2 dp + pu^2_x w_{pp} dp.$

Collecting terms, noting that the coefficients of dp equal D, which is defined in equation (7), leads to

$0 = dp[D] + dk\{f_p w_p[(1 - p)u^1_{ax} + pu^2_{ax} + k(f_p)^2[(1 - p)u^1_{aa} + pu^2_{aa}]$
$\quad\quad\quad\quad\quad + f_p[(1 + p)u^2_a - pu^1_a]\}.$

Solving for $\partial p/\partial k$, one obtains

(9) $\partial p/\partial k = -(1/D)\{f_p w_p[(1 - p)u^1_{ax} + pu^2_{ax}] + k(f_p)^2[(1 - p)u^1_{aa} + pu^2_{aa}]$
$\quad\quad\quad\quad\quad + f_p[(1 + p)u^2_a - pu^1_a]\}.$

If equation (7) is satisfied, D will be negative, implying that the sign of $\partial p/\partial k$ is the same as that of the term in parenthesis on the right side of equation (9). By assumption, the values of f_p, w_p, and k are positive, while u^1_a and u^2_a are negative. To assure that each of the component terms in the bracketed expression is nonpositive, one must impose three additional restrictions.

First, the two signs of the cross-partial terms u^1_{ax} and u^2_{ax} are assumed to be negative or zero. Equivalently, the partial derivative with respect to anxiety of the marginal utility of consumption is not positive. This assumption is quite plausible and was satisfied by the utility function in Section 5.2B.

The second restriction pertains to the second partials of the utility function with respect to a. If these are negative or equal to zero, the second term in the brackets will not be positive. Such a restriction also is needed to assure that the second-to-last term in the second-order condition (equation [7]) is negative, as is desired. In the usual instance, however, one would expect the marginal utility losses due to anxiety to be diminishing, so that u^1_{aa} and u^2_{aa} would be positive. For very large levels of these terms, $\partial p/\partial k$ may be positive, and the second-order condition for a maximum may be violated. This difficulty derives from the fact that if the utility loss due to anxiety diminishes at a sufficiently rapid rate, it may even be desirable to increase the level of anxiety, since doing so will result in a lower welfare loss than at lower levels of a. Aberrational patterns such as this do not appear sufficiently realistic to warrant significant attention.

The final restriction is that the negative term u_a^1 be greater than or equal to $[(1 + p)/p]u_a^2$. Thus, the marginal anxiety loss can exceed that in the injured state, but not by too great an amount.

Finally, it should be noted that some of the three terms comprising the expression in equation (9) can take on positive signs, provided that their magnitudes are not so large that they exceed the magnitude of the negative terms. Although the restrictions required to guarantee that $\partial p/\partial k$ is negative are more complicated than one would like, they do not appear implausible. The function relating the optimal value of p to the parameter k consequently should be negatively sloped. If the situation in which k equals zero represents the no-anxiety situation, and if a positive value of k, such as k equal to 1, represents the anxiety case, the introduction of anxiety into the worker's choice problem will reduce the optimal job risk.

APPENDIX F

EMPIRICAL ANALYSIS

F.1 SIMULTANEOUS EQUATION ESTIMATES

Throughout the empirical analysis, the equations in the system are treated as recursive, permitting the use of single-equation estimation techniques. This general approach was outlined in Chapter 12. The economic relationships being considered, however, clearly may involve a great deal of simultaneity. Fringe benefits and earnings can be viewed as components of a jointly determined pay package. The provision of fringe benefits may alter the job hazard a worker is willing to incur, while the risks posed by a worker's job may alter the worker's demand for and the employer's supply of fringe benefits. The simultaneity of job hazards and earnings can be described similarly.

To test for the empirical importance of this simultaneity, the FRINGE, EARNG, and DANGER equations for the Michigan Survey of Working Conditions data were each estimated using two-stage least squares (TSLS), a method that is appropriate for this overidentified system. The results are reported in Table F.1, where the starred values of variables represent estimated values of these endogenous variables.

The results are not particularly strong. Only one coefficient—that of FRINGE* in the DANGER equation—is larger than its standard error. Perhaps the most fundamental problem is the low explanatory power of the regressions used to estimate FRINGE* and DANGER* (both R^2's just exceed 0.2). This low explanatory power is due in large part to the use of individual data rather than aggregative statistics and the absence of reliable instruments to estimate FRINGE* and DANGER*. The net effect is that the estimated values used in the TSLS procedure may represent primarily random noise rather than systematic

Table F.1. TSLS Estimates of FRINGE, EARNG, and DANGER Equations

Dependent variable	Independent variable coefficients and standard errors			
	FRINGE*	EARNG*	DANGER*	R^2
FRINGE	—	$-.23E - 4$	$-.074$	.215
	—	$(1.02E - 4)$	(.129)	
EARNG	$-1,393.1$	—	$+212.94$	.638
	(6,365.9)	—	(927.64)	
DANGER	$+1.45$	$+.78E - 5$	—	.214
	(.76)	$(5.98E - 4)$	—	

Note: The starred variables indicate estimated values computed by regressing the original variable on all of the predetermined variables in the complete model. The variables used for each particular equation in the second stage of the procedure are the same as in the estimates in earlier chapters. In brief, all pertinent job characteristics and personal characteristics have been included. The danger equation has been estimated using OLS.

components related to the underlying variable of interest. It is for these reasons that the simpler recursive format has been followed.[1]

F.2 THE DETERMINANTS OF JOB CHARACTERISTICS

This section is devoted to analysis of the impact of exogenous variables in determining the characteristics of a worker's job. All job characteristics utilized in Chapters 13 through 16, other than DANGER, will be considered. The data source is the blue-collar worker subsample of the Michigan Survey of Working Conditions.

Table F.2 summarizes the pertinent OLS regression results. A personal characteristic of particular interest is BLACK. The only statistically significant effects are that black workers are more likely to be supervisors (SUPER) and less likely to be working in high injury-rate industries (INJRATE). Although the inability to identify any racial discrimination in terms of job attributes may be due in part to the small size of the sample (only 61 of the 496 individuals sampled were black), the results are consistent with the workers' own assessments of job discrimination and the impact of BLACK on DANGER—effects that have been discussed in Chapter 14. Moreover, a negative BLACK coefficient in the INJRATE equation is also borne out in National Longitudinal Survey data regressions (sample size 1,932) reported in Chapter 14.

The effect of unionization on job characteristics also is largely statistically

1. Alternatively, one might estimate the equations in the complete model using direct least squares. However, the results are not superior ro the recursive equations. For example, the positive FRINGE coefficient in the EARNG equation is more a reflection of the positive income elasticity of demand for fringes than any pay package trade-off. The inclusion of FRINGE in the DANGER equation has a negligible impact, since the coefficient is both small and exceeded by its standard error.

Table F.2. Regression Analysis of Job Characteristic Determinants, Blue-Collar Workers

Dependent variable	Independent variables						R², F
	AGE	FEMALE	BLACK	EDUC	UNION	TENURE	
INJRATE	-.027	-5.51	-2.80	-.010	+3.14	-.055	.201
	(.038)	(1.05)	(1.22)	(.146)	(.87)	(.049)	7.57
FAST	-.0045	+.222	-.0027	-.98E-3	+.012	+.0040	.182
	(.0022)	(.067)	(.068)	(8.15E-3)	(.050)	(.0028)	2.47
NODEC	-.93E-3	+.509	+.107	-.043	+.163	-.017	.200
	(4.96E-3)	(1.54)	(.156)	(.019)	(.116)	(.0064)	2.78
SECURITY	+.0018	-.106	-.059	-.0062	+.061	+.73E-7	.144
	(.0023)	(.071)	(.072)	(.0086)	(.053)	(2.93E-3)	1.86
PHYSC	-.0029	+.021	-.030	-.0019	+.046	+.44E-3	.166
	(.0022)	(.068)	(.069)	(.0083)	(.051)	(2.81E-3)	2.20
PHCOND	+.0039	-.094	+.072	-.0050	-.048	-.0010	.120
	(.0023)	(.071)	(.072)	(.0087)	(.054)	(.0029)	1.51
TRAIN	-.0033	-.020	+.089	+.014	+.048	+.0034	.271
	(.0021)	(.064)	(.065)	(.0077)	(.048)	(.0026)	4.12
CREAT	+.0022	-.482	-.094	+.026	-.113	+.0016	.160
	(.0055)	(.170)	(.173)	(.021)	(.128)	(.0070)	2.11
IRREG	-.46E-3	-.024	-.037	+.0040	-.0018	-.23E-3	.095
	(.93E-3)	(.029)	(.029)	(.0035)	(.022)	(1.19E-3)	1.16
OVERT	-.023	-.452	-.194	+.0021	+.301	+.017	.201
	(.0061)	(.189)	(.192)	(.023)	(.142)	(.0078)	2.79
SUPER	+.0030	-.131	+.101	+.026	-.059	+.0073	.189
	(.0021)	(.067)	(.068)	(.0081)	(.050)	(.0028)	2.57
MISTK	+.0014	-.104	+.159	-.036	+.107	-.0012	.117
	(.0049)	(.152)	(.154)	(.018)	(.114)	(.0063)	1.47

Note: Each equation also includes SIZE, SINGLE, HEALTH, NORTH, SOUTH, URBAN, OD, and ID. The industry dummy variables (ID) are omitted for the INJRATE equation.

insignificant. Unions do, however, increase the prevalence of overtime provisions. In addition, job injuries (INJRATE) are greater in unionized contexts. The analysis does not distinguish whether this influence is due to the impact of unions on job risks or whether the high level of hazards motivated unionization of the enterprise.

The most consistently significant of the explanatory variables is FEMALE. Women's jobs have the characteristics one would expect, given their orientation to lighter, lower-level blue-collar work. Their positions are less hazardous, require faster work, do not permit them to make decisions or be creative, and tend to involve less overtime work.

F.3 REGRESSION RESULTS FOR THE POOLED MICHIGAN SAMPLE

The analysis of the Michigan Survey of Working Conditions data in the text focused on the blue-collar subsample of this data set. The white-collar workers were excluded from consideration, since the job characteristic questions were not particularly pertinent for their kinds of jobs. This shortcoming of the survey questions is greatest for the compensating earnings differential equations since the absence of more appropriate job attribute variables limits the effort to disentangle the different determinants of worker income for white-collar workers. The quit intention, danger perception, and earnings regressions for the 951 workers in the pooled sample are reported in Tables F.3, F.4, and F.5. Definitions of variables and variable lists are the same as in the chapters presenting the corresponding blue-collar results.

The quit intention results reported in Table F.3 are quite similar to the blue-collar findings in Chapter 13.[2] Job dangers are an important determinant of workers' quit intentions, as the adaptive models predict. Older or more experienced workers are less likely to quit, as are those who have fringe benefits or job security. These findings also are consistent with rational adaptive behavior. Fringe benefits, for example, impose transactions costs on job changes that diminish the incentive to change jobs.

The danger assessment results in Table F.4 are also consistent with the adaptive models of job choice. The injury experience (EXPINJURY1) and weighted injury experience (EXPINJURY2) variables have the expected positive coefficients. Other job attributes, such as the physical effort required (PHYSC), the irregularity of the work (IRREG), the pleasantness of the physical work environment (PHCOND), and the industry injury rate (INJRATE), reflect influences that are consistent with Chapter 4's hypothesis that workers utilize different types of information pertaining to their jobs in forming their job hazard assessments. In short, the danger perception and quit intention results are consistent with the view that workers learn about job hazards through on-the-job experiences and quit if these experiences are sufficiently unfavorable.

The EARNG and LOGEARNG regressions in Table F.5 are less satisfactory. In particular, the DANGER coefficient has a varying sign and is statistically insignificant at the 5 percent level. This result is attributable to the fact that

2. The quit variables are somewhat different, QUIT1 is unchanged; QUIT2 is now QUIT4; the new QUIT2 = 0.5 (QUIT1 + QUIT2); and QUIT3 = 0.25(QUIT1) + 0.5(QUIT2).

Table F.3. Quit Intention Results, All Workers

Independent variables	Coefficients and standard errors			
	QUIT1	QUIT2	QUIT3	QUIT4
AGE	−.0030	−.0038	−.0030	−.0046
	(.0011)	(.0011)	(.0009)	(.0014)
FEMALE	−.042	−.037	−.026	−.031
	(.032)	(.032)	(.025)	(.039)
BLACK	+.033	+.081	+.073	+.130
	(.038)	(.038)	(.030)	(.047)
EDUC	$+.45E-3$	+.0020	+.0020	+.0037
	$(4.67E-3)$	(.0047)	(.0037)	(.0058)
HEALTH	+.033	+.045	+.037	+.058
	(.015)	(.015)	(.012)	(.019)
UNION	−.035	−.026	−.017	−.017
	(.027)	(.027)	(.021)	(.034)
TENURE	−.0029	−.0048	−.0041	−.0068
	(.0016)	(.0016)	(.0012)	(.0019)
EARNG	$-.28E-5$	$-.22E-5$	$-.15E-5$	$-.15E-5$
	$(.30E-5)$	$(.30E-5)$	$(.24E-5)$	$(.37E-5)$
DANGER	+.049	+.058	+.046	+.067
	(.025)	(.025)	(.020)	(.031)
FAST	+.084	+.051	+.030	+.017
	(.025)	(.025)	(.020)	(.031)
NODEC	+.014	+.0066	+.0031	$-.75E-3$
	(.013)	(.0128)	(.0101)	(.016)
SECURITY	−.081	−.100	−.080	−.120
	(.024)	(.024)	(.019)	(.030)
PHYSC	−.056	−.019	−.0044	+.019
	(.025)	(.025)	(.0200)	(.031)
PHCOND	−.026	−.051	−.044	−.076
	(.024)	(.024)	(.019)	(.030)
TRAIN	−.026	−.039	−.033	−.052
	(.025)	(.025)	(.020)	(.031)
CREAT	−.0016	$+.53E-3$	$+.94E-3$	+.0027
	(.0114)	(.011)	$(8.98E-3)$	(.014)
FRINGE	−.122	−.134	−.104	−.146
	(.043)	(.043)	(.034)	(.053)
Other variables	LIST1	LIST1	LIST1	LIST1
R^2	.168	.233	.238	.231
SEE	.334	.333	.264	.413

Table F.4. Regression of DANGER on All Pertinent Variables, All Workers

Independent variables	Coefficients and standard errors	
	(1)	(2)
AGE	−.0030 (.0014)	−.0029 (.0014)
FEMALE	−.050 (.036)	−.051 (.036)
BLACK	−.017 (.049)	−.015 (.048)
EDUC	−.0018 (.0057)	$-.93E-3$ (.0057)
HEALTH	+.011 (.019)	$-.74E-3$ (.020)
SIZE	$+.41E-4$ $(.16E-4)$	$+.40E-4$ $(.16E-4)$
UNION	+.017 (.033)	+.018 (.033)
INJRATE	+.0056 (.0019)	+.0055 (.0019)
TENURE	$+.28E-3$ (.0020)	$+.53E-3$ (.0019)
PHYSC	+.140 (.031)	+.142 (.031)
IRREG	+.305 (.084)	+.307 (.084)
PHCOND	−.114 (.030)	−.111 (.029)
MISTK	+.030 (.014)	+.030 (.014)
NODEC	−.030 (.015)	−.029 (.015)
OVERT	+.018 (.010)	+.019 (.010)
EXPINJURY1	+.248 (.047)	— —
EXPINJURY2	— —	+.083 (.015)
Other variables	LIST1	LIST1
R^2	.227	.231
SEE	.434	.433

Table F.5. EARNG and LOGEARNG Results, All Workers

Independent variables	Coefficients and standard errors	
	EARNG	LOGEARNG
AGE	+25.51	+.0032
	(12.73)	(.0012)
FEMALE	−3,723.1	−.501
	(336.4)	(.031)
BLACK	−139.87	−.031
	(429.8)	(.040)
EDUC	+375.20	+.042
	(50.43)	(.0047)
HEALTH	−206.12	−.027
	(170.24)	(.016)
SINGLE	−1,003.6	−.140
	(426.4)	(.039)
SIZE	+.546	+.39E − 4
	(.156)	(.14E − 4)
UNION	+158.31	+.095
	(298.25)	(.028)
TENURE	+38.71	+.0022
	(17.65)	(.0016)
DANGER	−181.86	+.015
	(284.43)	(.026)
SUPER	+694.88	+.062
	(290.44)	(.027)
FAST	+695.79	+.066
	(286.34)	(.026)
NODEC	−348.89	−.053
	(133.85)	(.012)
MISTK	−103.57	−.016
	(125.03)	(.012)
OVERT	−126.99	+.010
	(92.47)	(.0086)
PHYSC	−465.00	−.036
	(286.75)	(.027)
IRREG	+1,216.1	+.152
	(748.9)	(.069)
SECURITY	−246.29	+.030
	(262.03)	(.024)
TRAIN	+326.11	+.057
	(278.72)	(.026)
Other variables	LIST1	LIST1
R^2	.456	.612
SEE	3,779.6	.350

Table F.6. SWC Variable Definitions

Symbol	Definition
AGE	Age in years
BLACK	Black race d.v.[a]: 1 if worker is Negro; 0 otherwise.
CREAT	Job creativity d.v.: 3 if the statement that the job requires the worker to be creative is a lot like the worker's job; 2 if it is somewhat like the worker's job; 1 if it is a little like the worker's job; 0 if it is not at all like the worker's job.
DANGER	Job hazard perceptions d.v.: 1 if job exposes the worker to physical dangers or unhealthy conditions; 0 otherwise.
EARNG	Annual earnings in dollars from the worker's main job.
EDUC	Years of schooling completed.
EXPINJURY1	Injury experience d.v.: 1 if within the last three years the worker has had an illness or injury caused or made more severe by his present job; 0 otherwise.
EXPINJURY2	Weighted injury experience d.v.: 4 if an injury on the worker's present job in the last three years created a great problem; 3 if a sizable problem; 2 if a slight problem; 1 if no problem at all; 0 if EXPINJURY1 = 0.
FAST	Fast work speed d.v.: 1 if job requires worker to work very fast a lot; 0 otherwise.
FEMALE	Female sex d.v.: 1 if worker is female; 0 otherwise.
FRINGE	Fringe benefit d.v.: 1 if employer makes available sick leave, life insurance, medical insurance, pension, stock option, or profit-sharing fringe benefits; 0 otherwise.
HEALTH	Health limitations d.v.: 4 if limiting physical or nervous condition creates a great work problem; 3 if a sizable problem; 2 if a slight problem; 1 if no problem; 0 if worker has no limiting physical or nervous condition.
IRREG	Irregular work hours d.v.: 1 if worker expresses difficulty with respect to the regularity of work hours; 0 otherwise.
LIFEINS	Life insurance d.v.: 1 if employer provides life insurance that would cover death occurring for reasons not connected with the worker's job; 0 otherwise.
MEDINS	Medical insurance d.v.: 1 if employer provides medical, surgical, or hospital insurance that covers any injury that might occur to the worker while off the job; 0 otherwise.
MISTK	Job requires no mistakes d.v.: 1 if job requires that worker never make a mistake; 0 otherwise.
NODEC	No worker decisions on job d.v.: 4 if it is not at all true that job allows worker to make a lot of decisions on his own; 3 if a little true; 2 if somewhat true; 0 if very true.
NORTH	Northern regional d.v.: 1 if worker lives in northeastern U.S.; 0 otherwise.

(continued)

[a] d.v. = dummy variable

Table F.6. SWC Variable Definitions (*continued*)

Symbol	Definition
OVERT	Overtime work d.v.: 2 if worker often works overtime: 1 if once in a while; 0 otherwise.
PENSION	Pension plan d.v.; 1 if employer makes available a retirement program; 0 otherwise.
PHCOND	Pleasant physical conditions d.v.: 1 if very true of job that physical surroundings are pleasant; 0 otherwise.
PHYSC	Physical effort d.v.: 1 if the statement that the job requires a lot of physical effort is a lot or somewhat like the worker's job; 0 otherwise.
PROFIT	Profit-sharing plan d.v.: 1 if employer makes available a profit-sharing plan; 0 otherwise.
QUIT1	Strong quit intentions d.v.: 1 if worker is very likely to make a genuine effort to find a new job with another employer in the next year; 0 otherwise.
QUIT2	Strong and moderate quit intentions d.v.: 1 if worker is very likely or somewhat likely to make a genuine effort to find a new job with another employer in the next year; 0 otherwise.
SECURITY	Job security d.v.: 1 if it is very true that the worker's job security is good; 0 otherwise.
SICKLV	Sick leave d.v.: 1 if worker is allowed to take sick leave days with full pay; 0 otherwise.
SINGLE	Single marital status d.v.: 1 if worker is single; 0 otherwise.
SIZE	Enterprise size: the number of people employed at the location where the respondent works.
SOUTH	Southern region d.v.: 1 if worker lives in southeastern U.S.; 0 otherwise.
STOCK	Stock options d.v.: 1 if employer makes stock options available; 0 otherwise.
SUPER	Supervisor d.v.: 1 if worker supervises anybody as part of his job; 0 otherwise.
TENURE	Years of experience with the present employer.
TRAIN	Training program d.v.: 1 if employer makes available a training program to improve worker skills; 0 otherwise.
UNION	Unionization d.v.: 1 if worker belongs to a union or employees' association; 0 otherwise.
URBAN	Urban area d.v.: 1 if worker lives in a major SMSA; 0 otherwise.

lower-level white-collar jobs tend to be more hazardous. The DANGER coefficient consequently reflects more the relative rank of the white-collar jobs than compensation for a job attribute. In Chapter 14 this difficulty was ameliorated by considering only blue-collar workers, since the job attribute questions were more pertinent to them. Moreover, consideration of this subsample reduced the problems created by differences in worker ability or other characteristics not reflected in the personal background variables.

F.4 DATA SOURCES FOR THE AGGREGATIVE QUIT RATE REGRESSIONS

The data sources for the two-digit and three-digit industry quit-rate regressions in Chapter 13 are as follows. It should be noted that these are the sources for the data used to construct the variables, which often were transformed values of published data.

Two-Digit Data Sources: AGE16–24, from U.S. Bureau of the Census (1972), hereafter Census (1972), Table 34; AGE45+, from Census (1972), Table 34; EDUC, from Census (1972), Table 3; EMPLOY%, from U.S. Bureau of Labor Statistics (1972), hereafter BLS (1972), Table 38; FEMALE, from U.S. Bureau of Labor Statistics (1971), Table B-3; HIRES69, from BLS (1972), Table 55; INJRATE, from BLS (1972), Table 163; QUIT, from BLS(1972), Table 55; UNION, from BLS (1972), Table 150; WAGE, from BLS (1972), Table 99; WHITE, from Census (1972), Table 33;

Three-Digit Data Sources: AGE16–24, from Census (1972), Table 34; AGE 45+, from Census (1972), Table 34; EMPLOY%, HIRES71, HIRES72, HIRES73, HOURS, OVERT, PRODN, QUIT and WAGE from the U.S. Bureau of Labor Statistics, "Employment and Earnings" tape; FEMALE, from Census (1972), Table 32; INJRATE, U.S. Bureau of Labor Statistics (1976), hereafter BLS (1976), Table 155; INJRATE1, from BLS (1972), Table 13; INJRATE2, from BLS (1976), Table 155; UNION, developed using unpublished U.S. Dept. of Labor data by Richard Freeman and James Medoff, Harvard University.

Table F.7. Variable Definitions for NLS Survey of Young Men

Symbol	Definition
AGE	Age in years.
EARNG	Hourly wage rate.
EDUC	Highest grade completed.
HEALTH	Health limitation d.v.[a]: 1 if health limited work in 1970; 0 otherwise.
NONWHITE	Nonwhite d.v.: 1 if worker is not white; 0 otherwise.
QUIT1	Quit rate d.v.: 1 if worker changed employers voluntarily in 1969–1970; 0 otherwise.
QUIT2	Quit rate dummy variable: 1 if QUIT1 = 1 and worker quits because of working conditions; 0 otherwise.
QUIT3	Quit intention dummy variable: 1 if worker most dislikes the kind of work or working conditions; 0 otherwise.
UNION	Union dummy variable: 1 if worker's wages are set by a collective bargaining agreement; 0 otherwise.

Note: Unless otherwise indicated, all variables pertain to 1969.

[a] d.v. = dummy variable.

Table F.8. Variable Definitions for NLS Survey of Mature Men

Symbol	Definition
AGE	Age in years.
COTRAIN	Company training program d.v.[a]: 1 if worker participated in any company training program since 1969; 0 otherwise.
EARNG	Hourly wage rate in dollars.
EDUC	Highest grade completed in years.
HEALTH	Health limitation d.v.: 1 if worker's health limits the kind or amount of work he can perform; 0 otherwise.
NONWHITE	Nonwhite d.v.: 1 if worker is not white; 0 otherwise.
OTHTRAIN	Other training program d.v.: TRAIN - COTRAIN.
OVERT	Overtime d.v.: 1 if worker is covered by overtime provisions; 0 otherwise.
PENSION	Pension d.v.: 1 if worker is covered by a retirement plan; 0 otherwise.
QUIT1	Quit rate d.v.: 1 if worker changed employers voluntarily in 1969–1971; 0 otherwise.
QUIT2	Quit rate d.v.: 1 if QUIT1 = 1 or if worker sought an alternative job in 1966–1971; 0 otherwise.
TENURE	Years of experience with the present employer.
TRAIN	Training program dummy variable: 1 if worker participated in any training program since 1969; 0 otherwise.
UNION	Unionization dummy variable: 1 if worker's wages are set by a collective bargaining agreement; 0 otherwise.

Note: Unless otherwise indicated, all variables pertain to 1969.
[a] d.v. = dummy variable.

F.5 DETAILED VARIABLE DEFINITIONS

Tables F.6, F.7, and F.8 provide detailed definitions of all pertinent variables from the University of Michigan Survey of Working Conditions (SWC), the National Longitudinal Survey (NLS) of Young Men, and the NLS of Mature Men, respectively. Definitions of transformations of these variables that were employed in the text and subsidiary variables that were included in variable lists, such as the occupational dummy variables, are not presented in these tables.

The SWC includes a large number of dummy variables pertaining to the worker and his job. All dummy variables utilized as dependent variables or as explanatory variables of major interest are zero-one dummy variables. Six subsidiary dummy variables are quantitatively scaled somewhat differently, for example, by assigning integral values from 0 to 4 depending on the degree of health impairment.

Ideally, one would create a separate dummy variable for each of the qualitative responses. This approach was not adopted for two reasons. First, doing so would have consumed too many degrees of freedom. For example, the HEALTH variable alone would have required five dummy variables instead of one. Second, although one could test for the joint significance of the set of the dummy variables' coefficients, the individual coefficients could not have been interpreted readily, since the data were not rich enough to estimate all of the differing degrees of influence.

If an underlying quantitative scale exists that corresponds to the values assigned in creating the dummy variables, the resulting coefficients can be interpreted in a meaningful fashion. Otherwise, they should be regarded as subsidiary control variables for personal characteristics and nonpecuniary factors. It should be noted that while the weighted dummy variables performed somewhat better than their zero-one counterparts, none of the coefficients of the central hypotheses in this volume were sensitive to the formulation employed for these other variables.

BIBLIOGRAPHY

AKERLOF, GEORGE. 1970. The Market for "Lemons": Qualitative Uncertainty and the Market Mechanism. *Quarterly Journal of Economics* 84:488–500.

ARROW, KENNETH. 1969. The Organization of Economic Activity: Issues Pertinent to the Choice of Market Versus Nonmarket Allocation. In Joint Economic Committee, *The Analysis and Evaluation of Public Expenditures: The PPB System,* vol. 1. Washington, D.C.: U.S. Government Printing Office.

———1971. *Essays in the Theory of Risk-Bearing.* Chicago: Markham Publishers.

———1972. Models of Job Discrimination. In *Racial Discrimination in Economic Life,* ed. A. Pascal. Lexington: D. C. Heath.

———1973. Higher Education as a Filter. *Journal of Public Economics* 2:193–216.

ARROW, KENNETH, DAVID LEVHARI, AND EYTAN SHESHINSKI. 1972. A Production Function for the Repairman Problem. *Review of Economic Studies* 39:241–249.

ASHFORD, NICHOLAS. 1976. *Crisis in the Workplace: Occupational Disease and Injury.* Cambridge: MIT Press.

BECKER, GARY. 1964. *Human Capital.* New York: National Bureau of Economic Research.

———1965. A Theory of the Allocation of Time. *Economic Journal* 75:493–517.

BELLMAN, RICHARD. 1956. A Problem in the Sequential Design of Experiments. *Sankhya* 16:221–229.

———1961. *Adaptive Control Processes: A Guided Tour.* Princeton: Princeton University Press.

BEN-PORATH, YORAM. 1967. Production of Human Capital and the Life Cycle of Earnings. *Journal of Political Economy* 75:352–365.

BERRY, DONALD. 1972. A Bernoulli Two-Armed Bandit. *Annals of Mathematical Statistics* 43:871–897.

Bok, Derek, and John Dunlop. 1970. *Labor and the American Community.* New York: Simon and Schuster.

Brodeur, Paul. 1974. *Expendable Americans.* New York: Viking Press.

Burton, John, and John Parker. 1969. Interindustry Variations in Voluntary Labor Mobility. *Industrial and Labor Relations Review* 22:199–216.

Cheit, Earl. 1961. *Injury and Recovery in the Course of Employment.* New York: John Wiley & Sons.

DeGroot, Morris. 1970. *Optimal Statistical Decisions.* New York: McGraw-Hill.

Doeringer, Peter, and Michael Piore. 1971. *Internal Labor Markets and Manpower Analysis.* Lexington: D. C. Heath.

Dunlop, John. 1944. *Wage Determination under Trade Unions.* New York: Macmillan.

————1958. *Industrial Relations Systems.* Carbondale: Southern Illinois University Press.

Engels, Friedrich. 1968. *The Condition of the Working Class in England.* Stanford: Stanford University Press.

Feldman, Julian. 1963. Simulation of Behavior in the Binary Choice Experiment. *In Computers and Thought,* ed. E. Feigenbaum and J. Feldman. New York: McGraw-Hill.

Feldstein, Martin. 1973. *Lowering the Permanent Rate of Unemployment: A Study Prepared for the Use of the Joint Economic Committee.* Washington: U.S. Government Printing Office.

Feller, William. 1970. *An Introduction to Probability Theory and Its Applications,* vol. 1. New York: John Wiley & Sons.

Freeman, Richard. 1976a. Individual Mobility and Union Voice in the Labor Market. *American Economic Review* 66:361–368.

————1976b. Non-Wage Effects of Trade Unions on the Labor Market: An Exit-Voice Analysis. Unpublished paper, Harvard University.

Goldstein, Gerald, and Mark Pauly. 1976. Group Health Insurance as a Local Public Good. In *The Role of Health Insurance in the Health Services Sector,* ed. R. Rosett. New York: National Bureau of Economic Research.

Gordon, Jerome, Allan Akman, and Michael Brooks. 1971. *Industrial Safety Statistics: A Re-Examination.* New York: Praeger.

Gorman, W. M. 1967. Tastes, Habits, and Choices. *International Economic Review* 8:218–222.

Griliches, Zvi, ed. 1971. *Price Indexes and Quality Change.* Cambridge: Harvard University Press.

Griliches, Zvi, and William Mason. 1972. Education, Income, and Ability. *Journal of Political Economy* 80:S74–S103.

Griliches, Zvi, and V. Ringstad. 1971. *Economies of Scale and the Form of the Production Function: An Econometric Study of Norwegian Manufacturing Establishment Data.* Amsterdam: North-Holland Publishing Co.

Grossman, Michael. 1972. *The Demand for Health: A Theoretical and Empirical Investigation.* New York: National Bureau of Economic Research.

Haggstrom, Gus. 1974. Logistic Regression, Discriminant Analysis. Rand Corporation memorandum.

Hall, Robert. 1970. Why is the Unemployment Rate So High at Full Employment? *Brookings Papers on Economic Activity* 3:369–402.

HICKS, J. R. 1941. The Rehabilitation of Consumers' Surplus. *Review of Economic Studies* 9:108–116.

———1968. *The Theory of Wages.* London: Macmillan.

HIRSCHMAN, ALBERT. 1970. *Exit, Voice, and Loyalty.* Cambridge: Harvard University Press.

HIRSHLEIFER, JACK. 1971. The Private and Social Value of Information and the Reward to Inventive Activity. *American Economic Review* 61:561–574.

HOWARD, RONALD. 1960. *Dynamic Programming and Markov Processes.* Cambridge: MIT Press.

———1971. *Dynamic Probabilistic Systems,* vols. 1 and 2. New York: John Wiley & Sons.

ISKRANT, ALBERT, AND PAUL JOLIET. 1968. *Accidents and Homicide.* Cambridge: Harvard University Press.

KINNERSLY, PATRICK. 1973. *The Hazards of Work: How to Fight Them.* London: Pluto Press.

KRYTER, KARL. 1970. *The Effects of Noise on Man.* New York: Academic Press.

LAND, KENNETH. 1973. Identification, Parameter Estimation, and Hypothesis Testing in Recursive Sociological Models. In *Structural Equation Models in the Social Sciences,* ed. A. Goldberger and O. Duncan. New York: Seminar Press.

LEONTIEF, WASSILY. 1976. The Pure Theory of the Guaranteed Annual Wage Contract. *Journal of Political Economy* 54:76–79.

LEVHARI, DAVID, AND EYTAN SHESHINSKI. 1970. A Microeconomic Production Function. *Econometrica* 38:559–573.

LEWIS, H. G. 1963. *Unionism and Relative Wages in the United States.* Chicago: University of Chicago Press.

LUCAS, ROBERT. 1974. The Distribution of Job Characteristics. *Review of Economics and Statistics* 56:530–540.

McCALL, J. J. 1970. Economics of Information and Job Search. *Quarterly Journal of Economics* 84:113–126.

McFADDEN, DANIEL. 1973. Conditional Logit Analysis of Qualitative Choice Behavior. In *Frontiers in Econometrics,* ed. P. Zarembka. New York: Academic Press.

MALINVAUD, E. 1970. *Statistical Methods of Econometrics.* Amsterdam: North-Holland Publishing Co.

MANDLER, GEORGE. 1968. Anxiety. In *International Encyclopedia of the Social Sciences.* New York: Macmillan and the Free Press.

MARSHALL, ALFRED. 1949. *Principles of Economics.* London: Macmillan.

MARX, KARL. 1906. *Capital.* New York: Modern Library.

MEDOFF, JAMES. 1976. Layoffs and Alternatives under Trade Unions in American Manufacturing. Unpublished paper, Harvard University.

MICHIGAN, UNIVERSITY OF, INSTITUTE FOR SOCIAL RESEARCH. 1975. Survey of Working Conditions. SRC Study no. 45369. Ann Arbor: University of Michigan Social Science Archive.

MORTENSEN, DALE. 1970. A Theory of Wage and Employment Dynamics. In *Microeconomic Foundations of Employment and Inflation Theory,* ed. E. Phelps. New York: W. W. Norton.

———1975. The Turnover Implications of Learning about Attributes on the Job. Unpublished paper, Northwestern University.

NATIONAL SAFETY COUNCIL. 1972. *Supervisors Safety Manual.* Chicago: National Safety Council.

OI, WALTER. 1962. Labor as a Quasi-Fixed Factor. *Journal of Political Economy* 70:538–555.

———1973. An Essay on Workmen's Compensation and Industrial Safety. In *Supplemental Studies for the National Commission on State Workmen's Compensation Laws.* Washington: U.S. Government Printing Office.

———1974. On the Economics of Industrial Safety. *Law and Contemporary Problems* 38:669–699.

PAGE, JOSEPH, AND MARY-WIN O'BRIEN. 1973. *Bitter Wages.* New York: Grossman.

PARSONS, DONALD. 1972. Specific Human Capital: An Application to Quit Rates and Layoff Rates. *Journal of Political Economy* 80:1120–1143.

PENCAVEL, JOHN. 1970. *An Analysis of the Quit Rate in American Manufacturing Industry.* Princeton: Industrial Relations Section.

———1972. Wages, Specific Training, and Labor Turnover in U.S. Manufacturing Industries. *International Economic Review* 13:53–64.

POLLAK, ROBERT. 1970. Habit Formation and Dynamic Demand Functions. *Journal of Political Economy* 78:745–763.

PRATT, JOHN, HOWARD RAIFFA, AND ROBERT SCHLAIFER. 1975. *Introduction to Statistical Decision Theory.* New York: McGraw-Hill.

RAIFFA, HOWARD, AND ROBERT SCHLAIFER. 1961. *Applied Statistical Decision Theory.* Cambridge: MIT Press.

REDER, MELVIN. 1962. Wage Differentials: Theory and Measurement. In *Aspects of Labor Economics.* Princeton: Princeton University Press.

ROTHSCHILD, MICHAEL. 1974. A Two-Armed Bandit Theory of Market Pricing. *Journal of Economic Theory* 9:185–202.

ROTTENBERG, SIMON. 1956. On Choice in Labor Markets. *Industrial and Labor Relations Review* 9:183–199.

SALOP, JOANNE, AND STEVEN SALOP. 1976. Self-Selection and Turnover in the Labor Market. *Quarterly Journal of Economics* 90:619–627.

SCHELLING, THOMAS. 1968. The Life You Save May Be Your Own. In *Problems in Public Expenditure Analysis,* ed. S. Chase. Washington: Brookings Institution.

———1972. *Hockey Helments, Concealed Weapons, and Daylight Savings.* Discussion paper no. 9, Public Policy Program, Harvard University.

———1972. The Process of Residential Segregation: Neighborhood Tipping. In *Racial Discrimination in Economic Life,* ed. A Pascal. Lexington: D. C. Heath.

SCOTT, RACHEL. 1974. *Muscle and Blood.* New York: E. P. Dutton.

SIMON, HERBERT. 1957. *Models of Man.* New York: John Wiley & Sons.

SKINNER, B. F. 1953. *Science and Human Behavior.* New York: Free Press.

SLICHTER, SUMNER, JAMES HEALY, AND ROBERT LIVERNASH. 1960. *The Impact of Collective Bargaining on Management.* Washington: Brookings Institution.

SMITH, ADAM. 1937. *The Wealth of Nations.* New York: Modern Library.

SMITH, ROBERT. 1976. *The Occupational Safety and Health Act: Its Goals and Its Achievements.* Washington: American Enterprise Institute.

SPENCE, A. MICHAEL. 1974. Competitive and Optimal Responses to Signals: An

Analysis of Efficiency and Distribution. *Journal of Economic Theory* 7:296–332.

————1974. *Market Signaling: Informational Transfer in Hiring and Related Screening Processes*. Cambridge: Harvard University Press.

————1975. Monopoly, Quality, and Regulation. *Bell Journal of Economics* 6:417–429.

→ SPENCE, A. MICHAEL, AND RICHARD ZECKHAUSER. 1971. Insurance, Information, and Individual Action. *American Economic Review* 61:371–379.

STELLMAN, JAMES, AND SUSAN DAUM. 1973. *Work is Dangerous to Your Health*. New York: Vintage Books.

STIGLER, GEORGE. 1961. The Economics of Information. *Journal of Political Economy* 69:213–225.

STOIKOV, V., AND R. RAIMON. 1968. Determinants of Differences in the Quit Rate Among Industries. *American Economic Review* 58:1283–1298.

TERKEL, STUDS. 1974. *Working*. New York: Pantheon.

THALER, R., AND S. ROSEN. 1976. The Value of Saving a Life: Evidence from the Labor Market. In *Household Production and Consumption*, ed. Terleckyz. NBER Studies in Income and Wealth no. 40. New York: Columbia University Press.

THOMPSON, WILLIAM. 1933. On the Likelihood that One Unknown Probability Exceeds Another in View of Evidence of Two Samples. *Biometrika* 25:285–294.

TRUFFAUT, FRANCOIS. 1967. *Hitchcock*. New York: Simon and Schuster.

U.S. BUREAU OF THE CENSUS. 1973. *Industrial Characteristics*. Subject Report PC(2)-7B. Washington: U.S. Government Printing Office.

U.S. BUREAU OF LABOR STATISTICS. 1971. *Employment and Earnings*, vol. 17, No. 9.

U.S. BUREAU OF LABOR STATISTICS. 1972 and 1975. *Handbook of Labor Statistics*. Washington: U.S. Government Printing Office.

U.S. DEPT. OF LABOR, OCCUPATIONAL SAFETY AND HEALTH ADMINISTRATION. *Job Safety and Health*, selected issues.

→ VISCUSI, W. KIP. 1978. Labor Market Valuations of Life and Limb: Empirical Evidence and Policy Implications. *Public Policy* 26:359–386.

→ VISCUSI, W. KIP, AND RICHARD ZECKHAUSER. 1976. *Environmental Policy Choice under Uncertainty. Journal of Environmental Economics and Management* 3:97–112.

VON NEUMANN, JOHN, AND OSKAR MORGENSTERN. 1967. *Theory of Games and Economic Behavior*. New York: John Wiley & Sons.

WAGNER, HARVEY. 1969. *Principles of Operations Research*. Englewood Cliffs, N.J.: Prentice-Hall.

WALTERS, A. A. 1960. Marginal Productivity and Probability Distributions of Factor Services. *Economic Journal* 70:325–330.

WEISS, YORAM. 1976. The Wealth Effect in Occupational Choice. *International Economic Review* 17:292–307.

WILLIG, R. 1976. Consumer's Surplus without Apology. *American Economic Review* 66:589–597.

YAARI, MENAHEM. 1965. Uncertain Lifetime, Life Insurance, and the Theory of the Consumer. *Review of Economic Studies* 32:137–150.

YAKOWITZ, SIDNEY. 1969. *Mathematics of Adaptive Control Processes.* New York: American Elsevier.

→ ZECKHAUSER, RICHARD. 1970. Medical Insurance: A Case Study of the Tradeoff between Risk Spreading and Appropriate Incentives. *Journal of Economic Theory* 2:10–26.

———1974. Risk Spreading and Distribution. *In Redistribution through Public Choice,* ed. H. Hochman and G. Peterson. New York: Columbia University Press.

———1975. Procedures for Valuing Lives. *Public Policy* 23:419–464.

INDEX